THE PAST AND
FUTURE OF
AFFIRMATIVE
ACTION

The Past and Future of Affirmative Action

A Guide and Analysis for Human Resource
Professionals and Corporate Counsel

Ronald Turner

Quorum Books

New York • Westport, Connecticut • London

Library of Congress Cataloging-in-Publication Data

Turner, Ronald.
    The past and future of affirmative action: a guide and analysis for
human resource professionals and corporate counsel / Ronald Turner.
        p.   cm.
    Includes bibliographical references.
    ISBN 0-89930-511-3 (lib. bdg. : alk. paper)
    1. Affirmative action programs—United States. I. Title.
HF5549.5.A34T87   1990
331.13'3'0973—dc20   90-8393

British Library Cataloguing in Publication Data is available.

Library of Congress Catalog Card Number: 90-8393
ISBN: 0-89930-511-3

First published in 1990

Quorum Books, 88 Post Road West, Westport, CT 06881
An imprint of Greenwood Publishing Group, Inc.

Printed in the United States of America

The paper used in this book complies with the
Permanent Paper Standard issued by the National
Information Standards Organization (Z39.48-1984).

10 9 8 7 6 5 4 3 2 1

To Karen, Kadi, and Ronald

Contents

CONTENTS

Preface

Race and the question of discrimination are well-known and much discussed historical and contemporary issues of primary significance in our nation's history. These fundamental issues are the subject of social and public policy in all areas of life, including education, housing, voting rights, and employment. It is the latter area which is the subject of this book. Like other societal developments and problems, the issue of race has become and will remain an issue of and in the workplace. Given the history and legacy of discrimination on the basis of race, ethnicity, and gender that marks so much of the nation's political and social reality, private employers and public sector entities continue to face the task of ensuring that their practices and policies are nondiscriminatory. This task is not just of a moral imperative and dimension. While regulation and legislation of an individual's "heart" is a difficult if not impossible proposition, regulation of conduct through legislation is a more fruitful and hopefully attainable exercise. Thus, fair employment laws and constitutional protections for minorities underscore the question of discrimination and the quest for answers thereto. All members of society are affected by the emphasis given to this issue and the mechanisms put in place to combat discrimination as reflected by our laws and public policy.

This book focuses on the issue of affirmative action in employment and in public contracting as applied to racial minorities. In undertaking this project, it was my desire to describe what the law is—a step which is often overlooked in the rush to judge affirmative action as moral or immoral, right or wrong, constitutional or unconstitutional. That primary purpose is the goal of this endeavor, and it is hoped that the ensuing chapters will serve as a resource and guide through the maze of preferential treatment doctrine, United States Supreme Court decisions discussing the same, and agency regulations and practices.

Acknowledgments

Many individuals have knowingly and unknowingly contributed to my journey down a path which ultimately resulted in this and other works which have come to fruition in the past few years. Special thanks to Marvin Powell, Esq., for his encouragement and energetic efforts to convince me to pursue a career in law; to Howard Tolley and Steven Middleton for their demanding and rigorous curriculum and routine; Adam Thurschwell, Esq., for his friendship and intelligence; Herbert R. Northrup, professor emeritus of management and former director of the Industrial Research Unit of The Wharton School of the University of Pennsylvania, for extending significant opportunities to me; and to Philip Miscimara, Esq., for his friendship and example. In addition, Deborah Hild and Ceil Ziganta must be acknowledged for their work in the preparation of the manuscript.

I would be remiss if I did not thank Liliane H. Miller, acquisitions editor at Greenwood Publishing Group, for her efforts and energy expended in initiating this production.

Finally, and most important, my sincere thanks to my family for their continued support and patience.

Introduction

Affirmative action[1] has been and continues to be a volatile, complex, and hotly debated issue. The implementation of voluntary affirmative action programs and the imposition of judicially mandated race- and sex-conscious measures and remedies have fueled the ongoing debate regarding the legal, moral, and economic questions arising from preferential treatment of certain segments of society, and the conflict—both potential and real—between individual and societal rights and interests. Moreover, adjudication of affirmative action cases by the courts presents matters requiring a complex and still developing accommodation of rectification objectives and principles which affect both victims of unlawful discrimination, and "nonvictims" who are affected by the implementation of affirmative action measures.[2]

The debate reflects the sincere and strongly held beliefs of persons on both sides of the affirmative action question. On one side are persons who conclude that affirmative action programs are necessary and justifiable efforts to remedy the effects of undisputed past discrimination. Failure to remedy these effects, they argue, would deny to victims the fair and equal treatment to which they are entitled by law. On the other side are persons who believe that such programs and preferential treatment are unlawful and unconstitutional and will only result in further racial and sexual polarization and strife. Underlying their belief is a concern that affirmative action may unfairly disadvantage individuals who bear no responsibility, directly or indirectly, for the past or present discrimination practiced by others. Both sides of the debate can marshal sound arguments supporting their views and conclusions, a reality that makes resolution of the debate and an appropriate balancing of competing concerns all the more difficult.

Thus, the issue of whether and/or how public and private employers may or should consider race or sex in the context of affirmative action initiatives raises a host of fundamental and significant questions of equity, morality, and public policy. When, if ever, is affirmative action justified to remedy prior discrimination? Is there a constitutional duty to remedy the effects of a prior constitutional violation and, if so, what is the scope of that duty? Can discrimination be considered ''benign'' when a legislature acts to benefit minorities or women?[3] In the employment context, these questions include the following: May race or sex be considered? May race or sex be considered only when identifiable discrimination, and specific victims thereof, have been established? What temporal limitations, if any, apply to the use of race or sex as a determinative, influential, or ''plus'' factor in hiring, promotion, layoff, or termination decisions?[4] What must a public employer do to insure that federal, state, or local government affirmative action legislation is constitutional?

Governmental entities have also employed a distinct form of affirmative action, generally known as *set-aside programs*, in public contracting matters. Under such programs, states and other local bodies have determined that certain percentages of governmental purchases of goods and services will be made from minority or women business enterprises.[5] Typically, nonminority businesses are required to utilize the services of minority or women businesses as a condition of obtaining public contracts. Set-aside programs have been challenged in the courts on the grounds that such programs impose impermissible requirements on ''majority'' businesses, and grant unlawful preferential treatment to minority and women enterprises.

This book examines the judicial, legislative, and administrative record in the controversial and critical area of affirmative action. The underlying purpose of the book is twofold. First, this work will present a detailed examination of affirmative action. Second, a historical and prescriptive analysis of affirmative action doctrines will be offered. In examining this subject and related sub-issues, the book will be necessarily descriptive, for an accurate and complete analysis of court and agency rulings and regulations must be grounded in a careful explanation of complex and changing developments in this area.

The following chapters discuss affirmative action in several key areas. Chapter 1 discusses the origins and evolution of the affirmative action concept. Chapter 2 examines the affirmative action in employment jurisprudence of the United States Supreme Court and the application of the Court's rulings by the lower courts in selected cases. In Chapter 3, the requirements of Executive Order 11246, its implementing regulations, and the impact of the Order on federal contractors are detailed. Chapter 4 offers a brief review of the Equal Employment Opportunity Commission's affirmative action guidelines. In Chapter 5, judicial review of minority and women business enterprise set-aside programs is discussed, with particular emphasis on the Supreme Court's 1989 ruling in *City of Richmond v. J. A. Croson Company*,[6] which invalidated a minority business enterprise statute enacted by the City of Richmond, Virginia.

A preliminary point must be made. Affirmative action (both conceptually and as applied) cannot be neatly packaged into simply stated conclusions or notions of "right" or "wrong." Proponents of affirmative action may conclude that the use of preferential treatment is an indispensable means of remedying discrimination. However, that conclusion does not lessen the need for a careful review and analysis of affirmative action, nor does it mean that we should forego debate over, and discussion of, underlying and fundamental issues and assumptions regarding the costs of the use of affirmative action and the political, social, and moral questions arising therefrom.

On the other hand, opponents of affirmative action cannot merely rely on a deceptively simple argument against the legality of such measures such as: racial and sexual discrimination is illegal; certain forms of affirmative action discriminate against whites and males; therefore, affirmative action is illegal and/or unconstitutional.[7] The premises and assumptions made with respect to each element of this syllogism, and the specific matters encompassed by this argument, must be scrutinized before an accurate assessment of the conclusion as to the legality or constitutionality of affirmative action can be made.

By analyzing the record of the courts and legislative and administrative initiatives in affirmative action, this book attempts to go beyond a conclusory discussion of affirmative action and offers the type and level of analysis which this complex area demands. In so doing, one of the purposes and goals of this endeavor is to provide useful guidelines and information which will be helpful to all segments of the labor-management community involved in, and responsible for, affirmative action and preferential treatment of minorities and women.

NOTES

1. The term *affirmative action* has different meanings and definitions which flow, and are derived, from an individual's view of the legitimacy of the use of race-conscious or sex-conscious preferential remedies for unlawful discrimination. Alternative terminology used to define or describe affirmative action include "reverse discrimination," "affirmative discrimination," or "quotas." *See generally* R. DWORKIN, A MATTER OF PRINCIPLE 316–331 (1985); R. POSNER, THE ECONOMICS OF JUSTICE 364–407 (1983); T. SOWELL, CIVIL RIGHTS: RHETORIC OR REALITY? 37–60 (1984); T. SOWELL, KNOWLEDGE AND DECISIONS 249–260 (1980); Fallon and Weiler, *Firefighters v. Stotts: Conflicting Models of Racial Justice*, 1984 SUP. CT. REV. 1, 3 n. 10. *See also* Abram, *Affirmative Action: Fair Shakers and Social Engineers*, 99 HARV. L. REV. 1312 (1986) (contending that affirmative action contradicts constitutional principles).

The term *affirmative action* encompasses a broad spectrum of measures and initiatives which are utilized to "overcome the effects of past or present practices, policies, or other barriers to equal employment opportunity." EEOC Guidelines, *Affirmative Action Appropriate Under Title VII of the Civil Rights Act of 1964*, 29 C.F.R. § 1608.1(c) (1985). These initiatives include training programs, recruitment, changes in promotion and layoff procedures, and the elimination of adverse impact relative to an employer's selection criteria. *Id.*, § 1608.3(c); Office of Federal Contract Compliance Programs, Affirmative Action Programs, 41 C.F.R. §§ 60–2.1–2.32 (1987). *See also* Daly, *Some Runs, Some Hits, Some Errors—Keeping Score in the Affirmative Action Ballpark from* Weber *to* Johnson, 30 BOSTON COLLEGE L. REV. 1, 3 n. 1 (1988).

2. *See* Lilly v. City of Beckley, 797 F.2d 191 (4th Cir. 1986).

3. *See* G. STONE, L. SEIDMAN, C. SUNSTEIN and M. TUSHNET, CONSTITUTIONAL LAW 608–609 (1986).

4. *See* B. SCHLEI and P. GROSSMAN, EMPLOYMENT DISCRIMINATION LAW 775 (1983).

5. *See infra* Chapter 5.

6. 109 U.S. 706 (1989).

7. Judge Richard Posner notes the flaw in this argument in *Legal Formalism, Legal Realism, and the Interpretation of Statutes and the Constitution*, 37 CASE WEST. L. REV. 179, 184 (1986).

THE PAST AND
FUTURE OF
AFFIRMATIVE
ACTION

The Origins, Relevant Theories, and Evolution of the Concept of Affirmative Action

As noted in the introduction, the definition, concept, and use of affirmative action is a subject which continues to evoke strong responses and arguments between both proponents and opponents of preferential treatment measures. This chapter, which is no way intended to be exhaustive, provides a brief overview of certain legal developments and theories regarding the meaning and content of affirmative action (concentrating on race-conscious measures) to illustrate the difficulty in "identifying the roots of the concept,"[1] and to provide pertinent background for assessment of the affirmative action debate and analysis of the doctrine in employment and public contracting.

CONSTITUTIONAL AND STATUTORY RACE-CONSCIOUS MEASURES

For purposes of this discussion, the following definition of affirmative action, as phrased by Professor James Jones, is our point of reference: "public or private actions or programs which provide, or seek to provide, opportunities or other benefits to persons on the basis of, among other things, their membership in a specified group or groups."[2]

Although such race-conscious programs and measures are rooted in the legal history of the United States, recent attacks by opponents of certain uses of these measures rest on the notion that affirmative action is contrary to a principle and public policy of color-blind application of the Constitution and fair employment laws.[3] Thus, the argument goes, the color of an individual's skin should not and cannot have any bearing on the distribution of employment opportunities or benefits. The purpose of the recognition of color, whether benign or not, makes no difference and cannot legitimize the distinction.

The color-blind theory and principle is admirable and certainly one which posits an aspiration which society should and must recognize in its laws and the enforcement thereof. But, as noted below, color and race, like national origin and sex, have historically served as distinguishing characteristics which have been reflected in the history and laws of this nation.

The Historical Backdrop

Early Race-Conscious Governmental Initiatives. One problem with the color-blind position noted above is the well-known history of race relations and discrimination in the United States. That history shows, as noted by Professor Jones, that "from our nation's inception it has acted in a very color-conscious fashion."[4] It is this very history of national recognition of color as a ground for actions, which adversely affected racial minorities, that must be kept in mind when considering the origins of affirmative action and subsequent developments in the public policy of preferential treatment and any limitations thereon.

Of course, the American institution of slavery was based on color, with African Americans subjected to the degradation of a social and legal regime which denied to them basic human rights because of the color of their skin. Thus, slavery was color-consciousness in one of its most obvious forms. In 1863, President Abraham Lincoln issued an executive order, the Emancipation Proclamation,[5] which mandated the freedom of slaves in areas under the control of the Confederacy.[6]

Thereafter, the Federal Constitution was amended to address the issue of racial discrimination and the status and rights of the legally emancipated African Americans. The Thirteenth Amendment provides, *inter alia*, that "[n]either slavery nor servitude . . . shall exist within the United States, or any place subject to their jurisdiction."[7] The Fourteenth Amendment provides, *inter alia*, that all citizens are entitled to equal protection under law.[8] Under the Fifteenth Amendment, citizens cannot be denied the right to vote because of race, color, or previous condition of servitude.[9]

During that same general time period, Congress passed the Freedmen's Bureau Act—legislation which provided that the federal Bureau of Refugees, Freedmen, and Abandoned Lands would make available land, buildings, and funds for the "education of the freed people."[10]

In 1867 Congress made special provisions for disposing of claims for "pay, bounty, prize money or other moneys due . . . colored soldiers, sailors or marines, or their legal representatives." Congress also awarded federal charters to organizations established to support aged or destitute colored women and children. These organizations served as a bank for persons previously held in slavery or their dependents. An additional purpose was to educate and improve the moral and intellectual condition of the colored youth of the nation (these youths were also provided assistance in the form of funds and grants).

Express appropriations were made for relief of freedmen or destitute colored people in the District of Columbia and for the establishment of a hospital for freedmen in the District. No comparable federal programs existed—or were established—for whites.[11]

Another significant development occurred in 1875 when Congress enacted the Civil Rights Act.[12] This act, which was the first public accommodations act,[13] provided that all citizens were "entitled to the full and equal enjoyment of the accommodations, advantages, facilities, and privileges" of public conveyances, theaters, and places of "public amusement. . . ."[14] However, this Act was declared unconstitutional by the United States Supreme Court in *The Civil Rights Cases*.[15] Concluding that Congress had no power under either the Thirteenth or Fourteenth Amendments to enact the 1875 Act, the Court held that the Fourteenth Amendment did not authorize Congress to "create a code of municipal law for the regulations of private rights."

The Supreme Court's stance on racial matters in the late nineteenth century is perhaps best illustrated by its ruling in two well known and oft-discussed cases. In *Dred Scott v. Sandford*,[16] the Court declared that the Constitution itself pointed "directly and specifically to the negro race as a separate class of persons, and show clearly that they were not regarded as a portion of the people or citizens of the Government then formed."[17] In support of this statement, Chief Justice Taney's opinion for the Court stated that the Declaration of Independence, state and Congressional legislation, and federal executive action all led to the result reached by the Court.[18]

Near the close of the century in 1896, the Court decided in *Plessy v. Ferguson*[19] that the "separate but equal" approach to race relations was constitutional. Holding that a Louisiana statute providing for separate facilities for black and white passengers on trains did not violate the Fourteenth Amendment's ban on unequal protection of the law, the Court set forth its understanding of the Fourteenth Amendment: that amendment "was undoubtedly to enforce the absolute equality of the two races before the law, but in the nature of things it could not have been intended to abolish distinctions based upon color, or to enforce social, as distinguished from political, equality, or a commingling of the two races upon terms unsatisfactory to either."[20] Further, the Court made it clear that an African American was "not lawfully entitled to the reputation of being a white man."[21] Moreover, the Court concluded that it could not "say that a law which authorizes or even requires the separation of the two races in public conveyance is unreasonable. . . ."[22] This odious precedent persisted as the judicial foundation for constitutional color-consciousness and apartheid until 1954.[23]

The foregoing discussion reveals two significant points. First, the social and legal history of this nation is one which contains specific illustrations of race- and color-conscious constitutional provisions, and Supreme Court decisions which recognized and acted upon distinctions between whites and African Americans. Second, race- and color-conscious Presidential orders and Congressional statutes—including the Emancipation Proclamation, the Freedmen's Bureau Act, and the Civil Rights Act of 1875—serve as persuasive historical evidence supporting the proposition that preferential treatment of African Americans is not simply a contemporary development never before seen in this society. Rather, the nation's judicial, legislative, and political history is replete with examples of such treatment of African Americans as a legal remedy and response to racial discrimination and the vestiges of slavery.

The phrase *affirmative action* does not appear in the items discussed above. However, many of the items fall within the definition of affirmative action.[24] Governmental actions which sought to provide opportunities to individuals based on their membership in the African American group are affirmative acts taken for the purpose of affording preferential treatment to those individuals.

Of course, while these developments provide a backdrop for contemporary affirmative action analysis, it is conceded that the record of pre-1900 American law and jurisprudence does not answer the many questions relative to current preferential treatment of minorities. Nevertheless, it must be recognized that there is some linkage (direct or attenuated, depending upon one's view of affirmative action) between the history and disparate treatment of minorities, and the constitutionality and substance of a public policy which recognizes and seeks to remedy the effects of that history. Suffice it to say that the degree of the relevance and impact of that history are themselves the subject of debate—a debate capsulized in the current argument of some opponents of affirmative action that "innocent victims" should not be required to bear the brunt of remediation efforts for historical discrimination.

The New Deal Era. De jure segregation on the basis of race was a fundamental feature of American society which extended into the twentieth century and into another crucial period of United States history—the New Deal era. Among the legislative initiatives undertaken during that period to address the Depression and post-Depression economy, Congress enacted laws which contained anti-discrimination provisions. For example, the Unemployment Relief Act of 1933 provided that "in employing citizens for the purposes of this act, no discrimination shall be made on account of race, color, or creed. . . ."[25] In addition, the Civilian Conservation Corps,[26] the Civilian Pilot Training Act,[27] and the National Youth Administration Appropriation Act,[28] while providing for separate but purportedly equal treatment of African Americans, contained similar non-discrimination provisions.[29] Furthermore, prohibitions against employment discrimination on the basis of race were also found in regulations implementing the National Industrial Recovery Act of 1933, the Federal Housing Act of 1937, and the Public Works Administration's mandatory use of quotas in 1934.[30]

President Franklin Delano Roosevelt in 1941 issued the first executive order (Executive Order 8802) which prohibited employment discrimination on the basis of race and mandated the use of affirmative action in employment.[31] That order provided that the policy of the United States prohibited discrimination in employment because of "race, creed, color, or national origin,"[32] and further provided that employers and unions were to "provide for the full and equitable participation of all workers in defense industries without discrimination."[33] Although this order did not use the words *affirmative action*, the purpose of the order was one which called for an end to discrimination and a positive effort by management and labor to increase the employment opportunities of minorities and protected group members.

It is noteworthy that the phrase *affirmative action* was in fact contained in New Deal-Era federal legislation. The National Labor Relations Act of 1935 (NLRA)[34] expressly stated that the National Labor Relations Board (NLRB) was empowered to remedy unfair labor practices by the issuance of cease and desist, and reinstatement and back pay orders, and by ordering *affirmative action*[35] in effectuating the policies of the NLRA. Although the NLRB's authority is limited by the statutory requirement that its orders must effectuate the policies of the NLRA and must be remedial, not punitive,[36] the principle is one of governmental flexibility and authority to require affirmative acts by a party who has violated the law, so that an unlawful act is effectively remedied. Such affirmative acts include, *inter alia*, the employment of individuals who were not hired or were discharged for discriminatory reasons,[37] and, in cases involving unfair labor practice strikes, the reinstatement of striking employees even where the discharge of striker replacements would be necessary.[38] Interestingly, there is little or no evidence that the use and principle of affirmative action in the NLRA context had any bearing on or resemblance to the use of those words in the context of preferential treatment of minorities and women.[39]

The Brown Decision. In 1954, the Supreme Court addressed the issue of racial segregation in one of the most significant decisions in the Court's history, *Brown v. Board of Education of Topeka, Shawnee County, Kansas.*[40] In his opinion for a unanimous Court, Chief Justice Earl Warren stated that "we cannot turn the clock back . . . to 1896 when *Plessy v. Ferguson* was written."[41] Holding that segregation on the basis of race in public schools violated the Equal Protection Clause of the Fourteenth Amendment, the Chief Justice concluded that to separate black school children from others "of similar age and qualifications solely because of their race generates a feeling of inferiority as to their status in the community that may affect their hearts and minds in a way unlikely ever to be undone."[42] Expressly rejecting *Plessy v. Ferguson*,[43] the Court held that "[s]eparate educational facilities are inherently unequal."[44]

Thus, *Brown* serves as yet another fount for affirmative action, for the Court's opinion, read broadly, stands for the proposition that racial discrimination is a harmful feature of this society which must be remedied.[45] *Brown* presents and supports an argument of color-blind application of the Constitution in the sense that the benefits of society (there, public education) must be distributed and made available without any distinctions based on race, and that legal relief must be ordered to address and rectify any contravention of that principle. Such relief is inextricably intertwined with race, for the implementation of a remedy must take into account the adverse effects of the violation on those discriminated against, and formulate some plan or scheme which will effectively address the violation of the law. Whether, and how, these notions apply in the employment setting are questions which lurk in the background as the courts and agencies continue to grapple with the affirmative action question.

In 1960, the Committee on Government Contracts, chaired by then-Vice President Richard M. Nixon, issued a report to President Dwight D. Eisenhower which concluded, *inter alia*, that employer indifference to establishing a *"positive policy*" of non-discrimination hinders qualified applicants and employees from being hired and promoted on the basis of equality."[46] In the following year, President John F. Kennedy issued Executive Order 10925 in which, apparently, the words *affirmative action* first appeared in the context of race discrimination and employment.[47] That order, which established the President's Committee on Equal Employment Opportunity, provided that government contractors had to "take affirmative action to ensure that applicants ... and employees ... are treated ... without regard to race, creed, color, or national origin."[48]

Title VII of the Civil Rights Act of 1964[49] followed shortly thereafter. Section 706(g) of that statute, which provides that courts "may order such affirmative action as may be appropriate,"[50] is the subject and focus of important Supreme Court litigation, as detailed in Chapter 2.

In the year following the passage of Title VII, President Johnson issued Executive Order 11246.[51] That order, as amended, provides in pertinent part that government contracting agencies shall include in every government contract an agreement that the contractor will (1) not discriminate against any employee or applicant because of race, color, religion, or national origin, and (2) take affirmative action to ensure that applicants are employed and treated during employment without regard to their protected status. In addition, Executive Order 11246 granted authority to the federal Secretary of Labor to administer the order and ensure nondiscrimination in employment by federal contractors. The Office of Federal Contract Compliance Programs (OFCCP) was empowered to administer and enforce the order.[52]

Two significant employment discrimination statutes passed by Congress in the 1970s are relevant to this discussion. The Rehabilitation Act of 1973[53] requires federal contractors to take affirmative action to hire and promote qualified handicapped persons. And the Vietnam-Era Veterans' Readjustment Assistance Act of 1974[54] requires affirmative action by federal contractors in hiring and promoting Viet Nam-Era veterans as well as disabled veterans.

THEORIES OF EMPLOYMENT DISCRIMINATION AND THEIR RELEVANCE TO AFFIRMATIVE ACTION

Proponents of affirmative action typically argue that race-conscious remedies and treatment are necessary to eradicate the legacy of slavery and *de jure* and *de facto* discrimination. Adopting an "equal achievement" or "equal result" approach to affirmative action, they argue that affirmative action initiatives are presumptively valid, and that protected *groups* should be represented in the workplace in exact or approximate proportion to their availability in, or composition of, the relevant labor force.[55] Such an approach comports with a model of group justice in which discrimination, viewed from a group-based perspective, is to be addressed for remediation purposes by approaches which extend to the group and to the group's members.[56]

Opponents of group-based race-conscious treatment generally argue that such treatment is *per se* invalid.[57] Insisting upon a "color-blind" society and approach to enforcement of fair employment laws and the Constitution, individuals in this camp argue that all persons are entitled to "equal treatment," "equal opportunity," or "equal process" without regard to race or other protected status.[58] That approach, which is consistent with a model of individual justice in which any classification or practice based on race, sex, or membership in a protected group is disfavored,[59] recognizes no exceptions to anti-discrimination principles and is reflected in the affirmative action jurisprudence of several members of the current Supreme Court.

These opposing views, and their impact on judicial application and interpretation of Title VII and the Constitution, are discussed below.

The Disparate Treatment, Equal Process Analysis

As noted above, Title VII of the Civil Rights Act of 1964[60] prohibits discrimination in employment on the basis of race, color, sex, creed, religion, or national origin.[61] Under a disparate treatment theory, which the Supreme Court has described as "the most easily understood type of discrimination,"[62] an employer "simply treats some people less favorably than others because of their race, color, religion, sex, or national origin. Proof of discriminatory motive is critical. . . . "[63] Thus, preferential or differential treatment of individuals because of their race runs afoul of the statutory prohibition.

In a recent article, Professor Paul Cox posited four justifications for the disparate treatment theory: (1) race and gender classifications are *a priori* wrong; (2) race classifications may be founded on prejudice or hostility; (3) race and gender, when used as proxies for other characteristics deemed to be legitimate considerations, are inaccurate generalizations cast as irrebuttable presumptions; and (4) such classifications, even if used as accurate proxies, generate psychological harm and stigmatize disfavored persons.[64] Race, gender, or other protected status may not be used as employment criteria which directly cause an employment decision.[65] Thus, disparate treatment theory is "concerned with a narrow aspect of the *process* of employer decision making, rather than the *results* reached through that process."[66]

McDonnell Douglas Corporation v. Green[67] is the seminal case articulating and applying the disparate treatment theory under Title VII. Addressing the order and allocation of proof in an action alleging unlawful racial discrimination in hiring, a unanimous Supreme Court set forth the now familiar rules applicable to cases where there is no direct evidence of discrimination:

The complainant . . . must carry the initial burden under the statute of establishing a *prima facie* case of racial discrimination. This may be done by showing (i) that he belongs to a racial minority; (ii) that he applied and was qualified for a job for which the employer was seeking applicants; (iii) that, despite his qualifications, he was rejected; and (iv) that, after his rejection, the position remained open and the employer continued to seek applicants from persons of complainant's qualifications.[68]

If that initial burden was met by the plaintiff, the burden would then shift to the employer to "articulate some legitimate, nondiscriminatory reason for the employee's rejection."[69] Where that burden is met by the employer, the plaintiff must then show that the employer's articulated reason was a pretext for discrimination.[70] At all times, the burden of persuasion remains with the plaintiff.[71]

As can be seen, disparate treatment theory focuses on the employer's treatment of individuals, and requires that the process used in making employment decisions must be one of like treatment which is not influenced by race or gender.[72] Suppose, for example, that two individuals (one African American and one white, or one male and one female) apply for the same position with an employer. Under disparate treatment theory, the employer is required to treat both individuals equally (i.e., may not treat them in a dissimilar fashion because of their race);[73] must make available the same opportunity for employment to both individuals; and must follow the same process in considering both individuals for possible employment. Where any decision reached by the employer is based on grounds or factors independent of those grounds proscribed by Title VII, the statute is not violated and the employer has not engaged in unlawful disparate treatment.[74]

The Disparate Impact, Equal Results Analysis

Disparate treatment doctrine must be distinguished from Title VII disparate impact doctrine. In *Griggs v. Duke Power Company*,[75] the Supreme Court held that an employer's use of a high school completion requirement and general intelligence test violated Title VII, because neither requirement was shown to be demonstrably related to successful performance of the jobs for which the requirements were used.[76] Writing for the Court, Chief Justice Warren E. Burger declared that "[u]nder the Act, practices, procedures, or tests neutral on their face, and even neutral in terms of intent, cannot be maintained if they operate to 'freeze' the status quo of prior discriminatory employment practices."[77] In another passage, the Chief Justice stated:

[Title VII] proscribes not only overt discrimination but also practices that are fair in form, but discriminatory in operation. *The touchstone is business necessity.* If an employment practice which operates to exclude Negroes cannot be shown to be related to job performance, the practice is prohibited.[78]

Thus, the *Griggs* Court held that an employer could violate Title VII even in the absence of any intent to discriminate. "[G]ood intent or absence of discriminatory intent does not redeem employment procedures or testing mechanisms that operate as 'built-in-headwinds' for minority groups and are unrelated to measuring job capability."[79] The Court made it clear that Congress "directed the thrust of the Act to the *consequences* of employment practices, not simply the motivation."[80] Moreover, stated the Court, "Congress has placed on the employer the burden of showing that any given requirement must have a manifest relationship to the employment in question."[81]

Griggs has been hailed by some commentators as the most important judicial interpretation and contribution to the enforcement of Title VII.[82] The Court's decision and subsequent rulings[83] made it clear that the "touchstone" was business necessity, a requirement which called for a demonstration that the challenged employment criteria was job-related or had a "manifest relationship" to the employment in question.[84]

Under the *Griggs* analysis, the job-relatedness-manifest relationship requirement came into play only after a plaintiff had made a *prima facie* showing of disparate impact. Such proof, which is invariably quantitative,[85] could have been established by a statistical test which showed that a criterion or practice used by an employer to screen candidates for hiring or promotion was disproportionately excluding members of a group protected by Title VII. In assessing the question of exclusion and disparate impact, the racial and sexual composition of the relevant work force assumed critical significance. Suppose, for example, that minorities comprise 40 percent of the relevant geographical area and that the percentage of an employer's unskilled labor force was 10 percent. Under *Griggs*, a plaintiff could utilize those statistics to establish a *prima facie* case of disparate impact.

As a result of *Griggs*, employers also had to be cognizant of federal regulations, such as the Uniform Guidelines on Employee Selection Procedures,[86] that could be applied to selection procedures to determine whether those procedures had an adverse impact on minorities. Under the Uniform Guidelines, a test or other selection device will be deemed to have an adverse or disparate impact if it has a "selection rate for any race, sex, or ethnic group which is less than four-fifths (or 80 percent) of the rate for the group with the highest rate. . . ."[87] An example given by Sobol and Ellard[88] illustrates this point. Suppose that four hundred of five hundred white applicants (80 percent) are selected for employment. Suppose further that two hundred of five hundred black applicants (40 percent) are chosen. Dividing the black selection rate of 40 percent by the white selection rate of 80 percent results in an impact ratio of 50 percent, a figure which is less than the

80 percent bench mark of the Uniform Guidelines. Thus, adverse impact would be established.

The impact of *Griggs* and the focus on groups, and the percentage of members of those groups in the work force, had a predictable effect on employers which is directly related to, and provides justification for, affirmative action. As noted by Professor Blumrosen:

... *Griggs* provides the underlying justification for race conscious affirmative action programs under Title VII. Identification of "disparate impact" requires that employers be race conscious. Once disparate impact is identified, voluntary action to ameliorate it is necessary to avoid liability in the absence of business necessity. Affirmative personnel actions taken to *comply* with *Griggs* could not be held to violate the statutory restrictions on preferential treatment in Title VII.[89]

Recent decisions by the Supreme Court, while reaffirming the disparate impact theory, signal a fresh look at, and different view of, the underlying assumptions of the *Griggs* doctrine.[90] In 1988, the Court in *Watson v. Fort Worth Bank and Trust*[91] held that the disparate impact analysis may be applied to subjective or discretionary selection processes.[92] In so holding, a plurality of the Court also concluded that the risk of quotas and preferential treatment of minorities— measures which may have been taken to ensure that plaintiffs could not establish a *prima facie* case of disparate impact—required "a fresh and somewhat closer examination of the constraints that operate to keep [disparate impact] analysis within its proper bounds."[93]

If quotas and preferential treatment become the only cost-effective means of avoiding expensive litigation and potentially catastrophic liability, such measures will be widely adopted. The prudent employer will be careful to ensure that its programs are discussed in euphemistic terms, but will be equally careful to ensure that the quotas are met.[94]

The *Watson* plurality then determined that a disparate impact plaintiff should be responsible for isolating and identifying the "specific employment practices that are allegedly responsible for any observed statistical disparities."[95] If the practices are identified, the plaintiff must then show that the practices caused the exclusion of protected group members. If that is established, the employer would then be required to produce evidence that its "employment practices are based on legitimate business reasons. . . . "[96] To counter the employer's showing, stated the plurality, the plaintiff would be required to show that other tests or selection devices would serve the employer's legitimate business interests without the undesirable racial effect.[97]

Thus, the *Watson* plurality would increase the complexity of a plaintiff's initial showing of disparate impact by requiring specific isolation of allegedly unlawful practices and causation, a showing which required more than an initial presentation of group statistics relative to the relevant population and the employer's work force. At the same time, the plurality would reduce the employer's burden from one of persuasion to one of production of evidence that its practices are based on lawful business reasons.

In the following term, the Court returned to the burden allocation issue addressed in *Watson* in *Wards Cove Packing Company, Inc. v. Atonio*.[98] There, Justice Anthony M. Kennedy joined the *Watson* plurality and provided the fifth vote for a significant change in the burden allocation formula applicable to disparate impact cases.

The disparate impact issue addressed in *Atonio* involved a claim by minority, unskilled cannery workers that the employers' hiring and promotion policies were responsible for racial stratification in the work force, and that the cannery workers had been denied non-cannery jobs which were skilled and filled predominately with white employees. The United States Court of Appeals for the Ninth Circuit, holding, *inter alia*, that the plaintiffs had made out a *prima facie* case of disparate impact, relied solely on the employees' statistics which showed a high percentage of minority cannery workers and a low percentage of minority non-cannery workers.

The Supreme Court held that the Ninth Circuit's statistical analysis was erroneous. The "proper comparison [is] between the racial composition of the [at issue jobs] and the racial composition of the qualified . . . population in the relevant labor market."[99] Thus, the Ninth Circuit's comparison of the "internal" statistics relative to the employers' work force was flawed, in the Supreme Court's view, because the cannery work force did not reflect the pool of qualified job applicants or the qualified population in the labor force.[100]

The Court urged that the Ninth Circuit's theory would "mean that any employer who had a segment of his work force that was—for some reason—racially imbalanced, could be haled into court and forced to engage in the expensive and time-consuming task of defending the 'business necessity' of the methods used to select the other members of his work force."[101] In that circumstance, stated the Court, employers would adopt racial quotas to ensure that no portion of the work force deviated in racial composition from other portions of the work force; "this is a result that Congress expressly rejected in drafting Title VII."[102] Moreover, stated the Court, as long as there were no barriers or practices deterring qualified minorities from applying for cannery positions, the employers' selection mechanism probably did not operate with a disparate impact on minorities.[103]

Remanding the case for further proceedings, the Court addressed the questions of causation and the burden of proof applicable in disparate impact cases. Adopting the *Watson* plurality's statement of the law,[104] the Court concluded that a plaintiff "must demonstrate that it is the application of a specific or particular employment practice that has created the disparate impact under attack."[105] The Court opined that, on remand, the plaintiffs would be required to specifically show that each challenged practice (nepotism, separate hiring channels, rehire preferences, and so on) had a significantly disparate impact.

Noting that some would complain that this causation requirement is unduly burdensome on Title VII plaintiffs, the Court wrote that liberal discovery rules would give plaintiffs broad access to employer records which could be used to document their claims. In that regard, employers falling under the Uniform Guidelines on Employee Selection Procedures[106] are required to maintain records which would disclose the impact of its tests and selection procedures. Interestingly, seasonal jobs such as those held by the cannery workers in *Atonio* were exempt from certain record keeping requirements under the Uniform Guidelines.[107]

If the plaintiff meets the causation requirement, continued the *Atonio* Court, the case would shift to the employer's business justification for the use of the challenged practices. The two components of this phase are (1) the justification an employer offers for the use of the practices, and (2) the availability of alternative practices to achieve the same business ends with less adverse impact. As to the first component, the Court stated that the touchstone "is a reasoned review of the employer's justification for the use of the challenged practice."[108] "A mere insubstantial justification in this regard will not suffice. . . . At the same time, though, there is no requirement that the challenged practice be 'essential' or 'indispensable' to the employer's business for it to pass muster: this degree of scrutiny would be almost impossible for most employers to meet, and would result in a host of evils."[109]

Further, the Court held that the employers carried the burden of production of evidence for business justification, with the burden of persuasion remaining with the plaintiffs. In so holding, the Court expressly stated that this rule for disparate impact cases conforms to the rule in disparate treatment cases: that the plaintiff bears the burden of disproving an employer's assertion that an adverse employment action was based solely on legitimate, nondiscriminatory grounds.[110] The Court acknowledged that "some of our earlier decisions can be read as suggesting otherwise."[111] To the extent that those cases "speak of an employer's 'burden of proof' with respect to a legitimate business justification defense . . . they should have been understood to mean an employer's production—but not persuasion—burden."[112]

As to the second component, the Court opined that the plaintiffs could still prevail even when employers established a business justification defense. To prevail, the plaintiffs would be required to show that other tests or selection devices would serve the employers' interests without a similarly undesirable racial effect.[113] Those alternative practices "must be equally effective as [the employers'] chosen hiring procedures in achieving [the employers'] legitimate employment goals."[114] Moreover, stated the Court, cost factors and other burdens of the proposed alternative devices would be relevant in determining whether the alternatives are equally effective.[115] If equally effective devices are proposed and employers refuse to adopt the alternatives, "such a refusal would belie a claim . . . that their incumbent practices are being employed for nondiscriminatory reasons."[116]

As foreshadowed by *Watson*, *Atonio* represents a significant change in Title VII disparate impact doctrine. As noted above, *Griggs* and its progeny provided the underlying justification for preferential treatment of minorities and women under Title VII, because employers had to remain alert to the fact that statistical disparities in their work forces could establish a *prima facie* case of disparate impact discrimination. The prospects of such litigation, judicial review of the employer's personnel practices and procedures, and the employer's burden of establishing a business necessity for its selection processes, were matters that called for an ongoing review and awareness of the composition of the work force. Hiring and promotion decisions which favored minorities and women, and took into account race or sex, could be defended on the legal ground that Title VII required the employment of a certain level of qualified individuals from those groups.

The same concerns applied to federal contractors to the extent that the Office of Federal Contract Compliance Programs' concept of underutilization of minorities and women in a particular work force was based on, or patterned after, the *Griggs* disparate impact model.[117] Notions of group representation in the work force underlie the OFCCP's rules and regulations governing federal contractors and their eligibility to obtain federal contracts. Deficiencies in job categories, measured by statistical representation and numerical goals and timetables, flowed from the *Griggs* model.

At this juncture, any prediction with regard to the impact of *Atonio* on affirmative action would be both speculative and premature. The legal and practical questions which bear watching as the courts apply the *Atonio* analysis[118] are whether, and to what extent, employers view *Atonio* as a reason or signal to diminish or even discontinue any affirmative action initiatives currently in place at their companies. The answers to those questions depend on the litigation aversion preferences of a particular employer, and that employer's view of its role and responsibilities vis-a-vis the affirmative action question. Where a commitment to affirmative action is based on operational realities and the level of qualified minorities and women in a relevant geographical area, *Atonio* may have limited impact. But, where an employer's affirmative action policies were implemented due to an effort to insulate the entity from disparate impact liability, *Atonio* may remove a significant part of the legal incentive for affirmative action and result in the diminution or discontinuation of preferential treatment measures at such workplaces. Again, an accurate assessment of *Atonio's* impact in this area must await further developments.

Constitutional Analysis

Prior to 1989, there was no definitive resolution of the level of scrutiny applicable to race-conscious affirmative action measures taken by governmental bodies which implicated various portions of the Constitution. It was clear that racial classifications which operated to disadvantage African Americans and other racial minorities were suspect classifications subject to strict scrutiny by the courts.[119] No such clarity existed, however, with respect to the level of scrutiny applicable to remedial or "benign" race-conscious measures taken for the purpose of providing advantages and employment opportunities to racial minorities.[120]

City of Richmond v. J. A. Croson Company[121] (discussed in detail in Chapter 5) resolved the level of scrutiny issue in cases involving state and local governments. There, the Supreme Court held, *inter alia*, that strict scrutiny must be applied to *all* such governmental classifications by race. The *Croson* Court reviewed a city minority business set-aside plan which reserved 30 percent of public contracts to African Americans and other identified minorities. Writing for the Court, Justice O'Connor stated that absent "searching judicial inquiry into the justification for race-based measures, there is simply no way of determining what classifications are 'benign' or 'remedial' and what classifications are in fact motivated by illegitimate notions of racial inferiority or simple racial politics."[122] The Court held that the "standard of review under the Equal Protection Clause is not dependent on the race of those burdened or benefited by a particular classification."[123] In the Court's view, strict scrutiny would "smoke out" illegitimate uses of race by legislative bodies, and would ensure that the means chosen by the governmental body " 'fit' the compelling goal so closely that there is little or no possibility that the motive for the classification was illegitimate racial prejudice or stereotype."[124] In separate opinions, Justices Kennedy[125] and Scalia[126] agreed with the O'Connor analysis.[127] The impact of *Croson* is discussed in Chapter 5.

On June 27, 1990, the Court in *Metro Broadcasting, Inc. v. FCC*,[128] by a vote of 5–4 (Justices Brennan, White, Marshall, Blackmun, and Stevens in the majority), held that certain minority preference policies adopted by the Federal Communications Commission (FCC) did not violate nonminorities' rights to equal protection under the Fifth Amendment.[129] Initially noting that the FCC preference policies had been "specifically approved—indeed, mandated—by Congress,"[130] the Court held that benign race-conscious measures mandated by Congress "even if these measures are not 'remedial' in the sense of being designed to compensate victims of past governmental or societal discrimination— are constitutionally permissible to the extent that they serve important governmental objectives within the power of Congress and are substantially related to achievement of those objectives."[131]

Applying the aforementioned standard of review (which is a lower standard than the strict scrutiny standard applied in *Croson*), the Court first reasoned that the FCC's preference policies served the governmental objective of broadcast diversity and was a sufficient basis for the FCC's minority ownership policies.[132] Second, the Court concluded that the minority ownership policies were substantially related to the achievement of the government's interests. In so concluding, the Court accorded deference to the Congress' and FCC's judgment that there was a nexus between minority ownership and programming diversity.[133]

The result reached by the Court in *Metro Broadcasting* surprised many who awaited the Court's decision. Justice White, a member of the conservative ma-

jority in *Croson* and other affirmative action cases, voted with the Court's liberal
bloc and provided the swing vote for the validation of the FCC's policies. The
Court's ruling also made it clear that federal government affirmative action
measures are not analyzed under the same test applied to state and local government programs. Further, and significantly, the Court announced that Congressional race-conscious measures need not be remedial and tied to the compensation
of victims of discrimination. Thus, structural affirmative action—affirmative
action that focuses on the future and is taken for the purpose of promoting racial
diversity as a matter of affirmative public policy—has been endorsed by the
Court.

BAKKE

Before turning to the Supreme Court's affirmative action in employment decisions in the next chapter, the Court's seminal decision in *Regents of the University of California v. Bakke*[134] merits our attention. There, the Court held that
a special admissions program at the medical school of the University of California
at Davis, which reserved sixteen of one hundred positions in a class for "disadvantaged" minority students, was illegal, and ordered the admission of Alan
Bakke, a white applicant, into the medical school.

Announcing the judgment of the Court and authoring an opinion, Justice
Powell concluded, *inter alia*, that the special admissions program was undeniably
a classification based on race and ethnic background. "[W]hite applicants could
compete only for 84 seats in the entering class, rather than the 100 open to
minority applicants."[135] He noted that racial and ethnic discrimination of any
sort "are inherently suspect and thus call for the most exacting judicial examination. . . . "[136]

Reviewing the medical school's special admission program, Justice Powell
examined the purported purpose of the medical school's program. First, he stated
that if the purpose was to assure a specified percentage of a racial or ethnic
group within the student body, this "discrimination for its own sake" was
unconstitutional.[137] Second, Justice Powell wrote, a purpose of helping victims
of "societal discrimination" would not justify a classification that imposed disadvantages on nonminorities. Third, he rejected the argument that the purpose
of the program was to improve the delivery of health care services to under-
served communities, finding no evidence in the record supporting that purported
goal. Finally, Justice Powell concluded that the goal of the attainment of a
diverse student body was a constitutionally permissible goal for an institution
of higher learning—a goal grounded in the First Amendment. Powell cited the
experiences, outlooks, and ideas that a qualified medical student with a particular
ethnic, geographic, culturally advantaged or disadvantaged background could
bring to a professional school of medicine.[138]

In Powell's view, the problem with the special admissions program was its
focus solely on ethnic diversity. "[R]ace or ethnic background may be deemed

a 'plus' in a particular applicant's file, yet it does not insulate the individual from comparison with all other candidates for the available seats."[139] Where race is considered along with other factors (e.g., talents, maturity, a history of overcoming disadvantage), an unsuccessful applicant will not have been foreclosed from consideration for a seat because of color. Accordingly, Justice Powell concluded that a state could legitimately and constitutionally utilize a properly devised admissions program involving the "competitive consideration" of race and ethnic origin.[140]

Four justices (Brennan, White, Marshall, and Blackmun) concurred in the judgment in part and dissented in part. Agreeing with Justice Powell that the university could utilize race-conscious programs in the future, they concluded, *inter alia*, that racial classifications are not *per se* invalid under the Fourteenth Amendment. Further concluding that the medical school's goal of admitting disadvantaged minority students was sufficiently important to justify the use of race-conscious admissions criteria, and that the program was to address past discrimination, the four justices found no harm to nonminorities comparable to that imposed on racial minorities by exclusion or separation on grounds of race.[141] Thus, they would hold that the medical school program was constitutional and would not have ordered the admission of Bakke to the medical school.

Concurring in the judgment in part and dissenting in part, Justice Stevens (joined by Chief Justice Burger, and Justices Stewart and Rehnquist) concluded that the question of whether race could ever be a factor in an admissions policy was not at issue. Avoiding the constitutional issue and deciding the case on statutory grounds, Stevens urged that Title VI of the Civil Rights Act of 1964 applied.[142] The special admissions program violated Title VII by excluding Bakke because of his race, wrote Stevens, and Bakke should have been admitted to the medical school.[143]

Although Justice Powell announced the Court's judgment, a majority of the Court did not support the substantive sections of his opinion. On the questions of the constitutionality of the admissions program, Powell was outvoted four to one.[144] Powell was also the only justice calling for strict scrutiny. Thus, even though Bakke was admitted (by Powell's vote and the statutory analysis of Stevens, Burger, Stewart, and Rehnquist) *Bakke* discussed many of the issues which would arise in subsequent cases but did not definitively resolve the affirmative action question.

CONCLUSION

As set forth above, affirmative action does not exist in a vacuum. Rather, history, legal precedent, and statutes form the backdrop against which affirmative action must be viewed. None of these developments, standing alone or in conjunction, provides the definitive analysis or answer to the question of whether affirmative action is lawful and constitutional. That difficult question is one which must be answered by the courts through judicial interpretation of Title

VII and the Constitution. As we shall see in the next chapter, the Supreme Court has attempted to answer that question in a series of affirmative actions in employment decisions.

NOTES

1. Jones, *The Origins of Affirmative Action*, 21 U. CAL. DAVIS L. REV. 383, 385 (1988).

2. Jones, *The Genesis and Present Status of Affirmative Action in Employment: Economic, Legal, and Political Realities*, 70 IOWA L. REV. 901, 903 (1985); Jones, *supra* note 1, at 389.

3. *See* Jones, *supra* note 1, at 387 ("It is only recently that . . . programs have been artfully attacked as 'reverse discrimination' and labelled undesirable, illegal, and unconstitutional."). *See generally* Wright, *Color-Blind Theories and Color-Conscious Remedies*, 47 U. CHI. L. REV. 213 (1980).

4. Jones, *supra* note 1, at 387.

5. Proclamation of January 1, 1863, No. 17, 12 Stat. 1268 (1863).

6. *See* D. BELL, RACE, RACISM AND AMERICAN LAW 6 (2d ed. 1980).

7. U.S. Const., Am. XIII.

8. U.S. Const., Am. XIV.

9. U.S. Const., Am. XV.

10. *See generally* Act of July 16, 1866, ch. 200, 14 Stat. 173.

11. Jones, *supra* note 1, at 390. For a discussion of the Freedmen Bureau Laws, *see* Schnapper, *Affirmative Action and the Legislative History of the Fourteenth Amendment*, 71 VA. L. REV. 753 (1985).

12. *See* Ch. 114, §§ 3–5, 18 Stat. 336, 337 (1875).

13. Jones, *supra* note 1, at 391.

14. *See supra* note 12.

15. 109 U.S. 3 (1883).

16. 60 U.S. (19 How.) 393 (1857).

17. *Id.* at 405.

18. *Id.* at 411.

19. 163 U.S. 537 (1896).

20. *Id.* at 544.

21. *Id.* at 549.

22. *Id.* at 550.

23. *See* Brown v. Board of Education, 347 U.S. 483 (1954), discussed *infra* at notes 40–44 and accompanying text.

24. *See supra* note 2 and accompanying text.

25. Ch. 17, § 1, 48 Stat. 22, 23 (1933).

26. Ch. 383, § 8, 50 Stat. 319, 320 (1937).

27. Ch. 244, § 2, 53 Stat. 855, 856 (1939).

28. Ch. 428, § 20, 54 Stat. 580, 583 (1940).

29. Jones, *supra* note 1, at 392.

30. *Id.* at 393.

31. *See* Jones, *supra* note 1 at 393–394, citing 3 C.F.R. 957 (1938–1939 Comp.).

32. *Id.*

33. *Id.*

34. Now codified as amended at 29 U.S.C. § 151 *et seq. See generally* R. GORMAN, BASIC TEXT ON LABOR LAW, UNIONIZATION AND COLLECTIVE BARGAINING (1976).

35. The phrase *affirmative action* has been retained in subsequent amendments to the NLRA (*see supra* note 34) and is currently set forth in 29 U.S.C. § 160(c).

36. *See* J. HUNSICKER, J. KANE, and P. WALTHER, NLRB REMEDIES FOR UNFAIR LABOR PRACTICES 1, 5–13 (Rev. ed. 1986). NLRB orders are enforced by the federal courts of appeals.

37. Such conduct is prohibited by 29 U.S.C. §§ 158(a)(3) and 158(b)(2).

38. *See, e.g.*, Mastro Plastics Corp. v. NLRB, 350 U.S. 270 (1956); NLRB v. Fotochrome, 343 F.2d 631 (2d Cir. 1964), *cert. denied*, 382 U.S. 833 (1965).

39. *See* Andritzky and Andritzky, *Affirmative Action: The Original Meaning*, 17 LINCOLN L. REV. 249, 252–255 (1987).

40. 347 U.S. 483 (1954). In another case decided the same day as *Brown*, the Court in Bolling v. Sharpe, 347 U.S. 497 (1954), held that segregation imposed upon African-American school children in the District of Columbia deprived them of their constitutional rights to due process under the Fifth Amendment to the Constitution.

41. 347 U.S. at 492.

42. *Id.* at 494.

43. *See supra* notes 19–22 and accompanying text.

44. 347 U.S. at 495.

45. *Id.*

46. President's Committee on Government Contracts, *Pattern For Progress: Final Report to President Eisenhower* (1960).

47. 3 C.F.R. 448, 450 (1959–1963 Comp.). Abe Fortas, an attorney, and later Justice of the United States Supreme Court, is credited by President Johnson with drafting Executive Order No. 10925. *See* Jones, *supra* note 1, at 395 and 395 n. 57. Fortas' work and collaboration with Johnson on a host of domestic and foreign policies is detailed in B. MURPHY, FORTAS: THE RISE AND RUIN OF A SUPREME COURT JUSTICE (1987).

James Farmer, former president of the Congress of Racial Equality, has stated that President Johnson coined the phrase *affirmative action* in response to Farmer's request in 1962 for a policy of "compensatory preferential treatment" for blacks. *See* J. FARMER, LAY BARE THE HEART 222 (1985). Farmer's account has been challenged. Andritzky and Andritzky, *supra* note 39, at 251 and 251 n. 6.

48. *See* 26 Fed. Reg. 5184 (1961).

49. *See* 42 U.S.C. § 2000e *et seq.*

50. 42 U.S.C. § 2000e–5(g).

51. 3 C.F.R. 339 (1964–1965 Comp.).

52. For a full discussion of Executive Order 11246, *see infra* Chapter 3.

53. 29 U.S.C. § 701 *et seq.*

54. 38 U.S.C. § 2021 *et seq.*

55. *See* Sullivan, *Sins of Discrimination: Last Term's Affirmative Action Cases*, 100 HARV. L. REV. 78, 81 (1986).

56. *See* Fallon and Weiler, Firefighters v. Stotts: *Conflicting Models of Racial Justice*, 1984 SUP CT. REV. 1. *See also* Kennedy, *Persuasion and Distrust: A Comment on the Affirmative Action Debate*, 99 HARV. L. REV. 1327, 1327 n. 1 (1986) (affirmative

action refers to "policies that provide preferences based explicitly on membership in a designated group").

57. Sullivan, *supra* note 55, at 81.

58. *See* B. SCHLEI and P. GROSSMAN, EMPLOYMENT DISCRIMINATION LAW 775 n. 4 (2d ed. 1983).

59. Fallon and Weiler, *supra* note 56.

60. 42 U.S.C. § 2000e *et seq.*

61. Of course, discrimination on other grounds (*e.g.*, age, physical or mental handicap, etc.) are also prohibited by other federal laws. *See, e.g.*, the Age Discrimination in Employment Act, 29 U.S.C. § 621 *et seq.*

62. Teamsters v. U.S., 431 U.S. 324, 335 n. 15 (1977).

63. *Id.*

64. Cox, *The Supreme Court, Title VII and "Voluntary" Affirmative Action—A Critique*, 21 IND. L. REV. 767, 774–775 (1988).

65. *Id.* at 776.

66. *Id.* at 783 (emphasis in original and added; footnote omitted).

67. 411 U.S. 793 (1973).

68. *Id.* at 802 (footnote omitted).

69. *Id.*

70. *Id.* at 805.

71. *Id.* For further discussion of Title VII disparate treatment doctrine, *see* USPS Board of Governors v. Aikens, 460 U.S. 711 (1983); Texas Dept. of Community Affairs v. Burdine, 450 U.S. 248 (1981); Furnco Construction Corp. v. Waters, 438 U.S. 567 (1978). *See also* Note, *Indirect Proof of Discriminatory Motive in Title VII Disparate Treatment Claims After* Aikens, 88 COLUM. L. REV. 1114 (1988).

72. *See* Cox, *supra* note 64, at 772.

73. Both African American and white employees are protected from discrimination based on their race. McDonald v. Santa Fe Trail Transportation Company, 427 U.S. 273 (1976).

74. Cox, *supra* note 64, at 776.

75. 401 U.S. 424 (1971).

76. *Id.* at 431.

77. *Id.* at 430.

78. *Id.* at 431 (emphasis added).

79. *Id.* at 432.

80. *Id.* (emphasis in original).

81. *Id.*

82. *See, e.g.*, Blumrosen, *The Legacy of* Griggs: *Social Progress and Subjective Judgments*, 63 CHI–KENT L. REV. 1, 3–4 (1987) (*Griggs* "infused Title VII with extraordinary influence," caused employers to revise many practices so as to include minorities and women, and "laid the foundation for affirmative action programs." [footnote omitted]); Chambers and Goldstein, *Title VII: The Continuing Challenge of Establishing Fair Employment Practices*, 49 LAW AND CONTEMP. PROBS. 9, 16 (1986) (*Griggs* is the most important judicial interpretation of Title VII); Norton, *Equal Employment Law: Crisis in Interpretation—Survival Against the Odds*, 62 TULANE L. REV. 681, 691–692 (1988); Rutherglen, *Disparate Impact Under Title VII: An Objective Theory of Discrimination*, 73 VA. L. REV. 1297, 1297 (1987).

83. *See* Albemarle Paper Company v. Moody, 442 U.S. 405 (1975) (employer did

not establish the job relatedness of its testing program); Dothard v. Rawlinson, 433 U.S. 321 (1977) (height and weight requirements for law enforcement officers not job related); New York City Transit Authority v. Beazer, 440 U.S. 568 (1979) (employer regulations prohibiting the employment of users of narcotics was job related and therefore lawful); Connecticut v. Teal, 457 U.S. 440 (1982) (written test used for promotion purposes had disparate impact on African-American employees even though "bottom line" percentages showed that a number of African Americans had been promoted).

84. Federal appellate courts also recognized the business necessity hold of *Griggs*. *See, e.g.*, Chambers v. Omaha Girls Club, Inc., 834 F.2d 697 (8th Cir. 1987); Griffin v. Board of Regents of Regency Universities, 795 F.2d 1281 (7th Cir. 1986); Banch v. Ballard, 795 F.2d 384 (5th Cir. 1986); Williams v. Colorado Springs, Colorado School District #6, 641 F.2d 835 (10th Cir. 1981).

85. *See, e.g., Dothard*, 433 U.S. at 329; D. BALDUS and J. COLE, STATISTICAL PROOF OF DISCRIMINATION 47 (1980).

86. 29 C.F.R. Part 1607. *See generally* B. SCHLEI and P. GROSSMAN, *supra* note 58, at 93; AD HOC GROUP ON UNIFORM SELECTION GUIDELINES, A PROFESSIONAL AND LEGAL ANALYSIS OF THE UNIFORM GUIDELINES ON EMPLOYEE SELECTION PROCEDURES (1981).

87. 29 C.F.R. § 1607.4(d). For criticism of this rule, *see* Shoben, *Differential Pass-Fail Rates in Employment Testing: Statistical Proof Under Title VII*, 91 HARV. L. REV. 793 (1978).

88. Sobol and Ellard, *Measures of Employment Discrimination: A Statistical Alternative to the Four-Fifths Rule*, 10 INDUS. REL. L. J. 381, 389 (1988).

89. Blumrosen, *supra* note 82, at 6 (emphasis in original; footnote omitted).

90. This development is discussed in Turner, *The Rehnquist Court and Title VII Disparate Impact Theory*: Atonio's *Burden Allocation and the Retreat From* Griggs, OHIO N. U. L. REV. (forthcoming in 1990).

91. 108 S.Ct. 2777 (1988).

92. For pre-*Watson* discussion of this subject, *see* Blumrosen, *supra* note 82; Blumrosen, *Strangers in Paradise*: Griggs v. Duke Power Co. *and the Concept of Employment Discrimination*, 71 MICH. L. REV. 59 (1972); Rigler, *Title VII and the Applicability of Disparate Impact Analysis to Subjective Selection Criteria*, 88 W. VA. L. REV. 25 (1985).

93. 108 S.Ct. at 2788 (footnote omitted).

94. *Id.*

95. *Id.*

96. *Id.* at 2790.

97. *Id.*

98. 109 S.Ct. 2115 (1989).

99. *Id.* at 2121 (quoting Hazelwood School District v. U.S., 433 U.S. 299, 308 (1977)).

100. *Id.* at 2122.

101. *Id.*

102. *Id.* (citations omitted).

103. *Id.* at 2122–2123.

104. *See supra* notes 91–97 and accompanying text.

105. 109 S.Ct. at 2124.

106. 29 C.F.R. Part 1607.

107. 109 S.Ct. at 2125 n. 10; *id.* at 2133 n. 20 (Stevens J., dissenting).

108. *Id.* at 2126.

109. *Id.* (citation omitted).

110. *Id.*, citing Texas Dept. of Community Affairs v. Burdine, 450 U.S. 248, 256–258 (1981).

111. *Id.*

112. *Id.* (citation omitted).

113. *Id.*

114. *Id.* at 2127 (citation omitted).

115. *Id.*

116. *Id.* Justice Stevens joined by Justices Brennan, Marshall, and Blackmun, dissented. He argued, *inter alia*, that the majority blurred the distinction between the disparate impact and disparate treatment doctrines. The latter doctrine requires a showing of intent, a burden which remains on the employee at all times. In contrast, stated Stevens, intent plays no role in disparate impact cases. In those cases, he argued, the employer's justification for its practices is an affirmative defense to any sufficient proof of disparate impact. *Id.* at 2131 (Stevens, J., dissenting).

In addition, Stevens wrote that the Court's redefinition of the employees' burden of proof was troubling. The requirement of isolating and identifying specific employment practices that allegedly caused statistical disparities was unwarranted, in his view, because the "act need not constitute the sole or primary cause of the harm." *Id.* at 2132 (citations omitted). "[P]roof of numerous questionable employment practices ought to fortify an employee's assertion that the practices caused racial disparities." *Id.* at 2133 (footnote omitted).

117. *See infra* Chapter 3.

118. For examples of lower court application of *Atonio*, *see* Allen v. Seidman, 881 F.2d 375 (7th Cir. 1989); Evans v. City of Evanston, 881 F.2d 382 (7th Cir. 1989).

119. *See, e.g.*, Korematsu v. U.S., 323 U.S. 214 (1944).

120. *See, e.g.*, Wygant v. Jackson Board of Education, 476 U.S. 267, 279–280 (1986) (plurality view that standard of review under Equal Protection Clause is not dependent on the race of those burdened or benefited by the classification); *id.* at 301–302 (Marshall, J., dissenting) (calling for heightened, but not strict, scrutiny).

121. 109 S.Ct 706 (1989).

122. *Id.* at 721.

123. *Id.* (citations omitted).

124. *Id.*

125. *See id.* at 734 (Kennedy, J. concurring in part and concurring in the judgment) ("I accept the . . . rule contained in Justice O'Connor's opinion, a rule based on the proposition that any racial preference must face the most rigorous scrutiny by the courts.").

126. *Id.* at 735 (Scalia, J., concurring in the judgment) ("I agree . . . with [the Court's] conclusion that strict scrutiny must be applied to all governmental classifications by race, whether or not its asserted purpose is 'remedial' or 'benign.' ")

127. Justices Marshall, Brennan and Blackmun dissented.

128. 58 U.S.L.W. 5053 (1990).

129. The Court reviewed two FCC policies. One policy provided for consideration of minority ownership as one of several factors in FCC comparative proceedings for licenses to operate new radio or television broadcast stations. *Id.* at 5055. The second policy, the

so-called "distress sale" policy, allowed a broadcaster whose license had been designated for a revocation hearing, or whose renewal application had been designated for hearing, to assign the license to a minority enterprise approved by the FCC. *Id.*

130. *Id.* at 5057. The Court determined tht FCC appropriations legislation prohibiting the FCC from spending any appropriated funds to examine or charge its minority ownership policies were binding because they were passed by both Houses of Congress and signed by the President. *Id.* at 5056, 5061, n. 29.

131. *Id.* at 5057.

132. *Id.* at 5058.

133. *Id.* at 5058–59.

134. 438 U.S. 265 (1978). *See* Tribe, *Perspectives on* Bakke: *Equal Protection, Procedural Fairness, or Structural Justice*, 93 HARV. L. REV. 864 (1979).

135. 438 U.S. at 289 (opinion of Powell, J.).

136. *Id.* at 291 (opinion of Powell, J.).

137. *Id.* at 307 (opinion of Powell, J.).

138. *Id.* at 314 (opinion of Powell, J.).

139. *Id.* at 317 (opinion of Powell, J.).

140. *Id.* at 320 (opinion of Powell, J.).

141. *Id* at 374 (opinion of Brennan, White, Marshall, and Blackmun, J.).

142. 42 U.S.C. § 2000d. *See* § 601 of Title VI ("No person . . . shall, on the ground of race, color, or national origin, be excluded from participation in, . . . or be subjected to discrimination under any program or activity receiving Federal financial assistance.").

143. 438 U.S. at 421 (Steven, J., concurring in the judgment in part and dissenting in part).

144. G. STONE, L. SEIDMAN, C. SUNSTEIN, and M. TUSHNET, CONSTITUTIONAL LAW 601 (1986).

2

The Supreme Court
and Affirmative Action
in Employment

The United States Supreme Court has addressed and grappled with the issue of affirmative action in employment in a series of cases decided between 1979 and 1989.[1] In those cases, the Court produced numerous and lengthy opinions on various aspects of voluntary and court-mandated race- and sex-conscious measures. The Court's affirmative action in employment jurisprudence is characterized by the absence of a majority view and cohesive exposition of the law governing the conduct of employers, unions, and employees in this area—a reality which reflects the difficult nature of the issues arising from the question of preferential treatment of minorities and women in the workplace.

This chapter examines and details the legal "history" and evolution of the Supreme Court's affirmative action in employment jurisprudence, an undertaking made all the more timely by the 1987 retirement of Justice Lewis F. Powell from the Court, and the February 1988 appointment of Justice Anthony M. Kennedy as Powell's replacement. As noted *infra*, the Court's 1989 affirmative action decisions, with Justice Kennedy in the majority, signaled a discernible shift in the Court's direction and an emerging conservative Court majority. After a thorough review and assessment of the Court's rulings, this chapter examines lower court applications of the Court's rulings, and sets forth guidelines for employers who must operate within and under the affirmative action doctrine as enunciated by the Supreme Court.

VOLUNTARY AFFIRMATIVE ACTION IN THE PRIVATE SECTOR: *WEBER*

The Supreme Court's first and seminal affirmative action in employment decision is *United Steelworkers of America v. Weber*.[2] A master labor agreement between the Steelworkers and Kaiser Aluminum Chemical Corp., entered into in 1974, contained an affirmative action plan which was designed to eliminate conspicuous racial imbalances in Kaiser's craft work forces. Under the plan, 50 percent of nine openings in in-plant craft training programs were reserved for African-American employees. Applying the plan at its Gramercy, Louisiana plant, the company established a training program in which at least 50 percent of the craft trainees were to be African American until the percentage of black skilled craft workers in the Gramercy plant approximated the percentage of blacks in the local labor force.[3]

In 1974, thirteen craft trainees were chosen from the company's work force. Seven trainees were black and six were white, with the most senior black employees selected for training having less seniority than several white workers who applied for the program and were rejected. One of the rejected white employees, Brian Weber, filed a class action alleging that the affirmative action program discriminated against white employees in violation of Title VII of the Civil Rights Act of 1964 (Title VII).[4]

Ruling in Weber's favor, the district court held that the affirmative action plan violated Title VII and permanently enjoined the company and the union from denying Weber, and similarly situated employees, access to the training program on the basis of race. Affirming the district court, the United States Court of Appeals for the Fifth Circuit held that racial preferences incidental to affirmative action plans violated Title VII's ban on racial discrimination.[5]

The Majority Decision

By a 5–2 vote,[6] the Supreme Court reversed the Fifth Circuit. Writing for the majority, Justice William Brennan (joined by Justices Potter Stewart, Byron White, Thurgood Marshall, and Harry Blackmun) emphasized the narrowness of the Court's inquiry.

The only question before us is the narrow statutory issue of whether Title VII forbids private employers and unions from voluntarily agreeing upon bona fide affirmative action plans that accord racial preferences in the manner and for the purpose provided in the Kaiser-USWA plan.[7]

Thus, *Weber* did not involve nor address the issues of the legality of the plan under the Equal Protection Clause of the Fourteenth Amendment, nor the permissible remedies which a court could order in remedying proven violations of Title VII.[8]

Under Justice Brennan's analysis, because the company-union affirmative action plan was "voluntarily adopted by private parties to eliminate traditional patterns of racial segregation,"[9] a non-literal construction of §§ 703(a) and (d) of Title VII was appropriate.[10] Looking to the "spirit" of Title VII (an exercise which has been criticized by scholars of statutory interpretation),[11] Justice Brennan opined that the legislative history and historical context of Title VII showed that an interpretation of Title VII that prohibited all race-conscious affirmative action would "bring about an end completely at variance with the purpose of the statute" and, therefore, had to be rejected.[12]

The legislative history of Title VII reviewed by Justice Brennan included statements by Senators Humphrey, Kennedy, and Clark concerning the economic plight of blacks and the increasing rate of black unemployment,[13] and the message to Congress by President Kennedy when he introduced the Civil Rights Act of 1963 (which also referred to employment opportunities for blacks in occupations traditionally closed to them).[14] "[I]t was to this problem that Title VII's prohibition against racial discrimination in employment was primarily addressed."[15] Moreover, stated Justice Brennan, the House of Representatives Report accompanying the Civil Rights Act provided that federal legislation dealing with discrimination against minorities would "create an atmosphere conducive to voluntary or local resolution of other forms of discrimination."[16] Brennan thus concluded that Title VII "cannot be interpreted as an absolute prohibition against all private, voluntary, race-conscious affirmative action efforts to hasten the elimination" of the vestiges of historical discrimination.[17]

The *Weber* majority then turned to § 703(j) of Title VII[18] to buttress its conclusion. That section provides that nothing contained in Title VII "shall be interpreted to *require* any employer . . . to grant preferential treatment . . . to any group" because of that group's race due to a racial balance in an employer's work force.[19]

The section does *not* state that "nothing in Title VII shall be interpreted to *permit*" voluntary affirmative efforts to correct racial imbalances. The natural inference is that Congress chose not to forbid all voluntary race-conscious affirmative action.[20]

In Justice Brennan's view, § 703(j) was designed to preserve traditional management prerogatives and avoid undue federal regulation of private employers. "Clearly, a prohibition against all voluntary, race-conscious, affirmative action efforts would disserve those ends."[21]

The *Weber* Court did not define the "line of demarcation between permissible and impermissible affirmative action plans."[22] Holding that the Kaiser-Steelworkers affirmative action plan fell on the permissible side of the line, the Court noted four aspects of the plan which would be examined by courts reviewing affirmative action plans in subsequent cases:

1. The plan did not "unnecessarily trammel the interests of the white employees."[23]

2. The plan did not require the discharge of white workers and their replacement with new black hires.[24]

3. The plan did not create "an absolute bar" to the advancement of white employees since one-half of craft trainees would be white.[25]

4. The plan was temporary, was not intended to maintain racial balance, and was intended to eliminate a "manifest racial imbalance."[26] Once the percentage of black skilled craft workers approximated the percentage of blacks in the local labor force, the racial preference would end.

Accordingly, the Court concluded that the voluntarily adopted affirmative action plans "designed to eliminate conspicuous racial imbalance in traditionally segregated job categories"[27] did not violate Title VII.[28]

The Rehnquist Dissent

Dissenting, Justice (now Chief Justice) William H. Rehnquist quoted from Orwell's *Nineteen Eighty-Four*[29] in describing the majority's opinion. In his view, Title VII prohibited all racial discrimination in employment and proscribed discriminatory preferences for any group, minority or majority. Opining that the employer had a self-interest in retaining lucrative government contracts, Rehnquist stated that the employer entered into the labor agreement's affirmative action plan under pressure from the Office of Federal Contract Compliance, and with hope of deterring the filing of employment discrimination claims by minorities.[30] This perspective, which reflects a distrust of the motivations and realities of affirmative action initiatives which Rehnquist and other justices would express in subsequent cases, served as a preface to Rehnquist's analysis of *Weber*.

Rehnquist argued that Title VII prohibited the discrimination suffered by Brian Weber. Under §§ 703(a)(2), 703(d), and 703(j), "Kaiser's racially discriminatory admissions quota is flatly prohibited by the plain language of Title VII."[31] Reviewing the legislative history of Title VII (and getting the better of the debate),[32] Rehnquist concluded that §§ 703(a) and (d) plainly proscribe racial discrimination, while § 703(j) enjoins federal courts and agencies from interpreting Title VII to require employers to grant racial preferences to correct work force unbalances. "The section says nothing about voluntary preferential treatment of minorities. . . ."[33]

In a final passage, Justice Rehnquist left no doubt as to where he stood on the issue of affirmative action:

There is perhaps no device more destructive to the notion of equality than the *numerus clausus*—the quota. Whether described as "benign discrimination" or "affirmative action," the racial quota is nonetheless a creator of castes, a two-edged sword that must demean one in order to prefer another. . . . With today's holding, the Court introduces into Title VII a tolerance for the very evil that the law was intended to eradicate without offering even a clue as to what the limits on that tolerance may be. . . . By going not merely *beyond*, but directly *against* Title VII's language and legislative history, the Court has sown the wind. Later courts will face the impossible task of reaping the whirlwind.[34]

Weber's Significance

The significance of *Weber* cannot be overestimated. The majority's analysis evinces an equal achievement/group justice approach to the question of the legality of affirmative action plans under Title VII.[35] Proportional representation of African Americans in the craft work force of the employer's Gramercy, Louisiana plant was held to be a valid goal which could be pursued through voluntary affirmative action. This group-based perspective and analysis, applied in an area where the Court could validly take judicial notice of discrimination,[36] stands in direct contrast to the opposing view expressed by Justice Rehnquist which looks only to equal opportunity, and prohibits discrimination against minorities and nonminorities alike.

Weber also illustrates the effect of the justices' differing views on statutory construction. The majority did not hesitate to go beyond the literal terms of Title VII and divine the "spirit" of the statute as reflected in its purpose and legislative history. In contrast, Justice Rehnquist and Chief Justice Burger's dissents looked to the statutory text and legislative history, chiding the *Weber* majority for reaching a result which Rehnquist and Burger considered to be inconsistent with Title VII.

Although the Court declined to draw a definitive line between permissible and impermissible voluntary affirmative action plans, its endorsement of certain features of the Kaiser-USWA plan indicated basic requirements for such initiatives. Thus, a voluntary affirmative action plan must have a remedial purpose; must be temporary in duration and not intended to maintain racial balance; and must not "unnecessarily trammel" the interests of white employees by creating an absolute bar to their advancement.[37]

In sum, the Court answered in the negative the question whether a private employer's voluntary affirmative action plan which granted preferential treatment to minority workers violated Title VII. However, significant questions and concerns remained. *Weber* validated voluntary affirmative action in a context of discrimination so well established that the Court took judicial notice of exclusion of African Americans from the crafts category of workers. How would *Weber* be applied on other facts and in other contexts? In addition, Justices Powell and Stevens did not participate in *Weber*. How would they vote on affirmative action in employment cases?[38] Would the same result reached in *Weber* be reached in the event of a constitutional challenge to a voluntary affirmative action plan adopted by public employers? And what effect, if any, would changes in the membership of the Court have on this complex and hotly debated area of the law?

Subsequent to *Weber*, the Supreme Court accepted, but did not decide, two affirmative action in employment cases which could have shed some light on the foregoing questions and other issues. In *Minnick v. California Department of Corrections*,[39] white male correction officers brought a Fourteenth Amendment Equal Protection Clause challenge to an affirmative action plan which allegedly discriminated on the basis of race and sex. The Court declined to decide the case because of ambiguities in the record. In *Boston Firefighters Union, Local 718 v. Boston Chapter, NAACP*,[40] the Court remanded a case in which the lower courts held that the city of Boston, Massachusetts could not implement reductions in its firefighter work force in a manner that would reduce the percentage of minority employees below levels attained through the affirmative action provisions of a consent decree. During that same period, the Court denied *certiorari* in two cases involving affirmative action and the hiring and layoff of minority teachers.[41]

AFFIRMATIVE ACTION, CONSENT DECREES AND LAYOFFS: THE *STOTTS* DECISION

By 1984, only four of the nine Supreme Court justices had voted in favor of affirmative action in employment. Justices Brennan, White, Marshall, and Blackmun, members of the *Weber* majority, remained on the Court. Justice Stewart, the fifth vote in *Weber*, retired from the Court and was replaced by Justice Sandra Day O'Connor. Of the remaining four justices, two—Chief Justice Burger and Justice Rehnquist—had dissented in *Weber*,[42] and two—Justices Powell and Stevens—did not participate in *Weber*.[43]

Given the fact that a majority of the Court as constituted in 1984 had not voted in favor of affirmative action in employment, the Court's decision in *Firefighters Local Union No. 1784 v. Stotts*[44] was eagerly awaited by proponents and opponents of the doctrine. In that case, a district court approved and entered a consent decree in 1980 which, *inter alia*, established an interim annual goal of hiring qualified black applicants to fill 50 percent of job vacancies in the city of Memphis, Tennessee's Fire Department.[45] The decree also contained a goal of 20 percent of promotions in each job classification to blacks.[46] No provisions for layoffs, awards of competitive seniority, or reductions in rank were contained in the decree.

In 1981, the city announced layoffs based on a seniority-based "last hired, first fired" rule. The district court entered a temporary restraining order forbidding the layoff of any black employee. Even though the district court found that the consent decree did not contemplate the method to be used for layoffs or reductions in rank, and that the seniority-based layoff policy was not adopted with an intent to discriminate, the court entered an injunction which ordered that the city not apply seniority insofar as it would decrease the percentage of black employees in certain categories. The court then approved a modified layoff plan to protect black employees from layoff. As a result of the injunction and modified layoff scheme, non-minority employees with more seniority than minority employees were either laid off or demoted. The district court's actions were affirmed by the United States Court of Appeals for the Sixth Circuit.[47]

The Majority Opinion

Reversing the Sixth Circuit, the Supreme Court, by a 6–3 vote, held that the district court exceeded its powers in entering the injunction.[48] Writing for the Court, Justice White (joined by Chief Justice Burger and Justices Rehnquist, Powell, Stevens, and O'Connor) phrased the issue before the Court as "whether the district court exceeded its powers in entering an injunction requiring white employees to be laid off, when the otherwise applicable seniority system would have called for the layoff of black employees with less seniority."[49]

White emphasized that the consent decree did not mention layoffs or demotions, nor did it suggest any intention to depart from the existing seniority system or from the city's arrangement with the firefighter's union. "Had there been any intention to depart from the seniority plan in the event of layoffs or demotions, it is much more reasonable to believe that there would have been an express provision to that effect."[50] Moreover, stated Justice White, the agreed upon remedy of the decree did not include displacement of senior white employees by black employees. Further, stated White, neither the union nor the nonminority employees were parties to the suit which led to the consent decree. In the absence of their presence, the Court found it unlikely that the city would purport to bargain away nonminority rights under the seniority system.[51]

Having addressed the issue of the district court's powers to modify the consent decree, Justice White embarked upon an analysis of Title VII. Noting that § 703(h) of Title VII permits the application of a seniority system absent proof of discriminatory intent,[52] he opined that the city could not be faulted for following seniority as agreed to with and by the union. Citing the Court's 1977 decision in *Teamsters v. U.S.*,[53] White stated that individual members of a plaintiff class may be awarded competitive seniority if they demonstrate that they have been actual victims of discrimination. However, he continued, each individual must prove that the discriminatory practice had an impact on him or her. Because there had been no finding that the African-American employees protected from layoff had been victims of discrimination, and the parties had not identified any specific employee entitled to relief in the consent decree, Justice White concluded that the seniority provisions of the firefighter's labor agreement with the city could not be overridden.

Turning to § 706(g) of Title VII,[54] Justice White argued that the policy behind that section "is to provide make-whole relief only to those who have been actual victims of illegal discrimination. . . . "[55] He concluded, therefore, that a court was not authorized to give preferential treatment to nonvictims. Thus, the Court determined that the district court's order erroneously ignored *Teamsters* as well as the policy behind § 706(g).

The O'Connor and Stevens Concurrences

In her first opinion on the subject of affirmative action in employment, Justice O'Connor agreed with the Court that a district court cannot unilaterally modify a consent decree to provide retroactive relief that "abrogates legitimate expectations of other employees and applicants."[56]

A court may not grant preferential treatment to any individual or group simply because the group to which they belong is adversely affected by a bona fide seniority system. Rather, a court may use its remedial powers, including its power to modify a consent decree, only to prevent future violations and to compensate identified victims of unlawful discrimination.[57]

Opining that the district court had no authority to order the fire department to maintain its racial balance or provide preferential treatment to black workers, Justice O'Connor concluded that the lower court had abused its discretion.

Concurring in the judgment, Justice Stevens argued that *Stotts* did not involve any issue arising under Title VII. In his view, the issue was the administration of a consent decree. Noting two ways in which the district court's order was justifiable, Stevens found that neither way had been followed. First, the district court did not state that it was construing the decree and did not provide any indication of the portion of the decree upon which it relied.[58] Second, Stevens stated that the consent decree could have been modified upon a demonstration of changed circumstance. The adverse effect and layoffs on the level of African-American employment in the city's fire department were not a changed circumstance, reasoned Justice Stevens, since it was apparent at the time of the entry of the decree that future layoffs, based on seniority, would adversely affect blacks.

Blackmun's Dissent

Justice Blackmun, joined by Justices Brennan and Marshall, dissented. Under his analysis, the only issue before the Court was the validity of a preliminary injunction that prevented the city from conducting layoffs that would have reduced the number of blacks. Were that the issue, the settled standard—the black employees' likelihood of success on the merits, the balance of irreparable harm to the parties, and whether the injunction would be in the public interest[59]—and question on appellate review (whether the district court abused its discretion) would apply.

Instead, argued Justice Blackmun, the Court treated *Stotts* as a case involving a permanent injunction in addressing the question of whether the city's proposed layoffs violated the consent decree. He stressed that the only issue before the Court was the propriety of preliminary injunctive relief, which was a separate issue from the determination of the merits of the underlying legal claim.

Addressing the majority's discussion of Title VII, Blackmun took issue with the Court's statement that § 706(g) mandated victim-specific relief. The purpose of that relief was to remedy the class-wide effects of past discrimination rather than discrimination against identified members of the class, stated Blackmun. Accordingly, in his view, "individual beneficiaries of the relief need not show that they were themselves victims of the discrimination for which the relief was granted."[60] Blackmun wrote that it was unfair and improper for the Court to fault the plaintiffs for failing to identify specific victims of discrimination, since the case had not been tried and had been settled by consent decree. "The whole point of the consent decree in these cases—and, indeed, the point of most Title VII consent decrees—is for both parties to avoid the questions of liability and identifying the victims of discrimination."[61]

In addition, Justice Blackmun differed with the majority's interpretation of § 706(g). In his view, that section "merely prevents a court from ordering an employer to hire someone unqualified for the job, and has nothing to do with prospective class wide relief."[62]

Analyzing Stotts

The state of affirmative action in employment after *Stotts* was uncertain. The facts and context in which the case arose were unlike the facts and issues raised in *Weber*. *Weber* involved a voluntary affirmative action plan adopted by a private employer and union. *Stotts* involved a public employer and a decree entered without the consent or approval of a union. In fact, the *Stotts* majority did not cite *Weber*. Moreover, the Court noted, but did not decide, the question whether "the city, a public employer, could have taken this course without violating the law. . . ."[63]

As noted above, one of the significant aspects of *Stotts* involved the question of how the justices would align on the affirmative action issue. Chief Justice Burger and Justice Rehnquist cast votes against the district court's affirmative action consent decree, while Justices Blackmun, Brennan, and Marshall voted in favor of the decree. Justice White, a member of the *Weber* majority, joined Burger and Rehnquist in voting against the affirmative action measure, which was concededly different from the measure at issue in, and the facts of, *Weber*. And all three of the justices who had never cast a vote on the merits of an affirmative action in employment case voted to overturn the consent decree. Justice Powell, who did not participate in *Weber*, and Justice Stevens (albeit on a different rationale) joined the *Stotts* majority, as did Justice O'Connor in her first vote on, and analysis of, the issue. Her endorsement of victims-only relief under affirmative action measures was of particular significance.

Stotts offers an additional illustration of the disparate views of the justices with respect to the availability of group-based or individual relief in Title VII affirmative action litigation. Justice White's opinion (while technically *dicta*) rejected the notion that affirmative action measures are available to persons who have not been identified as actual victims of discrimination in employment dis-crimination litigation. In contrast, the *Stotts* dissenters argued that Title VII relief is not so limited, and is indeed available to persons within a protected group or class. If read broadly, *Stotts* and the majority's *dicta* would have had a significant and narrowing impact on the scope of affirmative action relief available under Title VII. Read narrowly, *Stotts* merely stood for the proposition that a federal court may not modify a consent decree so as to override a bona fide seniority system to prevent the layoff of minorities at the expense of senior white workers.

Commentators initially concluded that *Stotts* struck a devastating blow to proponents of affirmative action.[64] The Reagan Administration Justice Depart-ment espoused the same view. Former Assistant Attorney General of the De-partment's Civil Rights Division, William Bradford Reynolds, was of the view that *Stotts* appeared to hold that quotas or preferences for nonvictims were not permissible under Title VII.[65] Acting on that view after *Stotts* was decided, the Division reviewed outstanding Title VII decrees in which the United States was a party and sought modification of fifty-one court decrees—an initiative which was resisted by state and local governments and federal courts of appeals.[66] Despite the Department's initiative, *Stotts* did not have an immediate impact on Title VII affirmative action litigation, as the courts read *Stotts* narrowly and limited the decision to its facts.[67]

THE 1986 TRILOGY

On May 19 and July 3, 1986, the Supreme Court issued three affirmative action in employment decisions, thereby shedding additional light in this area while raising additional questions.

Affirmative Action, Layoffs, and the Constitution: The *Wygant* Decision

In *Weber* and *Stotts*, the Supreme Court addressed affirmative action under Title VII. The constitutionality of preferential treatment for racial minorities was at issue in *Wygant v. Jackson Board of Education*.[68] That case involved the question of the legality of the following provision contained in a collective bargaining agreement between the Jackson Board of Education and the Jackson Education Association:

In the event that it becomes necessary to reduce the number of teachers through layoff from employment by the Board, teachers with the most seniority in the district shall be retained, except at *no time will there be a greater percentage of minority personnel laid off than the current percentage of minority personnel employed at the time of the layoff.* In no event will the number given notice of possible layoff be greater than the number of positions to be eliminated. Each teacher so affected will be called back in reverse positions for which he is certificated maintaining the above minority balance.[69]

In 1974, the board of education did not comply with the above-quoted provision in laying off teachers, and the percentage of minority teachers fell below the percentage of such teachers employed at the time of the layoff. The union and two minority teachers who had been laid off brought suit in state court.[70] Holding for the plaintiffs, the state court found that the board had breached the labor agreement. That court also concluded that the board had not discriminated against minorities in its hiring practices. "The minority representation on the faculty was the result of societal racial discrimination."[71] Even though the contractual provision had a discriminatory effect on nonminority teachers, the state court held that the provision was a permissible attempt to remedy the effects of societal discrimination.

Future layoffs were in compliance with the contractual layoff provision. Adversely affected nonminority teachers brought suit in federal court alleging violations of the Equal Protection Clause, Title VII, and other federal and state statutes. Dismissing the suit, the district court held that findings of prior discrimination were not required grounds for the racial preferences. The racial preferences were permissible under the Equal Protection Clause, stated the court, as an attempt to remedy societal discrimination by providing "role models" for minority students.[72] The United States Court of Appeals for the Sixth Circuit affirmed.[73] The Supreme Court reversed in a 5–4 decision.

The Plurality Opinion. Justice Powell, joined by Chief Justice Burger and Justice Rehnquist and in part by Justice O'Connor, authored a plurality opinion which addressed the question "whether a school board, consistent with the Equal Protection Clause, may extend preferential protection against layoffs to some of its employees because of their race or national origin."[74]

At the outset, Justice Powell stated that "the level of scrutiny does not change merely because the challenged classification operates against a group that historically has not been subject to governmental discrimination."[75] Because the layoff provision classified by race and operated against whites and in favor of minorities, the preference "must necessarily receive a most searching examination,"[76] under a two-prong analysis. First, stated Powell, the racial classification must be justified by a compelling governmental interest. Second, the means chosen by the state to effectuate its purpose must be narrowly tailored to the achievement of that goal.[77]

In Justice Powell's view, the layoff provision's racial classification was not justified by a compelling state purpose. He rejected the district court and Sixth Circuit holdings that the board's interest in providing minority role models to alleviate the effects of societal discrimination was sufficiently important to justify the racial classification.

This Court never has held that societal discrimination alone is sufficient to justify a racial classification. Rather, the Court has insisted upon some showing of prior discrimination by the governmental unit involved before allowing limited use of racial classifications in order to remedy such discrimination.[78]

Powell also discussed the role model theory posited by the district court as a theory having no logical stopping point. "The role model theory allows the Board to engage in discriminatory hiring and layoff practices long past the point required by any legitimate remedial purpose."[79] Moreover, Powell stated, the role model theory could be used to justify a small percentage of black teachers by reference to a small percentage of black students.

The plurality also addressed the notion of societal discrimination as a predicate for affirmative action. "Societal discrimination, without more, is too amorphous a basis for imposing a racially classified remedy."[80] Reasoning that basing legal remedies on such discrimination was insufficient and overexpansive, and conceding that there has been "serious racial discrimination in this country," Powell stated that in the absence of particularized findings, "a court could uphold remedies that are ageless in their reach into the past and timeless in their ability to affect the future."[81]

Turning to the issue of evidentiary support for a conclusion that remedial action is warranted, Justice Powell instructed that a trial court must make a factual determination that the employer "had a strong basis in evidence" for such a conclusion, with the ultimate burden remaining with the nonminority employees to demonstrate the unconstitutionality of an affirmative action program.[82] Powell concluded that no factual determination that the school board had engaged in prior discriminatory hiring had been made—alleged discrimination which had been denied by the board in the earlier litigation concerning the layoff provision. "[A]ny statistical disparities were the result of general societal discrimination, not of prior discrimination by the Board."[83]

Finally, Justice Powell considered the legality of the layoff provision as a means to effectuate the board's asserted purpose. Stating that under strict scrutiny, the means chosen to accomplish the state's asserted purpose must be specifically narrowly formed to accomplish that purpose, Powell recognized that "in order to remedy the effects of prior discrimination, it may be necessary to take race into account."[84] Thus, continued Powell, "innocent persons may be called upon to bear some of the burden of the remedy."[85]

But the burden imposed by the contractual provision was the layoff of nonminority teachers with greater seniority than minority teachers who were retained—an area of concern noted in Stotts[86] and by the Weber Court.[87] Justice Powell distinguished layoffs from "valid hiring goals," writing that the latter diffuses the burden to be borne by innocent individuals among society, and does not impose the same kind of injury that layoffs impose. In contrast, stated Powell, "layoffs impose the entire burden of achieving racial equality on particular individuals, often resulting in serious disruption of their lives. That burden is too intensive."[88] Accordingly, he concluded that the layoff provision was not sufficiently narrowly tailored, and was therefore, unconstitutional, since less intrusive means of accomplishing "similar purposes—such as the adoption of hiring goals—are available."[89]

The O'Connor and White Concurrences. Concurring in part and concurring in the judgment, Justice O'Connor subscribed to Justice Powell's formulation of the strict scrutiny standard applicable to Equal Protection Clause analysis of racial classifications "because it mirrors the standards we have consistently applied in examining racial classifications in other contexts."[90] She noted that the Court was in agreement that "remedying past or present racial discrimination by a state actor is a sufficiently weighty state interest to warrant the remedial use of a carefully constructed affirmative action program. This remedial purpose need not be accompanied by contemporaneous findings of actual discrimination to be accepted as legitimate as long as the public actor has a firm basis for believing that remedial action is warranted."[91]

Further, stated O'Connor, "nothing the Court has said today necessarily forecloses the possibility that the Court will find other governmental interests which have been relied upon in the lower courts but which have not been passed on here to be sufficiently important or compelling to sustain the use of affirmative action policies."[92] And, she continued, the Court had agreed that a plan "need not be limited to the remedying of specific instances of identified discrimination for it to be deemed sufficiently 'narrowly tailored' or 'substantially related', to the correction of prior discrimination by the state actor."[93]

O'Connor agreed with the plurality that (1) societal discrimination ("that is, discrimination not traceable to its own actions")[94] was not sufficiently compelling to pass constitutional muster under strict scrutiny, and (2) the lower courts erred by using the role model theory.

Justice O'Connor then addressed the question of whether a contemporaneous finding of past discrimination was a constitutional prerequisite to a public employer's implementation of an affirmative action plan. Arguing that such a requirement would undermine public employers' incentive to meet their civil rights obligations, O'Connor reasoned that such a result would be at odds with the Court's and Congress's emphasis on the value of voluntary efforts to further the objectives of the law.[95] In her view, such a result would also be anomalous in that "what private employers may voluntarily do to correct apparent violations of Title VII . . . public employers are constitutionally forbidden to do to correct their statutory and constitutional transgressions."[96]

Justice O'Connor explained her conclusion that a public employer must have a "firm basis" for determining that affirmative action is warranted. This example was offered by O'Connor: Evidence of a disparity between the percentage of qualified blacks on a teaching staff and the percentage of qualified minorities in a relevant labor pool sufficient to support a *prima facie*, Title VII pattern or practice claim by minority teachers.[97] "Reverse discrimination" plaintiffs would then bear the burden of demonstrating that their rights had been violated because the employer's evidence did not support an inference of prior discrimination, or the plan was not sufficiently narrowly tailored.

Finally, O'Connor reached beyond the layoff issue and addressed the school board's hiring goal—a goal which she found was tied to the percentage of minority students and not to the percentage of qualified minority teachers in the relevant labor pool. The disparity between the minority teachers and minority students "is not probative of employment discrimination; it is only when it is established that the availability of minorities in the relevant labor pool substantially exceeded those hired that one may draw an inference of deliberate discrimination in employment."[98] Concluding that the layoff provision maintained minority hiring levels that had no relation to remedying employment discrimination, Justice O'Connor determined that the plan was not narrowly tailored to effectuate its remedial purpose.

Justice White authored a one-paragraph concurrence. In his view, the layoff position required the layoff of nonminority teachers solely on the basis of race.

Whatever the legitimacy of hiring goals and quotas may be, the discharge of white teachers to make room for blacks, none of whom has been shown to be a victim of any racial discrimination, is quite a different matter. I cannot believe that in order to integrate a work force, it would be permissible to discharge whites and have blacks until the latter comprised a suitable percentage of the work force. None of our cases suggests that this would be permissible under the Equal Protection Clause. Indeed, our cases look quite the other way. The layoff policy in this case—laying off whites who would otherwise be retained in order to keep blacks on the job—has the same effect and is equally violative of the Equal Protection Clause. I agree with the plurality that this official policy is unconstitutional and hence concur in the judgment.[99]

The Marshall and Stevens Dissents. In dissent, Justice Marshall (joined by Justices Brennan and Blackmun) argued, *inter alia*, that a public employer, with the agreement of its employees, should be permitted to preserve the benefits of a constitutional affirmative action plan while reducing its work force. Taking a historical approach, Justice Marshall noted that the first black teacher in the Jackson public schools was hired in 1954 and that by 1969 the faculty minority representation was approximately 4 percent. Marshall also noted that the National Association for the Advancement of Colored People had filed a complaint against the board with the Michigan Civil Rights Commission (MCRC) alleging that the board had engaged in discriminatory practices. After the MCRC concluded that the allegations had merit, the matter was settled and the board agreed to take affirmative steps to recruit, hire, and promote minority teachers and counselors. Two years later, the minority teacher percentage had risen to approximately 9 percent.[100]

Marshall also recounted the developments leading to the contractual layoff provision,[101] stating that the provision was a compromise which avoided placing the entire burden of layoffs on white or minority teachers, and was repeatedly ratified by a majority vote of the teachers (80 percent of whom were white).

The sole question posed by the case, stated Justice Marshall, was whether the Constitution prohibited a union and local school board from entering into a collective bargaining agreement that apportioned layoffs between two racial groups as a means of preserving the effects of an affirmative hiring policy. In his view, it did not matter which test—strict scrutiny, or a strict and searching inquiry[102]—the Court applied because the "history and application of Article XII" demonstrated that the provision passed constitutional muster."[103]

As to the purpose supporting the affirmative action initiative, Marshall identified the "need to preserve the levels of faculty integration achieved through the affirmative hiring policy adopted in the early 1970s."[104] Marshall agreed with the other justices that formal findings of past discrimination are not a necessary predicate to the adoption of affirmative action policies, and that the "scope of such policies need not be limited to remedying specific instances of identifiable discrimination."[105] Moreover, Justice Marshall concluded that the Court did not need to rely on societal discrimination in assessing the sufficiency of the school board's purpose. He listed racially motivated violence at the schools, apparent violations of the law, and substantial underrepresentation of minority teachers as found by the MCRC. "Since the district court did not permit submission of this evidentiary support, I am at a loss as to why Justice Powell so glibly rejects the obvious solution of remanding for the fact finding he appears to recognize is necessary."[106]

As the means chosen to achieve the school board's purpose, Justice Marshall again turned to the "history" of the contractual layoff position. Evidence contained in the lodgings submitted by the school board suggested to Marshall that the lack of some layoff protection would have crippled efforts to recruit minority applicants. Seniority concerns did not deter the justice citing Court precedent; he argued that courts may displace innocent workers by granting retroactive seniority to victims of employment discrimination;[107] that employee expectations arising from a seniority system may be modified to further a strong public policy interest;[108] and that labor agreements may go further than statutes and enhance the seniority of employees to foster legitimate interests.[109] And in *Weber*, the Court addressed and permitted a departure from the seniority principle.[110] Thus, stated Justice Marshall, protection from layoff was not unavailable as a tool for achieving societal goals.

The contractual layoff provision was sufficiently narrow in Justice Marshall's view. The burden was allocated proportionately between groups of blacks and whites; no one race was absolutely burdened or received absolute benefits; the hierarchy of seniority was preserved within certain confines; race was a factor, but was not dispositive; the protection of minorities from layoff was not a tool to increase minority representation; the provision was narrow in the temporal sense; and the provision did not modify contractual expectations related to merit or achievement.[111] Moreover, continued Marshall, the best evidence that the layoff provision was sufficiently narrow was that representatives of all affected parties had agreed to the provision six times since 1962. Accordingly, Justice Marshall would have vacated the Sixth Circuit's judgment and remanded the case to the district court for further proceedings.

In a separate dissent, Justice Stevens argued that, rather than analyzing the case as one involving a "remedy for sins that were committed in the past,"[112] the Court should ask whether the board's actions would advance the public interest in educating children for the future. Opining that race is not always irrelevant to governmental decision making, Stevens argued that, in the public education context, a "school board may reasonably conclude that an integrated faculty will be able to provide benefits to the student body that could not be forwarded by an all-white, or nearly all-white, faculty."[113] Stevens wrote that it is "one thing for a white child to be taught by a white teacher that color, like beauty, is only skin deep; it is far more convincing to experience that truth on a day-to-day basis during the routine, ongoing learning process."[114] Thus, Stevens concluded that multi-ethnic representation on a teaching faculty was a valid public purpose, a sound educational purpose, and a rational and legitimate basis for the school board's decision to enter into the labor agreement challenged by the nonminority teachers.

In his opinion, Justice Stevens discussed the difference between a decision to exclude a minority because of skin color and a decision to include minorities for that same reason. Exclusion "rests on the false premise that differences in race, or in the color of a person's skin, reflect real differences that are relevant to a person's right to share in the blessings of a free society."[115] Inclusion tends to dispel that illusion, wrote Stevens, and "is consistent with the principle that all men are created equal; the exclusionary decision is at war with that principle. One decision accords with the Equal Protection Clause of the Fourteenth Amendment; the other does not."[116] Stevens concluded that the board's valid purpose of inclusion was distinguishable from a case that would reinforce assumptions of inequality.

Assessing the harm to the disadvantaged nonminority teachers, Justice Stevens first assessed the fairness of the procedures used to adopt the layoff provision. The union negotiated the agreement and the membership ratified it. "[T]he race-conscious layoff policy here was adopted with full participation of the disadvantaged individuals and with a narrowly circumscribed berth for the policy's operations."[117] Acknowledging that every layoff is a loss to the affected individual, Justice Stevens concluded that the layoff was not based on a lack of respect for the nonminority teachers' race, or on blind habit and stereotype. Rather, stated Stevens, the nonminority teachers were laid off because of economic conditions and the preservation of the newly integrated character of the faculty in Jackson schools.

In addition, Stevens stated that the case involved layoffs and not hiring, which had no bearing on the equal protection question. In his view, the board's interest in employing more minority teachers justified their retention when the number of available jobs was reduced. He thus found wholly unpersuasive Justice Powell's suggestion that the difference between hiring and layoff was constitutionally significant. "[T]he distinction is artificial, for the layoff provision at issue in this case was included as part of the terms of the *hiring* of minority and other teachers under the collective-bargaining agreement."[118]

The Significance of Wygant. *Wygant* mandated that a public employer could not use affirmative action in the layoff context to remedy societal discrimination or to provide role models for minority students. Although *Wygant* did not definitively resolve the question of whether societal discrimination alone can ever be a suffi-

ciently compelling government interest to justify affirmative action,[119] Justice
White's negative response to affirmative action in his short concurrence only theoret-
ically withheld majority status of a rejection of that theory.[120]

It is noteworthy that the Court did not foreclose the use of affirmative action
in certain circumstances, such as hiring. Thus, under *Wygant*, a public employer
could constitutionally engage in some form of affirmative action which granted
preferential treatment to minorities. Moreover, it was still possible after *Wygant*
that a majority of the Court (O'Connor, Marshall, Brennan, Blackmun, and
Stevens) would consider educational and additional factors, other than past discrimination, as a valid constitutional predicate for race-conscious affirmative
action.[121] As to the required evidence of discrimination supporting the use of
affirmative action, *Wygant* did not definitively resolve that issue. The plurality
indicated that an employer must have a "strong basis in evidence" to justify its
conclusion that affirmative action remedies were necessary. Under that standard,
preferential treatment could be justified by something less than an admission by
the employer that it had engaged in unlawful discrimination. Justice O'Connor
would require a "firm basis" for constitutional affirmative action, relying on a
statutory analysis—the standards for a *prima facie* case under Title VII.

In several key respects, *Wygant* was an endorsement and continuation of *Stotts*,
albeit by a different analysis and rationale. In protecting senior white employees
from layoff, *Stotts* was grounded in the provision of Title VII which protects
bona fide seniority systems. *Wygant*, employing constitutional law analysis, also
protected senior white employees from layoff. The underlying principle shared
by both decisions is that affirmative action remedies should not be borne by
"innocent" employees to the extent that such remedies would result in the loss
of jobs of incumbent employees.

The layoff issue presented in *Wygant* and *Stotts* involved continued employment and expectations which had arisen from an individual's service with an
employer. That issue and scenario present a defined and focused picture of the
adverse impact of work force reduction which does not arise in the affirmative
action in hiring context. In the latter circumstance, it is easier to argue that the
burden of preferential treatment measures is diffused and does not disproportionately burden majority group employees. In the layoff context, the burden
falls on readily identifiable persons who may have worked for years, with ac-
complishments, achievements, and seniority. It is not surprising that the protection of less-senior minority employees in layoffs is met with resistance and
lawsuits by adversely affected majority employees.

Having addressed the constitutionality of affirmative action in *Wygant* (an
issue which the Court would again address in 1989), the Court returned to
construing Title VII in the two remaining cases of the 1986 Trilogy.

Consent Decrees and Relief for Nonvictims: *Firefighters Local 93*

Local Number 93, Firefighters v. City of Cleveland[122] presented the question
whether § 706(g) of Title VII[123] precluded the entry of a consent decree which

provided relief that may have benefited individuals who were not the actual victims of discriminatory practices. In 1980, the Vanguards of Cleveland, an organization of African-American and Hispanic firefighters, filed a class action complaint against their employer, the City of Cleveland, Ohio, alleging discrimination on the basis of race and national origin in hiring, assignments, and promotion in violation of the Thirteenth and Fourteenth Amendments to the Constitution and Title VII. The primary charge of the complaint was that the minority firefighters had been discriminated against in the fire departments' awarding of promotions, and that a written examination used for promotions was allegedly discriminatory.

The 1980 suit was not the first filed against the city in which race discrimination charges had been made. A 1972 action by African-American police officers against the city police department resulted in a district court finding in favor of the plaintiffs, and an order enjoining certain hiring and promotion practices and establishing minority hiring goals.[124] In 1977, the hiring goals were adjusted and promotion goals were established under a consent decree. An additional suit had been filed against the Cleveland Fire Department in 1975[125] and, in 1977, the court approved a plan governing hiring procedures for the fire department.

Rather than litigate the 1980 suit sought by the Vanguards, the city entered into settlement negotiations with the plaintiffs. In 1981, Local Number 93 of the International Association of Firefighters (the bargaining representative of a majority of the city's firefighters) successfully moved to intervene as a party-plaintiff.[126] Over the union's objections, the district court approved a consent decree in 1983 which stated, *inter alia*, that documents, statistics, and testimony presented at hearings on the decree revealed a historical pattern of racial discrimination in promotions in the fire department. Under the decree, which was to be in effect for four years, specific numbers of minority firefighters were to receive promotions.[127] The union appealed the district court's overruling of its objections. The United States Court of Appeals for the Sixth Circuit affirmed, finding that the relief ordered by the district court was justified by the statistical evidence and the city's admission that it had engaged in discrimination.[128]

The Majority Opinion. By a 6–3 vote, the Supreme Court affirmed the Sixth Circuit's decision. Writing for the Court, Justice Brennan (joined by Justices Marshall, Blackmun, Powell, Stevens, and O'Connor) wrote that "we hold that whether or not § 706(g) precludes a court from imposing certain forms of race-conscious relief after trial, that provision does not apply to relief awarded in a consent decree."[129]

Justice Brennan relied on *Weber* in his analysis and interpretation of § 706(g). *Weber* held that voluntary action available to employers and unions seeking to evaluate racial discrimination may include race-conscious relief benefiting persons who were not the actual victims of discrimination, stated Brennan. Although *Weber* involved a private contract rather than a consent decree, he did not see "any reason to distinguish between voluntary action taken in a consent decree and voluntary action taken entirely outside the context of litigation."[130]

The union, supported by the United States as *amicus curiae*, argued that §
706(g) established an independent limitation on courts. The last sentence of that
section provides that "[n]o order of the court shall require . . . the hiring, reinstatement, or promotion of an individual as an employee . . . if such individual
. . . was refused employment or advancement . . . for any reason other than discrimination on account of race. . . . "[131] In the union's and federal government's
view, a consent decree should be treated as an order within the meaning of §
706(g) because a consent decree looked like, and was entered as, a judgment;
courts retained the power to modify a consent decree; and noncompliance with
a consent decree was enforceable by a citation for contempt of court.[132]

Unpersuaded by that argument, Justice Brennan determined that a consent
decree is a hybrid of a judgment and a contract arrived at through the mutual
agreement of the parties. Turning to the legislative history of § 706(g), he
concluded that the section was drafted to address the concerns of business au-
tonomy and managerial prerogatives expressed by conservative proponents of
Title VII.[133] Thus, concluded Justice Brennan, "§ 706(g) by itself does not
restrict the ability of employers or unions to enter into voluntary agreements
providing for race-conscious remedial action."[134] Because the parties voluntarily
enter into consent decrees, Justice Brennan found it "readily apparent that consent decrees are not included among the 'orders' referred to in § 706(g). . . . "[135]
Consequently, he concluded that the limitations of § 706(g) do not apply to
obligations created by a consent decree.[136]

The Court also rejected the contention that, under *Stotts* and other precedents,
a consent decree could not provide greater relief than a court could have decreed
after a trial. Noting that the *Stotts* Court found a conflict between a consent
decree and the underlying statute,[137] Justice Brennan found no inconsistency
between § 706(g) and a consent decree providing race-conscious relief (even
though race-conscious relief by a court may be banned in disputed proceedings
to modify a consent decree) because § 706(g) was not concerned with voluntary
agreements by employers or unions to provide such relief.[138] Accordingly, the
Court held that § 706(g) did not bar the district court's approval of the consent
decree.

Justice O'Connor's Concurrence. Justice O'Connor, a member of the *Stotts*
majority, concurred. She wrote that the Court's holding was narrow: "Relief
provided in a consent decree need not conform to the limits on court-ordered
relief imposed by § 706(g), whatever those limits may be."[139] The validity of
a consent decree's race-conscious relief may be assessed under § 703 of Title
VII and, in the case of a public employer, the Fourteenth Amendment, stated
O'Connor; therefore, nonminority employees remain free to challenge race-
conscious measures contemplated by a consent decree.

Dissenting Views. Justice White authored a dissent. He opined that an employer
could not lose a Title VII case litigated to judgment unless it was proved that
the employer had discriminated within the meaning of § 703. "It is therefore
untenable to conclude, as the Court does, that a district court may nevertheless

enter a consent decree ordering an employer to hire or promote on a racial basis in a way that could not be ordered after a contested trial."[140]

Justice White argued that the consent decree was not immune from the mandate of § 706(g). Because none of the African-American firefighters was shown to have been a victim of discriminatory promotion practices, and none of the whites denied promotion was shown to be responsible for or implicated in the discriminatory practices recited in the decree, Justice White concluded that the race-conscious relief set forth in the decree could not have been ordered after a trial. Thus, he stated, relief was "no more valid when agreed to by the employer but contested by those who claim their right not to be discriminated against on racial grounds."[141]

In a separate dissent, Justice Rehnquist (joined by Chief Justice Burger) argued that *Firefighters* was governed by *Stotts*. Writing that five members of the *Stotts* Court concluded that § 706(g) barred the relief granted by the district court in *Firefighters*, Justice Rehnquist reasoned that the *Firefighters* majority's conclusion that § 706(g) was intended not to apply to consent decrees flew in the face of the language of that section, and conflicted with legislative history showing that § 706(g) also served to protect nonminority employees from the "evil of court-sanctioned racial quotas."[142]

Justice Rehnquist conceded that legislative history could be mustered in support of the majority's interpretation of § 706(g). However, he stated, the language of the statute was clear. "*No order of the Court* shall require promotion of an individual whose failure to receive promotion was for a reason other than discrimination prohibited by the statute."[143] Because the district court did not find that the minority firefighters who would be promoted were the victims of racial discrimination, Justice Rehnquist determined that the city of Cleveland's failure to advance them was not on account of race. In his view, an order of the Court entered by the consent of the parties is an adjudication and an order subject to the prohibitions of § 706(g).[144]

Analysis of Firefighters. *Firefighters* thus stands for the proposition that § 706(g) does not limit the race-conscious relief contained in consent decrees.[145] The case was significant in that the Court limited *Stotts* to cases involving court-ordered modifications of consent decrees.[146]

One issue which arose from *Firefighters* involves the question whether the consent decree would have a preclusive effect on any claims of the union and white employees. As noted by Professors Rutherglen and Ortiz, the Court assumed that the consent decree could be effective by binding only the parties to the decree itself, but not the union or the nonminority employees represented by the union.[147] It was certainly predictable that the success of any agreement between the city of Cleveland and its minority firefighters would be affected by the union's willingness to voluntarily abide by the terms of the decree, even in the face of opposition by nonminority firefighters who may have suffered the loss of promotions and other job benefits as a result of preferential treatment afforded to minorities. The Court did not pass upon the issue of the preclusive effect of the decree on the union; instead, it remanded that question to the district court.

Firefighters did not involve a constitutional challenge to the consent decree agreed to by a public employer. Thus, the Court was not required to apply a constitutional analysis which would have been stricter than the *Weber* standard relied on by Justice Brennan.[148] Nor was the Court required to decide significant issues concerning the limitations of § 703 of Title VII on an employer's ability to agree to race-conscious relief in a voluntary settlement that is not embodied in a consent decree, or what showing the employer would be required to make concerning possible prior discrimination on its part against minorities in order to defeat a challenge by nonminority employees based on § 703.[149]

Court Orders and Relief for Nonvictims: *Sheet Metal Workers*

Section 706(g) of Title VII was the focus in *Local 28, Sheet Metal Workers v. EEOC*,[150] a case decided by the Court on the same day that *Firefighters* was decided. In *Sheet Metal Workers*, the Court addressed the question whether § 706(g) "empowers a district court to order race-conscious relief that may benefit individuals who are not identified victims of unlawful discrimination."[151]

The facts of *Sheet Metal Workers* reveal a longstanding pattern of discrimination by a union which is only summarized here. In 1964, the New York State Commission for Human Rights found that Local 28 and the local's joint apprenticeship committee had excluded African Americans from the union and apprenticeship program in violation of state law. The commission's findings were affirmed by a state court in that same year.[152] In 1965 and 1967, the state court issued additional orders requiring the union to remedy its discrimination.[153]

The United States brought an action against the union in 1971 to enjoin the union's discriminatory patterns and practices against minorities. A consent order was agreed to early in 1974 which required the apprenticeship committee to admit up to forty minorities by September 1974. After a trial in 1975, the district court held that the union violated Title VII and New York law by discriminating against minorities in recruitment, selection, training, and admission to the union.[154] Among other things, the court established a 29 percent minority membership goal based on the percentage of minorities in the relevant New York city labor pool, to be achieved by July 1981.

The United States Court of Appeals for the Second Circuit affirmed the district court (with some modification) in 1976, upholding the membership goal.[155] Thereafter, the district court granted the union an additional year to meet the 29 percent membership goal, and approved a revised affirmative action program which the parties had been required to devise and implement under a court-appointed administrator. The revised program was affirmed by the Second Circuit in 1977.[156]

Five years later, New York city and state moved for an order holding the union in contempt, alleging that the union had not achieved the minority membership goal, and had committed numerous violations of the district court's order and judgment and the revised affirmative action program. Holding the union in civil contempt, the district court imposed a $150,000 fine to be used to fund an increase in minority membership in the union and apprenticeship program. At that time, the union's membership was approximately 11 percent minority; however, the district court did not rest its contempt finding on the union's failure to meet the membership goal.

An additional finding of civil contempt was entered against the union in 1983. The district court ordered the union to pay for a computerized record keeping system, and to fund a program enacted to increase the pool of qualified minority applicants for the apprenticeship program.[157] The court also modified the affirmative action program and established a 29.23 percent minority membership goal to be met by August 1987. On appeal, the Second Circuit affirmed the district court's contempt findings and affirmative action requirements with modifications.[158]

Justice Brennan's Plurality Opinion and Justice Powell's Concurrence. Although a majority of the Court affirmed the judgment of the Second Circuit in several respects,[159] Justice Brennan's plurality opinion required the vote of Justice Powell to muster a majority interpretation of § 706(g).

The union and the EEOC[160] argued that the minority membership goal, fund order, and other orders were prohibited by § 706(g) since these measures required the union to admit to membership and afford benefits to minorities who were not the identified victims of unlawful discrimination. Writing for himself and three other justices (Justices Marshall, Blackmun, and Stevens), Justice Brennan rejected that argument.

[We] hold that § 706(g) does not prohibit a court from ordering, in appropriate circumstances, affirmative race-conscious relief as a remedy for past discrimination. Specifically, we hold that such relief may be appropriate where an employer or a labor union has engaged in persistent or egregious discrimination, or where necessary to dissipate the lingering effects of pervasive discrimination.[161]

As in *Firefighters*, the union argued that the last sentence of § 706(g) prohibits a court from ordering an employee or union to affirmatively eliminate discrimination which may incidentally benefit individuals who were not the actual victims of discrimination.[162] Justice Brennan rejected that reading of the statute.

[Section 706(g)] does not . . . say that a court may order relief only for the actual victims of past discrimination. The sentence on its face addresses only the situation where a plaintiff demonstrates that a union (or an employer) has engaged in unlawful discrimination, but the union can show that a particular individual would have been refused admission, even in the absence of discrimination, for example, because that individual was unqualified. In these circumstances § 706(g) confirms that a court could not order the union to admit the unqualified individual. . . . In this case, neither the membership goal nor the Fund order required petitioners to admit to membership individuals who had

been refused admission for reasons unrelated to discrimination. Thus, we do not read §
706(g) to prohibit a court from ordering the kind of affirmative relief the district court
awarded in this case.[163]

In most cases, stated Justice Brennan, a court need only order an employer
or union to cease engaging in discriminatory practices and award make-whole
relief to victims of those practices. In cases of "particularly longstanding or
egregious discrimination," continued Brennan, "requiring recalcitrant employers or unions to hire and to admit qualified minorities roughly in proportion to
the number of qualified minorities in the work force may be the only effective
way to ensure the full enjoyment of the rights protected by Title VII."[164]

After reviewing the legislative history of Title VII,[165] Justice Brennan rejected
the union and EEOC arguments that Court precedent established that court-
ordered remedies under § 706(g) were limited to make-whole relief benefiting
actual victims of past discrimination.[166] The principal case cited by the union
and the EEOC was the Court's 1984 decision in Stotts.[167] Justice Brennan explained that the Stotts limitation on individual make-whole relief did not affect
a court's order to order race-conscious affirmative action.[168] Class relief was
central to his analysis:

The purpose of affirmative action is not to make identified victims whole, but rather to
dismantle prior patterns of employment discrimination in the future. Such relief is provided
to the class as a whole rather than to individual members; no individual is entitled to
relief; and beneficiaries need not show that they were themselves victims of
discrimination.[169]

Brennan therefore declined to read Stotts to prohibit judicial orders of race-
conscious affirmative relief that might benefit nonvictims.

In another significant passage, Justice Brennan set forth the legal principles
which would guide the judgment of courts in this area. In the majority of Title
VII cases, he stated, courts need only order employers and unions to cease
discriminatory practices and award make-whole relief to victims of those practices. Where an employer or union has engaged in "persistent or egregious
discrimination" or where it "may be necessary to dissipate the lingering effects
of pervasive discrimination,"[170] Justice Brennan opined that a court may have
to resort to race-conscious affirmative action. Courts should consider "whether
affirmative action is necessary to remedy past discrimination in a particular case
before imposing such measures," continued Justice Brennan, and "should also
take care to tailor its orders to fit the nature of the violation it seeks to correct."[171]

Under these principles, the district court and Sixth Circuit decisions were
affirmed. Justice Brennan determined that the union's pervasive and egregious
discrimination and longstanding resistance to court orders justified the membership goal fund order, and other race-conscious relief ordered by the lower courts.
With respect to the membership goal, Justice Brennan concluded that the district

court's flexible application of that goal, and the adjustments in deadlines for achieving it, indicated that the court was not using the goal to achieve and maintain racial balance. Rather, he stated, the goal was a bench mark which the court could consider in gauging the union's efforts to remedy its discrimination. And, citing *Weber*, Justice Brennan stated that the membership goal and fund order were temporary measures which would not unnecessarily trammel the interests of white employees.[172]

Further, Justice Brennan was not persuaded by the union's argument that the district court's order violated the equal protection component of the Due Process Clause of the Fifth Amendment.[173] Noting that the Court had not then agreed on the proper test applicable to the constitutionality of race-conscious measures,[174] Brennan concluded that the relief ordered by the district court passed even the most rigorous test because it was narrowly tailored to further the government's compelling interest in remedying past discrimination. The union had been found guilty of egregious violations of Title VII; the lower courts had determined that affirmative measures were necessary to remedy those violations; and the district court's orders were properly tailored to accomplish that objective.[175] Therefore, concluded Justice Brennan, the district court's orders did not violate the Constitution.

The crucial fifth vote was provided by Justice Powell. In a separate opinion, he agreed that § 706(g) did "not limit a court in all cases to granting relief only to actual victims of discrimination."[176] In his view, the "plain language of Title VII does not clearly support a view that all remedies must be limited to benefiting victims."[177] Powell then agreed with the plurality that "in cases involving particularly egregious conduct a district court may fairly conclude that an injunction alone is insufficient to remedy a proven violation of Title VII. This is such a case."[178]

Justice Powell also agreed that the court-ordered membership goal and fund order did not contravene the Due Process Clause of the Fifth Amendment, but under a different analysis than that employed in the plurality opinion. Quoting from his opinion in *Wygant*,[179] Justice Powell called for a two-prong examination of the constitutional question: (1) whether the racial classification was justified by a compelling governmental interest, and (2) whether the means chosen to effectuate the state's purpose was narrowly tailored to the achievement of that goal. The egregious violations of Title VII by the union established the compelling governmental interest. "It would be difficult to find defendants more determined to discriminate against minorities."[180]

As to the fund order, Justice Powell found that the order was supported by the governmental interest in eradicating the union's discriminatory practices, as well as the societal interest in compliance with federal court judgments. With respect to the membership goal, Justice Powell analyzed that issue by relying on the factors set forth by his concurrence in *Fullilove v. Klutznick*.[181] First, Powell stated that it was doubtful that the district court had available to it any other effective remedy, given the union's violations. Second, he stated, the goal was limited and not permanent. Third, the goal was directly related to the percentage of minorities in the relevant work force. Fourth, Justice Powell determined that the flexible application of the goal demonstrated that it was not a means to achieve racial balance, noting that the original deadline for the goal was 1981 and had been changed to 1987. Finally, Justice Powell emphasized that nonminorities would not be directly burdened, if at all, since no layoffs of nonminority workers would be required.

Justice O'Connor's Opinion. Concurring in parts of the Court's opinion, Justice O'Connor dissented from the Court's judgment insofar as it affirmed the use of "mandatory quotas." Declining to reach the constitutional claims, she concluded that the membership goal and fund order were impermissible quotas under § 706(g) as read in light of § 703(j). The latter section provides that "[n]othing contained in this title shall be interpreted to require" an employer or union to grant preferential treatment to any individual or to any group because of race.[182] In Justice O'Connor's view, § 703(j) applies to the interpretation of any provision of Title VII, including § 706(g). "Therefore, when a court interprets § 706(g) as authorizing it to require an employer to adopt a racial quota, that court contravenes § 703(j) to the extent that relief imposed as a purported remedy for a violation of Title VII's substantive provisions in fact operates to require racial preferences 'on account of [a racial] imbalance.' "[183]

Justice O'Connor explained her view of the difference between an impermissible quota and a permissible goal.

To be consistent with § 703(j), a racial hiring or membership goal must be intended to serve merely as a benchmark for measuring compliance with Title VII and eliminating the lingering effects of past discrimination, rather than as a rigid numerical requirement that must unconditionally be met on pain of sanctions. To hold an employer or union to achievement of a particular percentage of minority employment or membership, and to do so regardless of circumstances such as economic conditions or the number of available qualified minority applicants, is to impose an impermissible quota. By contrast, a permissible goal should require only a good-faith effort on the employer's or union's part to come within a range demarcated by the goal itself.[184]

O'Connor reasoned that the membership goal ordered by the district court operated as a strict racial quota that the union was required to attain, in that the union's racial composition was to mirror the relevant labor pool by August 1987, without regard to the number of qualified minority applicants or new apprenticeships needed. "The District Court plainly stated that '[i]f the goal is not attained by that date, defendants will face fines that will threaten their very existence.' "[185]

Justice O'Connor did not question that the union engaged in egregious violations of Title VII and exhibited inexcusable recalcitrance. But, she stated, the timetable of the membership goal was unrealistic and could not be met by the union's good-faith efforts. "In sum, the membership goal operates as a rigid membership quota, which will in turn spawn a sharp curtailment in the opportunities of nonminorities to be admitted to the apprenticeship program."[186]

The White and Rehnquist Dissents. In a one-paragraph opinion, Justice White dissented. The author of the majority opinion in *Stotts*, Justice White agreed with the majority that "§ 706(g) does not bar relief for nonvictims in all circumstances."[187] However, like Justice O'Connor, he argued that the cumulative effect of the orders against the union established a strict racial quota that the union was required to attain during an economic downturn in the construction industry, and a declining demand for the union's skills. For all practical purposes, stated Justice White, the Court had insisted that the union comply even if nonminorities had to be replaced by minorities.[188]

Justice Rehnquist (joined by Chief Justice Burger) also dissented. Relying on his dissent in *Firefighters, Local 93 v. City of Cleveland*,[189] he concluded that § 706(g) does not sanction the granting of relief to nonvictims at the expense of innocent nonminority workers injured by racial preferences.[190] Arguing for reversal of the Second Circuit's judgment solely on statutory grounds, Justice Rehnquist did not reach the equal protection question.

Analysis. Sheet Metal Workers is significant in that six justices concluded that § 706(g) does not prohibit race-conscious relief which benefits nonvictims, and which may be ordered by the courts in certain circumstances. In addition to the *Sheet Metal Workers'* plurality (Justices Brennan, Marshall, Blackmun, and Stevens), Justices Powell and White agreed that § 706(g) does not preclude relief for nonvictims in all instances.

CHANGES IN THE COURT'S MEMBERSHIP

On June 16, 1986, Chief Justice Burger announced his retirement from the Court after a seventeen-year tenure. President Ronald Reagan nominated Justice Rehnquist to assume the Chief Justiceship and also nominated Antonin Scalia, a judge on the United States Court of Appeals for the District of Columbia Circuit. The confirmation of Rehnquist as the nation's sixteenth Chief Justice and Scalia as an associate justice were of some concern to both proponents and opponents of affirmative action, but did not portend substantive changes in the results of the Court's affirmative action decisions. While Rehnquist's views against affirmative action were well established, it was predicted that Scalia (who had expressed his opposition to affirmative action in an earlier writing)[191] would replace the vote against affirmative action consistently cast by Chief Justice Burger. That prediction was ultimately borne out by Scalia's votes in subsequent cases.

THE 1987 CASES

Promotion Quotas and the Constitution: *Paradise*

In *U.S. v. Paradise*,[192] the Court addressed the question whether a one-black-for-one-white promotion requirement ordered by a court was permissible under the Equal Protection Clause of the Fourteenth Amendment.[193]

Paradise involved litigation which commenced in 1972, and the facts are only summarized here. In that year, the NAACP sued the Alabama Department of Public Safety (Department) alleging that the Department excluded African Americans from employment. The United States was joined as a party plaintiff and Philip Paradise intervened on behalf of a class of black plaintiffs. Determining that the Department had engaged in blatant and continuous discrimination (there had never been an African-American trooper in the history of the patrol), the district court ordered the Department to hire one black trooper for each white trooper hired until blacks constituted approximately 25 percent of the state trooper force.[194]

The plaintiffs returned to the district court in 1977 for relief with regard to the Department's promotion practices. Thereafter, in 1979, the district court approved a partial consent decree in which the Department agreed to develop a promotion procedure within one year for the rank of corporal. Another consent decree was approved by the court in 1981 in which the Department reaffirmed its commitment made in the 1979 decree.

The plaintiffs returned to the court in 1983 and sought enforcement of the 1979 consent decree. The plaintiffs requested the promotion of African Americans to corporal at a one-black-for-one-white rate. The district court noted that of six majors, twenty-five captains, thirty-five lieutenants, and sixty-five sergeants, not one was an African American. Of sixty-six corporals, four were black.[195] It then held that, for a "period of time," at least 50 percent of promotions to corporal had to be awarded to qualified African-American troopers. In addition, the district court imposed a 50 percent promotional quota to upper ranks if there were qualified black applicants, if the rank were less than 25 percent black, and if the Department had not developed and implemented a promotion plan without adverse impact on blacks.

In February 1984, the Department promoted eight blacks and eight whites to corporal. Four months later, the district court suspended the one-for-one requirement for the corporal rank, and suspended the quota for the sergeant rank in October 1984 after approving the Department's new selection procedures for that rank. Further, the Department was allowed to promote only white troopers to lieutenant and captain because no African Americans had qualified for promotion to those ranks.[196]

On appeal, the United States Court of Appeals for the Eleventh Circuit affirmed.[197] Granting *certiorari*, the Supreme Court affirmed in a 5–4 decision.

The Plurality Opinion. Writing for a four-justice plurality, Justice Brennan (joined by Justices Marshall, Blackmun, and Powell) initially discussed the Court's failure to reach a consensus on the appropriate constitutional analysis. He concluded, however, that the promotion quota survived even strict scrutiny analysis, for it was narrowly tailored to serve a compelling governmental purpose. "[T]he pervasive, systematic, and obstinate discriminatory conduct of the Department vented a profound need and a firm justification for the race-conscious relief ordered by the district court in both hiring and promotions."[198] The order was "also supported by the societal interest in compliance with the judgment of federal courts."[199]

The plurality then concluded that the promotion requirement was narrowly tailored for several reasons. First, Justice Brennan wrote that the requirement was necessary to remedy the Department's long term and pervasive discrimination, and that alternative remedies would not have effectuated the court's purposes. One alternative suggested to the Court by the Solicitor General (which was never proposed to the district court) was the imposition of fines and fees on the Department. Justice Brennan noted that the Department had been ordered to pay the plaintiff's attorneys' fees and costs. "In addition, imposing fines on the defendant does nothing to compensate the plaintiffs for the long delays in implementing acceptable promotion procedures."[200]

Second, continued Brennan, the one-for-one requirement was flexible and could be varied if no qualified black candidates were available. In that regard, he noted that the requirement had been suspended for the corporal and sergeant ranks when the Department submitted promotion procedures, and that the Department had been permitted to promote only whites to upper ranks.

Third, the plurality rejected the Solicitor General's argument that the one-for-one requirement was arbitrary because it was not related to the 25 percent relevant minority labor pool. "This argument ignores that the 50% figure is not itself the goal; rather, it represents the speed at which the goal of 25% will be achieved."[201] In Brennan's view, the use of the 50 percent requirement was constitutionally permissible given the ineffectiveness of the district court's deadlines and the district court's determination that it should compensate for past delay and prevent future recalcitrance.

Fourth, Justice Brennan concluded that the promotion requirement did not unacceptably burden innocent third parties. The requirement was temporary and limited; 50 percent of those promoted were white; the layoff or discharge of whites was not required; the promotions of qualified whites were only postponed and were a diffuse burden; and the fact that promoted black troopers must be qualified meant that qualified white candidates simply had to compete with qualified black candidates.[202]

Finally, Justice Brennan concluded that the district court properly balanced the individual and collective interests at stake in shaping the remedy. The court's "proximate position and broad equitable powers mandate substantial respect for this judgment."[203]

Justice Powell's Concurrence. Agreeing with the plurality, Justice Powell reasoned that the protracted history of the litigation justified the conclusion that the promotion requirement was appropriate. Relying on his five-factor analysis set forth in *Sheet Metal Workers* and *Fullilove*,[204] Justice Powell determined that the district court's order was flexible and fair because it applied only to qualified black candidates and was suspended when the Department proposed valid promotion procedures. Further, Justice Powell concluded that the effect of the order on innocent white troopers was likely to be relatively diffuse in that it did not impose the entire burden of achieving racial equality on particular individuals, and did not "disrupt seriously" the lives of innocent individuals.[205] Therefore, Justice Powell joined the plurality's opinion.

The Stevens Concurrence. Providing the fifth vote affirming the Eleventh Circuit's judgment, Justice Stevens, relying on school desegregation precedent, viewed the case as one involving a district court's broad and flexible authority to remedy an egregious violation of the Equal Protection Clause. Citing and discussing *Swann v. Charlotte-Mecklenburg Board of Education*,[206] Justice Stevens rejected the notion that the Court should craft special rules for reviewing judicial decrees in racial discrimination cases. "A party who has been found guilty of repeated and persistent violations of the law bears the burden of demonstrating that the chancellor's efforts to fashion effective relief exceed the bounds of 'reasonableness.' "[207] Finding no showing that the district court abused his discretion in shaping a remedy, Justice Stevens concurred in the Court's judgment.

Dissenting Opinions. Justice O'Connor, joined by Chief Justice Rehnquist and Justice Scalia, dissented. Conceding that the Department had engaged in pervasive and systematic discrimination which the district court had a compelling interest in remedying, she concluded that the district court unquestionably had the authority to remedy the Department's "egregious history of discrimination."[208]

Justice O'Connor parted company with the majority on the issue of the tailoring of the district court's order. In her view, the district court's order was not manifestly necessary to achieve compliance with the court's orders. The only purpose of the district court's order, stated O'Connor, was to compel the Department to develop a promotion procedure that would not have an adverse impact on blacks. She therefore rejected the suggestion that the purpose of the order was to eradicate the effects of the Department's delay in producing a promotion procedure. In her view, the promotion quota would end when the Department developed a promotion procedure in compliance with the consent decrees. If the order was designed to eradicate the effects of the Department's delay, stated O'Connor, the district court would have continued the quota after the Department complied with the consent decrees.

Moreover, stated Justice O'Connor, the quota was not justified. The one-for-one promotion quota "far exceeded the percentage of blacks in the trooper force, and there is no evidence in the record that such an extreme quota was necessary to eradicate the effects of the Department's delay."[209] Speed was not an adequate justification "because it has no stopping point; even a 100% quota could be defended on the ground that it merely 'determined how quickly the Department progressed toward' some ultimate goal."[210] Thus, absent compelling justification, Justice O'Connor would require that a racial goal not substantially exceed the percentage of minority group members in the relevant population or work force.

Applying strict scrutiny, Justice O'Connor concluded that the district court order could not be justified. Other alternatives were available which, in her view, could have been used: the appointment of a trustee to develop a promotion procedure; contempt of court findings; the imposition of stiff fines or penalties. Arguing that the district court did not expressly evaluate alternative remedies, and determining that the alternatives would have compelled Department compliance with the consent decrees, she concluded that the district court could not survive strict scrutiny.

The fourth dissenting vote was cast by Justice White in a short, one-paragraph dissent that agreed with "much of what" Justice O'Connor had written.[211] He found it "evident that the District Court exceeded its equitable powers in devising a remedy in this case."[212]

Analysis. The *Paradise* Court's holding that the one-for-one promotion requirement was constitutional was understandable and defensible given the long-standing discrimination by the Alabama Department of Public Safety against African Americans. However, the 5–4 vote for affirmance of the Eleventh Circuit's judgment revealed that the dissenting justices were only one vote short of a majority which would not hold such a requirement constitutional, even where there was no dispute that the employer had violated the Constitution by engaging in pervasive and egregious discrimination. Instead, the dissenting justices would require express evaluation and consideration of alternatives prior to the imposition of a race-conscious quota.

One of the most interesting aspects of *Paradise* is the dispute between the majority and the dissent over the speed of the promotion requirement. Under the majority analysis, the speed was not anchored to, nor limited by, the percentage of minorities in the relevant labor pool. Thus, under *Paradise*, a district court would enjoy considerable flexibility and discretion in establishing percentage increase requirements and the time in which such requirements must be satisfied. In contrast, the dissenting justices argued that the speed of a "quota" should be tied to the percentage of the relevant minority labor pool. While that view offers some standard by which percentage requirements could be measured, this view would also limit district court discretion in setting percentages at a level which best responds to the particular discrimination being remedied by the court.

It is thus apparent that the central question in *Paradise* and like cases will not center on liability, for there was no question with respect to whether or not the Constitution was violated. The question is one of the proper scope and level of relief and how far the lower courts can go in remedying discrimination. That question is far from settled. With the subsequent departure of Justice Powell, one of the five votes for the result in *Paradise* is no longer on the Court.

Voluntary Affirmative Action in the Public Sector: Johnson

An additional and significant affirmative action in employment case decided by the Supreme Court in 1987 was *Johnson v. Transportation Agency, Santa*

Clara County, California.[213] In that case, the Court considered the question whether the county transportation agency violated Title VII by taking into account the sex of an applicant for a promotion.[214]

In 1979, the agency announced a vacancy for a promotional position of road dispatcher. Twelve employees applied for the promotion, and nine were deemed qualified for the job. Interviews of the applicants were conducted by a two-person board; seven applicants received a score above seventy on the interview (the scores ranged from seventy to eighty) and were certified as eligible for promotion.[215]

Among the seven employees certified were Paul Johnson and Diane Joyce. Johnson, who tied for second in the interview with a score of seventy-five, began working for the county in 1974 as a road yard clerk after working in the private sector as a supervisor and dispatcher. Johnson had unsuccessfully applied for a road dispatcher position in 1974, worked as a road maintenance worker, and occasionally worked as a dispatcher.[216] Joyce, who scored seventy-three on the interview, had worked for the county since 1970. Joyce worked as an account clerk until 1975, had unsuccessfully applied for a road dispatcher position in 1974, had become the first woman to assume a road maintenance worker position in 1975, and occasionally worked as a road dispatcher.[217]

A second interview was conducted by three supervisors who recommended that Johnson receive the promotion. Before her second interview, Joyce contacted the county affirmative action officer because she feared that she would not receive a disinterested review.[218] The officer contacted the agency's affirmative action coordinator, who was responsible for keeping the director of the agency informed of opportunities for the agency to accomplish its objectives under its affirmative action plan.[219] Of the seven eligible employees, the director chose Joyce for the promotion. In selecting Joyce, the director testified that he attempted to look at the "whole picture, the combination of her qualifications, and Mr. Johnson's qualifications, their test scores, their expertise, their background, affirmative action matters, things like that. . . . ''[220]

Johnson brought suit, alleging that he had been denied the promotion on the basis of sex in violation of Title VII. The district court found in his favor, concluding that Johnson was more qualified than Joyce, that sex was the determining factor in her selection, and that the agency's affirmative action plan did not satisfy *United Steelworkers of America v. Weber*[221] because the plan was not temporary. The United States Court of Appeals for the Ninth Circuit reversed, holding that the absence of a termination date in the plan was not dispositive.[222] The Ninth Circuit also concluded that consideration of Joyce's sex was lawful, and that the plan had been adopted to address a conspicuous imbalance in the agency work force.

The Majority Opinion. By a 6–3 vote, the Supreme Court affirmed the Ninth Circuit. Justice Brennan (joined by Justices Marshall, Blackmun, Powell, and Stevens) wrote the majority opinion. Initially noting that Johnson bore the burden of establishing the invalidity of the affirmative action plan,[223] Justice Brennan instructed that the assessment of the legality of an affirmative action plan must be guided by *Weber*. Thus, stated Brennan, "we must determine whether the effect of the Plan on males and nonminorities is comparable to the effect of the plan in [*Weber*]."[224]

The first issue addressed by the Court was whether consideration of the sex of applicants was justified by the existence of a "manifest imbalance" that reflected underrepresentation of women in traditionally segregated job categories. To determine whether that imbalance existed, Justice Brennan stated that where jobs required "no special expertise" it is appropriate to compare the percentage of minorities or women in the employer's work force with the percentage in the area labor market or general population.[225] Where jobs require special training, wrote Brennan, "the comparison should be with those in the labor force who possess the relevant qualifications."[226]

The manifest imbalance need not support a *prima facie* case "since we do not regard as identical the constraints of Title VII and the Federal Constitution on voluntarily adopted affirmative action plans."[227] Application of the *prima facie* standard in Title VII cases would be inconsistent with *Weber's* focus on statistical imbalance, stated Brennan, and could create a "significant disincentive for employers to adopt an affirmative action plan."[228] Justice Brennan made it clear that "as long as there is a manifest imbalance, an employer may adopt a plan even where the disparity is not so striking, without being required to introduce the nonstatistical evidence of past discrimination that would be demanded by the '*prima facie*' standard."[229]

Women were egregiously underrepresented in the skilled craft category, concluded Justice Brennan; none of the 238 positions was occupied by a woman. At the time of Joyce's promotion in 1980, the agency had not yet established short-term goals. (In 1982, the agency did establish a short-term goal of approximately 6 percent for the craft worker category.) The fact that only long-term goals were in place at the time of Joyce's promotion did not make the director's choice of Joyce inappropriate. Justice Brennan wrote that the agency's plan did not authorize blind hiring, but expressly directed that numerous factors be taken into account in making employment decisions. "The fact that only the long-term goal had been established for this category posed no danger that personnel decisions would be made by reflective adherence to a numerical standard."[230] Given the obvious imbalance in the craft category, Justice Brennan concluded that it was not unreasonable for the agency to consider the sex of Joyce as one factor in making the promotion decision.

Justice Brennan then considered whether the agency's plan unnecessarily trammeled the interests of male employees or created an absolute bar to their advancement. Contrasting the agency plan to the plan in *Weber*[231] and the consent decree in *Firefighters*,[232] he noted that the plan set aside no positions for women. Rather, it only authorized consideration of affirmative action concerns when evaluating qualified applicants. Moreover, women were required to compete with all other qualified applicants. And, stated Brennan, Johnson had no absolute entitlement to the road dispatcher job. "Thus, denial of the promotion unsettled no legitimate firmly rooted expectation on the part of [Johnson]."[233] Furthermore, Johnson retained his employment at the same salary and seniority, and remained eligible for other promotions. Finally, Justice Brennan concluded that the plan was intended to attain, and not maintain, a balanced work force.[234]

Holding that the agency's affirmative action plan "represents a moderate, flexible case-by-case approach to effecting a gradual improvement in the representation of minorities and women in the Agency's work force,"[235] the Court affirmed the Ninth Circuit's judgment.[236]

Justice O'Connor's Concurrence. Concurring in the judgment in light of the Court's precedents, Justice O'Connor argued that the majority had chosen to follow "an expansive and ill-defined approach to voluntary affirmative action by public employers despite the limitations imposed by the Constitution and by the provisions of Title VII. . . . "[237]

In Justice O'Connor's view, the initial inquiry in this Title VII case was no different from that required by the Constitution.

[T]he employer must have had a firm basis for believing that remedial action was required. An employer would have such a firm basis if it can point to a statistical disparity sufficient to support a prima facie claim under Title VII by the employee beneficiaries of the affirmative action plan of a pattern or practice claim of discrimination.[238]

Justice O'Connor made it clear that this firm basis did not require employers to prove that they actually discriminated against women or minorities. Such a contemporaneous finding of discrimination would discourage voluntary affirmative remedies, she stated. Thus, evidence sufficient for a *prima facie* case against the employer suggested to O'Connor that the absence of women or minorities in the work force cannot be explained by societal discrimination alone.[239]

Applying these principles in *Johnson*, Justice O'Connor determined that the agency plan satisfied *Weber* and *Wygant*. She noted that, at the time the plan was adopted, no women were employed in the employer's 238 skilled craft positions. Opining that the plan would have violated Title VII if its long-term goals had been applied to hiring decisions,[240] she stated that the long-term goals are merely a stated aspiration with no operational significance. Instead, the employer was guided by short-term goals which the plan provided "should not be construed as 'quotas' that must be met."[241]

In addition, Justice O'Connor found that the agency had a firm basis for adopting the affirmative action plan. Although the district court did not find any discrimination against women, in fact, no women were employed as skilled craft workers. Noting that women constituted approximately 5 percent of the local labor pool of skilled craft workers in 1970, Justice O'Connor determined that the statistical disparity between the "inexorable zero" and the availability percentage would have been sufficient for a *prima facie* Title VII case. Accordingly, she concurred in the Court's judgment.

The Dissenting Opinions. Continuing his pattern of one-paragraph dissents,

Justice White urged that *Weber* should be overruled. A member of the *Weber* majority, White stated he understood that the phrase "traditionally segregated jobs" used in *Weber* referred to intentional and systematic exclusion of blacks by employers and unions. "The Court now interprets it to mean nothing more than a manifest imbalance between one identifiable group and another in an employer's labor force. As so interpreted, that case, as well as today's decision, is a perversion of Title VII."[242]

Authoring his first opinion in an affirmative action in employment case, Justice Scalia (joined by Chief Justice Rehnquist and in part by Justice White) wrote a heated dissent. In his view, the majority ruling "effectively replace[d] the goal of a discrimination-free society with the quite incompatible goal of proportionate representation by race and by sex in the work place."[243] He further stated that the majority's decision also established the proposition that racial or sexual discrimination is permitted under Title VII when it is "intended to overcome societal attitudes, not the employer's discrimination," a proposition which he concluded contradicted the Court's decision in *Wygant*.[244]

Moreover, continued Scalia, the majority's opinion went beyond eliminating the effects of prior societal discrimination. The agency's road maintenance position was traditionally segregated not in the *Weber* sense, he stated, "but in the sense that, because of longstanding social attitudes, it has not been regarded *by women themselves* as desirable work."[245]

There are, of course, those who believe that the social attitudes which cause women themselves to avoid certain jobs and to favor others are as nefarious as conscious, exclusionary discrimination. Whether or not that is so (and there is assuredly no consensus on the point equivalent to our national consensus against intentional discrimination), the two phenomena are certainly distinct. And it is the alteration of social attitudes, rather than the elimination of discrimination, which today's decision approves as justification for state-enforced discrimination. This is an enormous expansion, undertaken without the slightest justification or analysis.[246]

Justice Scalia also argued that *Weber* should be overruled. In his view, "*Weber* rewrote the statute it purported to construe" and "disregarded the text of the statute, invoking instead its 'spirit'...."[247] *Weber* could not be saved by the doctrine of *stare decisis*, stated Scalia.[248] First, he stated, *stare decisis* doctrine had been applied less rigorously by the Court to civil rights statutes than to other laws. Second, *Weber* was a dramatic departure from the Court's prior Title VII precedent and could not be said to be beyond question. Third, Scalia continued, *Weber* should be overruled because it appeared beyond doubt that the decision misapprehended the meaning of Title VII.[249]

Johnson's impact was clear to Justice Scalia. Employer discrimination through affirmative action offers "a threshold defense against Title VII liability premised on numerical disparities. Thus, after today's decision, the *failure* to engage in reverse discrimination is economic folly, and arguably a breach of duty to shareholders or taxpayers, wherever the cost of an anticipated Title VII litigation exceeds the cost of hiring less capable (though still minimally capable) workers."[250] The incentive would be greatly magnified, in his view, by governmental contracting agencies.[251] In a final shot, Justice Scalia wrote that the "only losers in the process are the Johnsons of the country. . . . "[252] "The irony is that these individuals—predominantly unknown, unaffluent, unorganized—suffer the injustice at the hands of a Court fond of thinking itself the champion of the politically impotent."[253]

The Impact of Johnson. In reaffirming *Weber*, the *Johnson* Court went beyond the type of voluntary affirmative action contained in the Steelworkers-Kaiser collective bargaining agreement and endorsed voluntary affirmative action which was not linked to traditional job segregation in the *Weber* sense. The discrimination and intentionally exclusionary practices addressed in *Weber* were so well established that the Court took judicial notice of the exclusion of African Americans from craft positions. *Johnson* did not present that factual scenario. Instead, the Court concluded that underutilization of women as reflected in work force and population statistics was a sufficient predicate for the agency's voluntary affirmative action plan. Incidents or evidence of specific past discrimination was not at issue; rather, the Court noted that the underrepresentation stemmed from the fact that women were not traditionally employed in road dispatcher jobs and did not seek employment in such positions.

The exact level of underrepresentation was not decided by the Court. As noted above, *Johnson* involved the inexorable zero—no women were employed in the skilled trades by the agency before Diane Joyce was hired as a road dispatcher. While it was clear that a majority of the Court determined that the underrepresentation did not have to rise to the level of a *prima facie* case under Title VII, it was unclear what types and levels of "manifest imbalance" would satisfy *Johnson*.[254]

The *Johnson* Court also established that the plaintiff bore the burden of proving that an employer's justification for affirmative action was unlawful and a pretext for discrimination. Given the Court's holding that underutilization can support a plan and that sex (or race) may be considered as "a" factor in certain employment decisions, it would be exceedingly difficult for a plaintiff to successfully challenge an affirmative action plan which met the *Johnson* standards. In addition, *Johnson* resolved the question whether public employers would be permitted the same flexibility under Title VII with respect to voluntary affirmative action as enjoyed by private employers. In sum, *Johnson's* majority affirmance of the agency's affirmative action plan stood as an important endorsement of *Weber* and voluntary affirmative action.

Although some commentators argued that any question of the future viability of such affirmative action had been definitively resolved,[255] a closer look at *Johnson* reveals that that argument may be premature. True, *Johnson* was a 6–3 decision. However, the Court split 5–1–3 on the issue of the statistical underrepresentation required to support a plan. With the departure of Justice Powell in 1987, only four justices remained on the Court who voted for the manifest imbalance standard. Justice O'Connor voted for the application of a Title VII *prima facie* standard as sufficient support for such initiatives. Under certain scenarios, the following result could be reached in a future case: four justices (Brennan, Marshall, Blackmun, and Stevens) could vote for voluntary affirmative action under Brennan's manifest imbalance standard; one justice (O'Connor) could vote against a plan because the statistical evidence did not rise to a *prima facie* case standard; and four justices (Rehnquist, White, Scalia, and Kennedy) could vote against voluntary affirmative action and seek to overrule *Weber*. Thus, a 5–4 vote against voluntary affirmative action is not inconceivable.

JUSTICE POWELL'S DEPARTURE AND THE APPOINTMENT OF JUSTICE ANTHONY M. KENNEDY

A major development which was sure to have a substantive impact on the Court's affirmative action jurisprudence occurred at the close of the Court's 1987 term. At that time, Justice Powell announced his departure from the Court. Given the fact that Justice Powell had voted with the majority in every affirmative action case decided by the Court and the narrow margins of victory for both proponents and opponents of preferential treatment in those cases, it was readily apparent that Justice Powell's replacement would cast crucial votes in affirmative action and other cases.

In July 1987, former President Reagan nominated Robert H. Bork, then a judge for the United States Court of Appeals for the District of Columbia Circuit. The Bork nomination was not approved by the United States Senate,[256] however, and Reagan nominated Douglas Ginsburg, also a judge for the District of Columbia Circuit. Ginsburg withdrew from consideration less than two weeks later.[257]

President Reagan then nominated Anthony M. Kennedy, a judge on the United States Court of Appeals for the Ninth Circuit. Kennedy was unanimously confirmed by the Senate in February 1988,[258] and would later cast votes with an emerging conservative majority of the Court in affirmative action cases.

THE 1989 CASES

The Application of Strict Scrutiny to Affirmative Action: *Croson*

In January 1989, the Supreme Court decided *City of Richmond v. J. A. Croson Company*,[259] wherein the Court held that a city program could set aside at least 30 percent of the dollar amount of city construction contracts to minority business enterprises (MBEs). Although this case (which is discussed in detail in Chapter 5)[260] is not an employment case, the Court's ruling on certain aspects of affirmative action and preferential treatment of minorities is directly relevant to the constitutionality of affirmative action in the employment context.

The city of Richmond, Virginia adopted an MBE program in 1983 which required nonminority prime contractors to subcontract at least 30 percent of the dollar amount of the contract to one or more MBEs. Challenging the program, which expired in June 1988, the J. A. Croson Company brought suit against the city alleging that the program was unconstitutional on its face and as applied. The district court upheld the program in all respects. But the United States Court of Appeals for the Fourth Circuit struck down the program as violative of the Equal Protection Clause of the Fourteenth Amendment.[261]

The Court Applies Strict Scrutiny. Among other things, a majority of the Supreme Court applied the strict scrutiny standard of review to an affirmative action program designed to benefit minorities. Writing for the Court on that point, Justice O'Connor (joined by Chief Justice Rehnquist and Justices White and Kennedy) concluded that strict scrutiny was the proper standard. In a separate opinion, Justice Scalia agreed that strict scrutiny must be applied to all governmental racial classifications.

Justice O'Connor wrote that the Richmond program "denies certain citizens the opportunity to compete for a fixed percentage of public contracts based solely upon their race."[262] Opining that strict scrutiny must be applied, she stated:

Absent searching judicial inquiry into the justification for such race-based measures, there is simply no way of determining what classifications are "benign" or "remedial" and what classifications are, in fact, motivated by illegitimate notions of racial inferiority or simple racial politics. Indeed, the purpose of strict scrutiny is to "smoke out" illegitimate uses of race by assuring that the legislative body is pursuing a goal important enough to warrant use of a highly suspect tool. The test also ensures that the means chosen "fit" this compelling goal so closely that there is little or no possibility that the motive for the classification was illegitimate racial prejudice or stereotype.[263]

Justice O'Connor thus reaffirmed the *Wygant* plurality's view[264] that "the standard of review under the Equal Protection Clause is not dependent on the race of those burdened or benefited by a particular classification."[265]

Justice O'Connor then concluded that heightened scrutiny was appropriate because African Americans comprised approximately 50 percent of the population of the city of Richmond and held five of the nine seats in the city council. "The concern that a political majority will more easily act to the disadvantage of a minority based on unwarranted assumptions or incomplete facts would seem to militate for, not against, the application of heightened judicial scrutiny in this case."[266]

Applying strict scrutiny, Justice O'Connor found that the factual predicate offered in support of the Richmond program was defective. In her view, the 30 percent quota was not tied to any injury suffered by anyone.[267] Because the city did not point to identified discrimination in the Richmond construction industry, the Court held that the city had failed to demonstrate a compelling interest in apportioning public contracting opportunities on the basis of race. Further, Justice O'Connor wrote that it was impossible for the Court to assess whether the Richmond program was narrowly tailored to remedy prior discrimination. Race-neutral means to increase MBE participation in city contracting were apparently not considered, stated O'Connor, and the 30 percent quota ''cannot be said to be narrowly tailored to any goal, except outright racial balancing.''[268]

An additional vote for application of the strict scrutiny standard of review was provided by Justice Scalia. He agreed ''with much of the Court's opinion, and, in particular, with its conclusion that strict scrutiny must be applied to all governmental classification by race, whether or not its asserted purpose is 'remedial' or 'benign.' ''[269]

Croson thus brings into majority status the *Wygant* plurality's views on the level of scrutiny to be applied in constitutional challenges to affirmative action in employment measures. While the impact of that development is not yet clear, it would appear that employers and other entities formulating affirmative action plans and initiatives must prepare those measures to withstand harsh and skeptical judicial examination.

Collateral Attacks on Consent Decrees: The *Wilks* Decision

The most recent affirmative action in employment decision by the Court, *Martin v. Wilks*,[270] offered an additional setback to proponents of affirmative action. Addressing the technical issue of the collateral attack doctrine,[271] the Court held, in a 5–4 decision, that a district court holding precluding white firefighters from challenging employment decisions taken pursuant to consent decrees contravened ''the general rule that a person cannot be deprived of his legal rights in a proceeding to which he is not a party.''[272]

The facts of *Wilks* present another illustration of the lengthy litigation characteristic of affirmative action cases. In 1974, the NAACP and seven African-American individuals filed separate class action suits against the city of Birmingham, Alabama and the Jefferson County Personnel Board. Those suits alleged that the city and the board had engaged in discriminatory hiring and promotion practices. After a bench trial, but before judgment, the individual black employees entered into separate consent decrees with the city and the board, which included long-term and interim yearly goals for the hiring of blacks as firefighters, and also provided goals for the promotion of blacks in the fire department.

Provisional approval of the consent decrees was granted by the district court, and notice of fairness hearings was published in two local newspapers. The Birmingham Firefighters Association (Association) appeared at the hearing and filed objections. After the fairness hearing, and before the decrees were finally approved, the Association and two Association members moved to intervene, asserting that their rights were adversely affected by the decrees. The district court denied the motions as untimely, and the decrees were approved.[273] A complaint against the city and the board was then filed by seven white firefighters who sought to enjoin enforcement of the decrees. The district court denied injunctive relief, and the district court's denial of intervention and injunctive relief was affirmed by the United States Court of Appeals for the Eleventh Circuit.[274]

An additional suit was then brought by another group of white firefighters against the city and the board. In that suit, the plaintiffs alleged that they were denied promotions in favor of less qualified black firefighters. Subsequent to a trial on that complaint, the district court granted the defendant's motion to dismiss, concluding that the city's promotion of black employees under the consent decree would not constitute illegal racial discrimination against whites.[275] However, the Eleventh Circuit reversed the district court.[276] Rejecting the doctrine of impermissible collateral attack which would immunize parties to a consent decree from discrimination charges by nonparties, the Eleventh Circuit held that the public policy in favor of voluntary affirmative action must yield to the policy against "requiring third parties to submit to bargains in which their interests were either ignored or sacrificed."[277]

The Court's Decision. In a 5–4 decision, the Supreme Court affirmed the Eleventh Circuit. Chief Justice Rehnquist's opinion for the Court (joined by Justices White, O'Connor, Scalia, and Kennedy) began by noting that it is a "principle of general application in Anglo-American jurisprudence that one is not bound by a judgment *in personam* in a litigation in which he is not designated as a party or to which he has not been made a party by service of process."[278] With certain exceptions which were not applicable, stated Chief Justice Rehnquist, a judgment or decree among parties does not conclude the rights of nonparties.

The Chief Justice rejected the argument that the white firefighters' challenge was an impermissible collateral attack because they failed to timely intervene in the initial proceedings. Although the majority of the federal courts of appeals had endorsed that view,[279] the Chief Justice rejected it as inconsistent with the Federal Rules of Civil Procedure (Federal Rules) "[A] party seeking a judgment binding on another cannot obligate that person to intervene; he must be joined."[280] Rule 24 of the Federal Rules provides for intervention as of right ("[u]pon timely application anyone shall be permitted to intervene") or by permission ("[u]pon timely application anyone may be permitted to intervene").[281] Rule 19(a) of the Federal Rules provides for a mandatory joinder where a judgment rendered in the absence of an individual may leave "persons already parties subject to a substantial risk of incurring . . . inconsistent obligations. . . . "[282] Where an interested party is absent, Rule 19(b) of the Federal Rules sets forth the factors to be considered by the courts in deciding whether an action should proceed.[283] Joinder, not intervention, was the procedural mechanism required by the Court.

Joinder as a party, rather than knowledge of a lawsuit and an opportunity to intervene, is the method by which potential parties are subjected to the jurisdiction of the court and bound by a judgment or decree. The parties to a lawsuit presumably know better than anyone else the nature and scope of relief sought in the action, and at whose expense such relief might be granted. It makes sense, therefore, to place on them a burden of bringing in additional parties where such a step is indicated, rather than placing on potential additional parties a duty to intervene when they acquire knowledge of the lawsuit. The linchpin of the "impermissible collateral attack" doctrine—the attribution of preclusive effect to a failure to intervene—is therefore quite inconsistent with Rule 19 and Rule 24.[284]

The Chief Justice conceded that requiring joinder of affected parties will present difficulties. In that regard, the city argued that potential adverse claimants may be numerous and difficult to identify and that judicial resources will be needlessly consumed in relitigating the same question. In his view, those difficulties "arise from the nature of the relief sought and not because of any choice between mandatory intervention and joinder."[285] Nor was he convinced that joinder was likely to produce more relitigation of issues than would the converse rule.

The Chief Justice also concluded that the Court's decision would not hinder the federal policy favoring the voluntary settlement of employment discrimination claims. "A voluntary settlement in the form of a consent decree between one group of employees and their employer cannot possibly 'settle,' voluntarily or otherwise, the conflicting claims of another group of employees who do not join in the agreement."[286] For the foregoing reasons, the Court affirmed the Eleventh Circuit and remanded the case for trial of the reverse discrimination claims.

The Dissent. Four justices dissented in an opinion by Justice Stevens (joined by Justices Brennan, Marshall, and Blackmun). In Justice Stevens' view,

there was no reason why the consent decrees might not produce changes in conditions at the white firefighters' place of employment that, as a practical matter, may have a serious effect on their opportunities for employment or promotion even though they are not bound by the decrees in any legal sense. The fact that one of the effects of a decree is to curtail the job opportunities of nonparties does not mean that the nonparties have been deprived of legal rights or that they have standing to appeal from that decree without becoming parties.[287]

Noting that the white firefighters were not parties to the consent decrees and that they were not bound by the decrees, Justice Stevens stated that the "judgments did, however, have a practical impact on respondents' opportunities for advancement in their profession."[288] For that reason, he stated, the white employees had standing to collaterally challenge the validity of the decrees under limited grounds, such as lack of court jurisdiction, or a judgment obtained through corruption, fraud, collusion, or mistake.[289] A retrial of the case was not required, opined Stevens, since broad collateral review would "destroy the integrity of litigated judgments, would lead to an abundance of vexatious litigation, and would subvert the interest in comity between courts."[290]

Justice Stevens found no collusion or fraud in connection with the consent decrees, and further found that the decree was the product of genuine arm's length negotiations. Furthermore, he concluded that the relief ordered in the decree was consistent with the Court's approach to affirmative action. And, Justice Stevens noted, the white employees did not claim mistake, duress, or lack of jurisdiction which would serve as a basis for collaterally attacking the decree. In the absence of such claims, "it would be 'unconscionable' to conclude that obedience to an order remedying a Title VII violation could subject a defendant to additional liability."[291]

The impact of the decree and remedy on nonminorities was also discussed by Justice Stevens. In his view, the white firefighters were the beneficiaries of the discriminatory practices to be remedied by the decree, and any remedy would necessarily have an adverse impact on whites because of the sharing of jobs and promotion opportunities with blacks. "Just as white employees in the past were innocent beneficiaries of illegal discriminatory practices, so is it inevitable that some of the same white employees will be innocent victims who must share some of the burdens resulting from the redress of the past wrongs."[292] Taking the position that compliance with the terms of a valid consent decree cannot itself violate Title VII or the Equal Protection Clause, Justice Stevens would have vacated the Eleventh Circuit's judgment and remanded the case.

Analysis. The *Wilks* Court's rejection of the impermissible collateral attack doctrine, a doctrine which had been accepted by the vast majority of the federal courts of appeals, introduces an additional factor which has to be considered by parties to consent decrees—the joinder of potential parties and the possibility that decrees would be subsequently attacked by nonparties, claiming that their interests or rights were adversely affected by the settlement of employment discrimination litigation. The joinder requirement and the consequent burden placed on litigants will present practical difficulties of identification of potential adverse claimants and the expansion of litigation. By permitting collateral attacks, settlements which were thought to be final and binding may be tentative agreements subject to additional litigation brought by parties affected by the operation of the decree. In the employment and affirmative action context, it is likely that reverse discrimination suits will be filed where whites are adversely affected by hiring, promotion, or other employment actions required by decrees. Thus, joinder of unions and the identification of the pool or segment of a work force which will, or may be, affected by operation of a decree is now a necessary and critical aspect of affirmative action litigation.

Even if collateral attacks are not successful, the litigation costs of defending attacks by nonparties and the uncertain permanence of the decree raise concerns which must be recognized. Whether and how those concerns will hinder the federal policy of voluntary settlement of employment discrimination claims is an issue which warrants ongoing scrutiny as *Wilks* is applied by the lower courts.

RECENT LOWER COURT DECISIONS

The best illustration of the impact and meaning of the Supreme Court's rulings discussed above is the application of the Court's decisions by the lower courts. Selected decisions reveal the ongoing dispute with respect to what the Court meant in its fractured decisions, and the underlying factors which render preferential treatment measures lawful or unlawful.

Different panels of the United States Court of Appeals for the District of Columbia Circuit have issued decisions which highlight this point. In *Ledoux v. District of Columbia*,[293] (later vacated) a three-member panel remanded a district court decision rejecting nonminority and male employees' challenge to, and upholding, a police department's affirmative action plan. Writing for the panel, Judge Harry T. Edwards reviewed the Supreme Court's affirmative action in employment decisions, including *Weber*, *Wygant*, and *Johnson*. In his view, those cases established that the validity of an affirmative action plan must be judged by two factors: (1) whether there was an adequate factual predicate justifying the use of affirmative action, and (2) if justified, whether the employer's plan unnecessarily trammelled the legitimate interests of nonminority or male employees.[294] Under both Title VII and the Constitution, stated Judge Edwards, the burden is on the plaintiff to establish the invalidity of plan.[295]

Judge Edwards concluded that the department's plan was valid under Title VII. Holding that the plan was justified by a "manifest imbalance in traditionally segregated categories" within the meaning of *Weber* and *Johnson*, he noted that women held six of eight hundred and seven positions at or above the rank of sergeant, with blacks holding one hundred and seventy-four of those positions. Under either the District of Columbia or Standard Metropolitan Statistical Area labor markets,[296] Edwards concluded that "these figures plainly demonstrate a manifest imbalance . . . justifying some effort at voluntary affirmative action."[297]

Further, Edwards determined that the plan did not unnecessarily trammel the legitimate interests of nonminority or male employees. He stated that the plan did not call for the displacement or layoff of nonminorities or males; did not authorize the promotion of unqualified blacks and women; and did not seek to "establish in perpetuity a work force whose racial or sexual composition mirrors that of the area labor force."[298] In his view, the plan was virtually identical to the plan in *Johnson*, for the consideration of race or sex as a factor in choosing among qualified employees was authorized with a long-term goal of achieving (not maintaining) racial and sexual balance in the work force.[299]

A different result was reached in *Hammon v. Barry*.[300] There, the panel majority reversed a district court ruling that an affirmative action plan of the District of Columbia fire department was valid. The panel's decision denying the District's petition for rehearing will be focused upon here. Then Judge (now United States Solicitor General) Kenneth Starr applied *Johnson* in reviewing the fire department's race-conscious hiring plan. Judge Starr noted that the fire department had hired blacks for entry level positions at a rate of 50 percent per year since 1969, and that since 1981 over 75 percent of new firefighter hires were black.[301] And, as of April 1984, 37 percent of the District's firefighting force was black.

Conceding that the fire department was officially segregated in the 1950s, Starr found a "rather obvious and substantial temporal gap between the time of the Korean Conflict . . . and the present day. . . ."[302] He then applied *Johnson* and relied on this area labor force bench mark: the relevant labor force consisted of persons twenty to twenty-eight years of age in the Washington metropolitan area. Approximately 29 percent of that metropolitan area was black. Thus, stated Starr, the fire department work force had a greater percentage of blacks than the black percentage in the area labor force. Moreover, the average percentage of black hires was greater than the percentage of blacks in the hiring pools referred to by the district court. Under this analysis, Judge Starr found no manifest imbalance in the fire department.[303]

Distinguishing the district's plan from the plan validated in *Johnson*, Judge Starr found that the District's requirement of at least 60 percent blacks in each entering class of firefighters was a rigid quota and blind hiring by the numbers. In addition, Judge Starr concluded that the District's hiring plan was not narrowly tailored because available race-neutral alternatives were not considered.[304] Accordingly, he concluded that the plan violated Title VII.[305]

Dissenting, Judge Mikva urged that the majority was oblivious to the district court's findings that there was a manifest imbalance in the racial composition of the fire department's uniformed work force; that there was a history of overt discrimination in the department; and that there was evidence of recent discrimination. He rejected the majority's use of the racial composition of the Washington metropolitan area as the appropriate bench mark; rather, he would use the District of Columbia work force for assessing whether there was a manifest imbalance.[306] Moreover, stated Judge Mikva, the applicant pool was an appropriate bench mark because the applicant pool had been predominantly black since the 1970s, yet only 37 percent of the District's fire force were African Americans.[307]

In another Title VII case, *Higgins v. City of Vallejo*,[308] the court upheld a city's affirmative action plan under Title VII and the Constitution. The plaintiff, a white male firefighter, filed a reverse discrimination suit alleging that the promotion of an African-American male to a firefighter engineer position was unlawful and unconstitutional. At the time the position was available, the plaintiff ranked first on the basis of competitive examinations with a score of 94.17. The African American promoted ranked third with a score of 93.09. The fire department chief recommended that the plaintiff receive the promotion. The city manager instead promoted the black firefighter in 1983 because that selection was consistent with the city's affirmative action plan. The plaintiff was subsequently promoted in 1986.[309]

Affirming the district court's summary judgment to the city, the Ninth Circuit held, *inter alia*, that the plaintiff did not carry his burden under *Johnson* and

Weber. The court found that the city had satisfied the "manifest imbalance" requirement. In support of this finding, the court stated that the city had implemented its affirmative action plan after, and as a result of, the California Fair Employment Practices Commission's determination that minorities were conspicuously lacking in the work force. That report, issued in 1973, found that the city's population was approximately 30 percent minority and 11.4 percent of the city work force was minority; that 17 percent of the population was black and 7.3 percent of the municipal work force was black; and that the city's employment practices facilitated the discrimination. Within the city fire department, stated the court, blacks were not hired until 1964; two other blacks received fire department jobs between 1964 and 1973; five blacks were among the forty-seven firefighters hired between 1972 and the end of 1983; one black individual was promoted to fire captain in that same period (with thirty-five others promoted to captain); and three blacks had held the position of firefighter/engineer in the history of the fire department.

Further, the court held that the plan did not unnecessarily trammel the rights of nonminorities. Applying *Johnson*, the Ninth Circuit determined, first, that the City of Vallejo's plan was free of rigid quotas and discriminatory exclusions, with only qualified employees considered for promotions and all applicants entitled to compete against each other. Race was taken into account once a pool of qualified applicants was assembled.[310] Second, the court concluded that the plaintiff had no absolute entitlement to the promotion because, under the city charter, the city manager had discretion to choose one of the top three applicants. Third, the court noted that the plaintiff retained his job, salary, and seniority and retained his eligibility for future promotions (which he obtained in February 1986). Finally, the court noted that the affirmative action plan stated that the city intended to "accomplish" the goal of equal employment opportunity.[311] Thus, the city's plan was designed to attain, not maintain, racial balance.

As to the plaintiff's equal protection challenge, the *Higgins* court held that the city's plan passed the most rigorous test applicable in analyzing whether race-conscious remedial measures are constitutional. The city's compelling interest was satisfied by the aforementioned state report indicating that the city's work force was racially imbalanced and that the imbalance was caused, at least in part, by the city's employment practices. In the court's view, the city's plan was narrowly tailored to achieve racial balance. Under the plan, race was only a "plus" factor because it was one of several factors considered by the city manager when deciding which of three certified applicants to promote. Moreover, stated the court, the city's plan did not use layoffs to achieve its goals. Thus, the court concluded that the city's plan for promoting qualified minorities was a minimally intrusive means to achieve racial balance and a narrowly tailored remedy.[312]

Janowiak v. Corporate City of South Bend[313] provides another contemporary example of statutory and constitutional analysis in this area. The question addressed in that case was whether the city could adopt an affirmative action program for its police and fire departments based solely upon a finding of a disparity between the percentage of minorities in the city's population (14.1 percent) and the percentage of minorities in the departments (in the fire department, 5.3 percent).[314]

A minority recruitment task force, emphasizing that the city's hiring practices were reasonable and should be continued, recommended the adoption of a preferential hiring plan to reflect the city's minority composition. Thereafter, a minority recruitment review committee recommended that the departments use separate lists to rank minority and nonminority applicants and that a three-member panel recommend the number of applicants to be hired from each list. This recommendation was adopted by the city's Board of Public Safety, and one nonminority and four minority applicants were appointed to the fire department in November 1980. Timothy Janowiak, who ranked second of twenty-two nonminority applicants, was not selected for appointment. He brought suit challenging the city's affirmative action program.

The Seventh Circuit, reversing the district court's summary judgment for the city, held that *Johnson* holding for *Janowiak* was clear.

In a case such as this one, in which the City has proffered no evidence of an "inexorable zero" and absolutely no other evidence of past discrimination, any proffered statistical comparison must establish a manifest imbalance between the relevant qualified area labor pool and the employer's work force.[315]

The city's affirmative action plan failed to pass Title VII muster, stated the court, because the statistical comparison upon which the city based its affirmative action program focused not on the relevant qualified area labor pool, but on general population statistics.

If a job category requires that applicants possess minimum qualifications, the City's proffered statistical comparison must narrow its focus to those actually qualified for the position. Because the City here did not offer any evidence of a statistical disparity between the number of minorities in the fire department and the number of qualified minorities in the area labor pool, it failed to establish the manifest imbalance required by *Johnson*.[316]

Accordingly, the court held that the city was not entitled to summary judgment; that its plan did not violate Title VII.

Turning to the constitutional question, the Seventh Circuit applied what it termed the bench mark standards of *Wygant*: (1) the plan must be justified by a compelling governmental interest, and (2) the means chosen by the government must be narrowly tailored to effectuate the plan's purpose.[317] Formulating a "lowest common denominator holding" of *Wygant*,[318] the court held that a statistical comparison upon which an affirmative action plan is based "must compare the percentages of minorities in [the] employer's workforce with the percentage of minorities in the qualified area labor pool before it can establish the predicate past discrimination required to justify an affirmative action remedy under the fourteenth amendment."[319] Because the city's statistical comparison focused on general population statistics alone, the court held that the plan ran afoul of the Equal Protection Clause.[320]

A significant, *en banc* decision by the Seventh Circuit merits consideration. In *Britton v. South Bend Community School Corporation*,[321] a plurality held that the Equal Protection Clause was violated by a labor agreement's layoff provision under which no African-American teachers would be laid off until all white teachers were laid off.[322] Judge Richard Posner's opinion for the plurality noted, *inter alia*, that the racially preferential layoff plan went further than the plan struck down in *Wygant*, and that the goal advanced by the school board— correcting a discrepancy between the percentage of black teachers and black students—had been held to be not probative of employment discrimination in *Wygant*.[323] That goal also led the court to conclude that the plan was not narrowly tailored.

Judge Posner stated that the court could not exclude the possibility that the South Bend School Board had discriminated against black teachers in hiring. "One would think, however, that if this were so, the board would have argued the point in the district court; for while *Wygant*, decided later, withdrew certain justifications for such provisions, it did not create a new one (correcting previous discrimination)."[324] And, continued Posner, the plan erected an absolute racial preference for blacks—"no matter how recently hired a black was, he was placed on the seniority ladder above every white teacher."[325]

A December 1989 decision by the Ninth Circuit offers yet another illustration of judicial application of the Supreme Court's affirmative action rulings. In *Davis v. San Francisco Fire Fighters Local 798*,[326] a union challenged a consent decree[327] executed by plaintiff intervenors and the city and county of San Francisco which settled Title VII class action litigation by setting certain hiring and promotion goals. The decree was addressed in a fairness hearing and approved by court order. The union participated in the hearing, objected to the terms of the decree, and did not sign it.[328]

Analyzing the decree under Title VII, the Ninth Circuit relied on *Johnson's* manifest imbalance standard. In its view, determination of whether an imbalance had occurred required a comparison of the "percentage of minorities or women in the employer's work force with the percentage in the area labor market or general population."[329] Where an agreement is voluntary, the imbalance "need not be sufficient to support a *prima facie* case of racial discrimination 'since we do not regard as identical the constraints of Title VII and the Federal Constitution on voluntarily adopted affirmative action plans.' "[330] Finding an imbalance on the facts of the case, the court concluded that the manifest imbalance test had been met.

The court then examined the question of whether the decree unnecessarily trammeled the interests of white employees or created an absolute bar to their advancement. Holding that the decree was lawful under Title VII, the court rejected the union's argument that the decree was invalid because it did not require the promotion of whites. "Affirmative relief may be implemented only to remedy harm caused by past discrimination."[331] Absent discrimination against nonminority or male firefighters, the decree need not and could not mandate their promotion. And, stated the court, the advancement of nonminorities was not absolutely barred since nonminorities received promotions in addition to minorities promoted under the consent decree. Because preferential promotions were awarded to minorities in the relevant labor force—the fire department—nonminorities would be able to compete for a "large number" of remaining positions.[332]

The decrees also passed constitutional muster and strict scrutiny review under *Wygant* and *Croson*. In the court's view, there was sufficient evidence to justify the decree's affirmative action provisions, given the statistical disparities between the number of minorities and women hired in the fire department and the number of minorities and women residing in the city of San Francisco, and given the fact that all hiring was entry level and nonskilled. Moreover, stated the court, the decree was narrowly tailored to meet its objectives.

While the decree in *Davis* passed muster under *Croson*, the United States Court of Appeals for the Eleventh Circuit recently vacated a district court ruling dismissing a plaintiff's challenge to a consent decree, and requested the district court to consider the applicability of *Croson*.[333] Acknowledging that *Croson* was distinguishable because the affirmative action program before it was implemented under the auspices of a federal district court, the Eleventh Circuit reasoned that language set forth in *Croson*[334] "may be applicable to race-based classifications imposed by Congress, and *a fortiori* to any such classification practiced by an inferior branch of federal or state government."[335] In remanding, the court did not decide whether the city's plan should be reviewed as a judicially imposed plan, as a plan adopted by a local government, or as a hybrid of the two.

The foregoing cases illustrate the factors and features of affirmative action plans which are essential to judicial assessment of the validity of such plans under Title VII and the Constitution. In that regard, a clear understanding of *Weber*, *Johnson*, *Wygant*, and *Croson* is key. As noted in this chapter's discussion of those decisions, courts will search for the appropriate statistical comparison and factual predicate for an employer's affirmative action initiative, and will assess the impact of that initiative on nonminorities and males. As to the latter, the absence of rigid quotas and goals which seek to maintain a particular composition of a work force are required features of lawful preferential treatment of minorities and women.

SUMMARY AND GUIDELINES

The following guidelines and principles may be gleaned from the Supreme Court's affirmative action decisions.

The Basis for the Affirmative Action Plan or Program

Affirmative action programs must rest upon a sufficient showing or predicate of past discrimination which must go beyond the effects of societal discrimination, do more than provide role models to or for minorities.

Further, plans must be formulated and implemented for the purpose of remedying past discrimination and attaining, not maintaining, racial or sexual balance in the work force. Where the past discrimination is egregious, as found by a court, the Court has upheld the employer's affirmative action. In "non-egregious" cases, affirmative action may be upheld where the disparity between the percentage of minorities or women in the work force and their availability in the relevant labor force are significant. Under Title VII, a *prima facie* showing of unlawful discrimination is not required. Under the Constitution, statistics which are sufficient to establish a *prima facie* case may be required.

The Impact on Nonminority and Male Employees

The Supreme Court's decisions make it clear that affirmative action plans calling for the termination or layoff of white or male employees are not favored. Thus, plans which call for hiring, promotion, or other employment goals which diffuse the effects of affirmative action are preferred. Also, plans which provide employment opportunities to all qualified employees and do not totally favor or prefer minorities or nonminority candidates will be helpful in defending the affirmative action plan against reverse discrimination challenges, for employers will then be able to argue that plans did not unnecessarily trammel nonminorities or males, or serve as an absolute bar to their opportunities.

Plans and consent decrees which override or otherwise modify bona fide seniority systems without the consent of a labor organization and its constituent members are open to attack. Where those nonconsenting parties or individuals are not joined in the litigation, lawsuits challenging a decree or plan may be brought; a possibility that may affect an employer's incentive to adopt plans or enter into consent decrees in settlement of litigation.

The Duration and Flexibility of a Plan

Affirmative action plans with definite ending or termination dates are preferred. The absence of such a date in a plan is not fatal, however, as long as the plan is temporary in the sense that it is adopted to attain, and not maintain, a certain percentage of minority and female employment (as determined by the relevant labor force) and will end once those percentages are attained.

The use of short-term goals and good-faith effort, not inflexible quotas, are key. In that regard, goals which call for the employment or advancement of qualified minorities or females with race or sex as one factor (a plus factor) and not *the* determinative factor, should be included in plans. Again, non-minority and male employees should not be excluded from employment opportunities, but should receive consideration along with qualified minorities and women.

CONCLUSION

This chapter sets forth the Supreme Court's affirmative action in employment jurisprudence and the Court's analysis of Title VII and the Constitution as applied to affirmative action. The series of decisions by the Court offers extensive discussion of both sides of the legal questions raised therein, and frameworks and principles which govern the use of voluntary affirmative action plans, consent decrees, and judicial orders. By detailing the views of the justices for the reader it is hoped that the principles and guidelines unearthed from the mountain of opinions, concurrences, and dissents which have been issued by the Court are made clear and shed light on the many questions arising from the legal "history" and public policy of affirmative action.

NOTES

1. The affirmative action in employment cases decided by the Court are: Martin v. Wilks, 109 S.Ct. 2180 (1989) (white firefighters who failed to intervene in proceedings in which consent decree was entered may bring suit challenging employment decisions taken pursuant to those consent decrees); Johnson v. Transportation Agency, Santa Clara County, California, 480 U.S. 616 (1987) (Court held that a public employer's consideration of the sex of an employee as one factor in promoting her over a qualified male employee under an affirmative action plan did not violate Title VII of the Civil Rights Act of 1964); U.S. v. Paradise, 107 S.Ct. 1053 (1987) (50 percent promotion requirement was permissible under the Equal Protection Clause of the Fourteenth Amendment of the Constitution); Local Number 93, Firefighters v. City of Cleveland, 478 U.S. 501 (1986) (consent decree requiring promotion of specific number of minorities was not barred by Title VII, even though decree may have benefitted persons who were not actual victims of discrimination); Local 28, Sheet Metal Workers International Association v. EEOC, 478 U.S. 421 (1986) (court order imposing a nonwhite membership goal on a union and establishing a fund to be used in remedying discrimination was authorized by Title VII, and was not violative of the equal protection component of the Due Process Clause of the Constitution); Wygant v. Jackson Board of Education, 476 U.S. 267 (1986) (the layoff of nonminority teachers under a labor agreement which was designed to preserve an affirmative action hiring policy was violative of the Equal Protection Clause where minority teachers with less seniority were retained); Firefighters Local Union No. 1784 v. Stotts, 467 U.S. 561 (1984) (district court order enjoining city from following seniority system in layoffs exceeded the court's powers and was an invalid modification of a consent decree); United Steelworkers of America v. Weber, 443 U.S. 193 (1979) (private employer's voluntary affirmative action plan which granted preference to African-American employees over more senior white employees in admission to a craft training program was not violative of Title VII).

In addition, the Court has decided two cases in the area of minority business set-asides *(see infra* Chapter 5) which involve voluntary affirmative action by federal, state, and local governments to increase minority contracting opportunities. *See* City of Richmond v. J. A. Croson Company, 109 S.Ct. 706 (1989) (in holding that the city of Richmond, Virginia's minority business set-aside program was unconstitutional, a majority of the Court applied strict scrutiny analysis to affirmative action measures designed to benefit minorities); Fullilove v. Klutznick, 448 U.S. 448 (1980) (Court held that federal minority business set-aside program was constitutional).

In addition, For the Court's discussion of affirmative action in the educational context, *see* Regents of the University of California v. Bakke, 438 U.S. 265 (1978).

2. 443 U.S. 193 (1979).

3. Prior to 1974, 1.83 percent of skilled craft workers at the company's Gramercy facility were African Americans, while the Gramercy area work force was approximately 39 percent African American. *Id.* at 198–199.

4. 42 U.S.C. § 2000e *et seq.*

5. *See* 563 F.2d 216 (5th Cir. 1977). Judge Wisdom dissented from the Fifth Circuit panel's ruling. In his view, the appeals court's decision would hinder voluntary compliance with Title VII and require an employer to walk a "high tightrope without a net." *Id.* at 230 (Wisdom, J., dissenting). Wisdom reasoned that a requirement of employer admission of past discrimination as justification for affirmative action programs would expose an employer to liability to those persons harmed by such discrimination. An employer would also risk exposure to liability, continued Judge Wisdom, if it adopted an affirmative action plan but did not admit that it had engaged in prior discrimination. *Id.* To avoid this dilemma, Judge Wisdom articulated an "arguable violation" test under which reasonable affirmative action programs adopted in response to an employer's arguable violation of Title VII would be lawful. *Id.* This view was later adopted by Justice Blackmun in his concurrence in *Weber. See* 443 U.S. at 210–211; *see infra* note 28.

6. Justices Lewis F. Powell and John Paul Stevens did not participate. 443 U.S. at 209.

7. *Id.* at 200. The narrow question addressed by the *Weber* Court was noted, but not decided, in McDonald v. Santa Fe Trail Transportation Company, 427 U.S. 273, 281 n. 8 (1976).

8. 443 U.S. at 200.

9. *Id.* at 201.

10. Section 703(a) of Title VII, 42 U.S.C. § 2000e–2(a), provides:

It shall be an unlawful employment practice for an employer—
  (1) to fail or refuse to hire or to discharge any individual, or otherwise to discriminate against any individual with respect to his compensation, terms, conditions, or privileges of employment, because of such individual's race, color, religion, sex, or national origin; or
  (2) to limit, segregate, or classify his employees or applicants for employment in any way which would deprive or tend to deprive any individual of employment opportunities or otherwise adversely affect his status as an employee, because of such individual's race, color, religion, sex, or national origin.

Section 703(d) of Title VII, 42 U.S.C. § 2000e–2(d), provides:

It shall be an unlawful employment practice for any employer, labor organization, or joint labor-management committee controlling apprenticeship or other training or retraining, including on-the-job training programs to discriminate against any individual because of his race, color, religion, sex, or national origin in admission to, or employment in, any program established to provide apprenticeship or other training.

11. Justice Brennan's reliance on the "spirit" of Title VII and his rejection of a literal interpretation of that statute was controversial to some commentators. *See, e.g.,* Farber and Frickey, *Legislative Intent and Public Choice*, 74 VA. L. REV. 423, 452 (1988); Eskridge, *Dynamic Statutory Interpretation*, 135 U. PA. L. REV. 1479, 1488–1491 (1987).

12. 443 U.S. at 202.

13. *Id.* at 202–203.

14. *Id.* at 203.

15. *Id.*

16. *Id.* at 204, quoting H.R. Rep. No. 914, 88th Cong., 1st Sess., pt. 1, p. 18 (1963).

17. *Id.* at 204.

18. Section 703(j) of Title VII, 42 U.S.C. § 2000e–2(j), provides, in pertinent part:

Nothing contained in this subchapter shall be interpreted to require any employer, employment agency, labor organization, or joint labor-management committee subject to this subchapter to grant preferential treatment to any individual or to any group because of the race, color, religion, sex, or national origin of such individual or group on account of an imbalance which may exist with respect to the total number or percentage of persons of any race, color, religion, sex, or national origin employed by any employer, referred or classified for employment by any employment agency or labor organization, admitted to membership or classified by any labor organization, or admitted to, or employed in, any apprenticeship or other training program, in comparison with the total number or percentage of persons of such race, color, religion, sex, or national origin in any community, State, section, or other area, or in the available work force in any community, State, section, or other area.

19. 443 U.S. at 204.

20. 443 U.S. at 206 (emphasis in original).

21. *Id.* at 207.

22. *Id.* at 208.

23. *Id.*

24. *Id.*

25. *Id.*

26. *Id.*

27. *Id.* at 209.

28. Concurring, Justice Blackmun expressed some misgivings with respect to the majority's legislative history analysis. He noted that the Kaiser-Steelworker affirmative action plan was established after critical reviews from the then-Office of Federal Contract Compliance regarding Kaiser's past hiring practices. *Id.* at 210 (Blackmun, J., concurring).

Blackmun argued for adoption of the narrow "arguable violation" theory articulated by Judge Wisdom in his dissent in the Fifth Circuit's *Weber* decision. *See* 563 F.2d 216, 230 (5th Cir. 1977); *supra* note 5. Thus, employers and unions who had committed arguable violations of Title VII would be free to make a reasonable response, including preferential hiring, to remedy the arguable violation. The advantages of that theory, stated Blackmun, are its response to a practical problem not anticipated by Congress, and its predictability and effectuation of the purposes of Title VII. 443 U.S. at 211.

Blackmun was disturbed by the majority's more expansive "traditionally segregated job categories" approach; however, he concluded that the Court's reading of the statute was acceptable. *Id.* at 213.

29. G. ORWELL, NINETEEN EIGHTY-FOUR (1949).

30. 443 U.S. at 222–223, 223 n. 2. (Rehnquist, J., dissenting).

31. *Id*. at 228.

32. *See id*. at 230–252.

33. *Id*. at 253.

34. *Id*. at 254–255 (Rehnquist, J., dissenting) (emphasis in original and citations omitted). In a separate dissent, Chief Justice Burger stated that the Court reached "a result I would be inclined to vote for were I a Member of Congress considering a proposed amendment of Title VII." *Id*. at 216 (Burger, C.J., dissenting). He did not join the Court's judgment, however, because, in his view, it was contrary to the explicit language of Title VII, and the Court had rewritten the statute to achieve what it regarded as a desirable result.

35. *See* Chapter 1, notes 55–59 and accompanying text.

36. The *Weber* Court found that "[j]udicial findings of exclusion from crafts on racial grounds are so numerous as to make such exclusion a proper subject for judicial notice." 443 U.S. at 198 n. 1 (citations omitted).

37. *See supra* notes 23–26 and accompanying text.

38. Justices Powell and Stevens did cast votes on affirmative action in the context of education in Regents of the University of California v. Bakke, 438 U.S. 265 (1978). Powell provided the fifth vote for the Court's holding that a medical school admission's program which set aside sixteen of one hundred available seats for minorities was unconstitutional, and that the denial of admission to a white applicant because of his race was constitutionally suspect. Powell also provided the fifth vote for the Court's ruling that race may be considered as a "plus" factor in the admissions process. *See id*. at 317–318, 318 n.52, 320 (opinion of Powell, J.).

Justice Stevens, joined by Chief Justice Burger and Justices Stewart and Rehnquist, concurred in the judgment in part and dissented in part in *Bakke*. Stevens determined that the question whether race can ever be used as a factor in admissions decisions was not an issue in that case. Nor was the constitutionality of the admissions program addressed by Stevens; instead, he concluded that the program violated Title VI of the Civil Rights Act of 1964, 42 U.S.C. § 2000d.

For a full discussion of the *Bakke* case, *see* T. O'NEILL, BAKKE AND THE POLITICS OF EQUALITY: FRIENDS AND FOES IN THE CLASSROOM OF LITIGATION (1984).

39. 452 U.S. 105 (1981).

40. 461 U.S. 477 (1983).

41. *See* Arthur v. Nyquist, 712 F.2d 816 (2d Cir. 1983) (court held that school board had to hire minorities and nonminorities on a one-to-one ratio until the percentage of minority faculty reached a certain level), *cert. denied sub nom*. Buffalo Teachers Federation v. Arthur, 466 U.S. 936 (1984); Morgan v. O'Bryant, 671 F.2d 23 (1st Cir. 1982) (court held that layoff could not operate so as to reduce the percentage of minorities on a school's faculty), *cert. denied*, 459 U.S. 827 (1983).

42. *See supra* notes 29–34 and accompanying text.

43. *See supra* note 6.

44. 467 U.S. 561 (1984).

45. *Id*. at 566.

46. *Id*.

47. *See* 679 F.2d 591 (6th Cir. 1982).

48. The initial issue addressed by the Court was the claim by the plaintiff class that the case was moot because all white employees laid off or demoted as a result of the injunction had been returned to work and their former positions. The Court rejected that claim for three reasons. First, stated the Court, it appeared that the injunction was still in force and would govern future layoffs unless set aside. Second, unless overturned, the city would have to obey the modified consent decree under the district court and Sixth Circuit rulings. Third, continued the Court, white employees laid off or demoted, even though reinstated, had not been made whole with respect to back pay and lost seniority. Thus, stated the Court, it would be unreasonable to expect the city to pay money to which employees had no legal right. Moreover, the loss of competitive seniority could determine promotions, transfers and order of layoffs in future reductions in force. 467 U.S. at 568–572.

Disagreeing with the Court on the mootness issue, Justice Blackmun argued that the Court could vacate the judgment below and remand the cases with directions to dismiss them as moot. Upon vacating, "the legal rights of the parties would return to their status prior to the entry of the preliminary injunction." *Id.* at 595 (Blackmun, J., dissenting).

49. *Id.* at 572–573 (footnotes omitted).

50. *Id.* at 574.

51. *Id.* at 575.

52. Section 703(h), 42 U.S.C. § 2000e–2(h), provides in pertinent part:

[I]t shall not be an unlawful employment practice for an employer to apply different standards of compensation, or different terms, conditions, or priveleges of pursuant to a bona fide seniority or merit system . . . provided that such differences are not the result of an intention to discriminate . . .

53. 431 U.S. 324 (1977).

54. Section 706(g) of Title VII, 42 U.S.C. § 2000e–5(g), provides:

No order of the court shall require the admission or reinstatement of an individual as a member of a union, or the hiring, reinstatement, or promotion of an individual as an employee, or the payment to him of any back pay, if such individual was refused admission, suspended, or expelled, or was refused employment or advancement or was suspended or discharged for any reason other than discrimination on account of race, color, religion, sex, or national origin or in violation of section 2000e–3(a) of this title.

55. 467 U.S. at 580.

56. *Id.* at 587 (O'Connor, J., concurring) (citations omitted).

57. *Id.* at 587–588 (O'Connor, J., concurring) (citations omitted).

58. *Id.* at 591 (Stevens, J., concurring in the judgment).

59. *See id.* at 601 (Blackmun J., dissenting), citing University of Texas v. Camenisch, 451 U.S. 390 (1981); Doran v. Salem Inn, Inc., 422 U.S. 922 (1975).

60. *Id.* at 613.

61. *Id.* at 615. Justice Blackmun also sought to distinguish *Teamsters* as a case concerned with individual relief rather than the class wide relief at issue in *Stotts*. *See id.* at 616–617.

62. *Id.* at 618.

63. *Id.* at 583.

64. *See, e.g.*, Fallon and Weiler, Firefighters v. Stotts: *Conflicting Models of Racial Justice*, 1984 SUP. CT. REV. 1, 2 (*Stotts* represents perhaps the "biggest defeat" in Title VII litigation for the civil rights movement); *id.* at 2 n.8 (authors state that former

Solicitor General Rex Lee characterized *Stotts* as a "slam dunk," and "perhaps one of the greatest decisions of all time!").

65. *See* Reynolds, *The Reagan Administration and Civil Rights: Winning the War Against Discrimination*, 1986 U. ILL. L. REV. 1001, 1015.

66. *Id.* at 1015. *See, e.g.*, Deveraux v. Geary, 765 F.2d 268 (1st Cir. 1985), *cert. denied*, 478 U.S. 1021 (1986); Turner v. Orr, 759 F.2d 817 (11th Cir. 1985).

67. *See, e.g.*, Pennsylvania v. Operating Engineers, 770 F.2d 1068 (3d Cir. 1985), *cert. denied*, 474 U.S. 1060 (1986); Paradise v. Prescott, 767 F.2d 1514 (11th Cir. 1985) (*aff'd sub nom.* U.S. v. Paradise, 480 U.S. 149 (1987); Turner v. Orr, 759 F.2d 817 (11th Cir. 1985); Diaz v. AT&T, 752 F.2d 1356 (9th Cir. 1985); Van Aken v. Young, 750 F.2d 43 (6th Cir. 1984); Wygant v. Jackson Board of Education, 746 F.2d 1152 (6th Cir. 1984), *rev'd on other grounds*, 476 U.S. 267 (1986); Kromnich v. School District of Pennsylvania, 739 F.2d 894 (3d Cir. 1984), *cert. denied*, 469 U.S. 1107 (1985); Grann v. City of Madison, 738 F.2d 786 (7th Cir.), *cert. denied*, 469 U.S. 918 (1984); Deveraux v. Geary, 596 F. Supp. 1481 (D. Mass. 1984), *aff'd*, 765 F.2d 268 (1st Cir. 1985); NAACP v. Detroit Police Officers Association, 591 F. Supp. 1194 (E.D. Mich. 1984).

68. 476 U.S. 267 (1986).

69. *Id.* at 270–271 (emphasis added and citation omitted).

70. The union and minority teachers initially brought suit in federal court alleging, *inter alia*, that the board's noncompliance with the labor agreement violated the Equal Protection Clause of the Fourteenth Amendment and Title VII. The district court concluded that it lacked jurisdiction over the case. *Id.* at 271.

71. *Id.* at 272 (citation omitted).

72. *Id.*

73. *See* 746 F.2d 1152 (6th Cir. 1984).

74. 476 U.S. at 269.

75. *Id.* at 273, citing Mississippi University for Women v. Hogan, 458 U.S. 718 (1982); Regents of University of California v. Bakke, 438 U.S. 265 (1978); Shelley v. Kraemer, 334 U.S. 1 (1948); A. BICKEL, THE MORALITY OF CONSENT (1975). This view was ultimately adopted by a majority of the Court in City of Richmond v. J. A. Croson Company, 109 S.Ct. 706 (1989), discussed *infra* and in Chapter 5.

76. 476 U.S. at 273.

77. *Id.* at 274.

78. *Id.*

79. *Id.* at 275.

80. *Id.* at 276.

81. *Id.*

82. *Id.* at 277.

83. *Id.* at 278. The school board argued that it could establish the existence of prior discrimination on its part. Justice Powell declined to consider that question. *Id.*

84. *Id.* at 280.

85. *Id.* at 281.

86. *See* Firefighters v. Stotts, 467 U.S. 561, 574–576 (1984).

87. *See* United Steelworkers of America v. Weber, 443 U.S. 193, 208 (1979) ("The plan does not require the discharge of white workers and their replacement with new black hirees").

88. 476 U.S. at 283.

89. *Id.* at 284.

90. *Id.* at 285 (O'Connor, J., concurring in part and concurring in the judgment).

91. *Id.* at 286 (citations omitted).

92. *Id.*

93. *Id.* at 287 (citations omitted).

94. *Id.* at 288.

95. *Id.* at 290.

96. *Id.* at 291.

97. *Id.* at 292.

98. *Id.* at 294.

99. *Id.* at 295.

100. *Id.* at 297–298 (Marshall, J., dissenting). Many of the facts related by Justice Marshall were contained in "submissions" lodged with the Court by both parties. *Id.* at 295.

101. *See supra* note 69 and accompanying text.

102. 476 U.S. at 301–302.

103. *Id.* at 303.

104. *Id.* (citations omitted).

105. *Id.* at 305 (citations omitted).

106. *Id.* at 306 (citations omitted).

107. *Id.* at 308, citing Franks v. Bowman Transportation Co., 424 U.S. 747, 775 (1976).

108. *Id.*, citing *Franks*, *supra* note 107, at 778.

109. *Id.*, citing Ford Motor Co. v. Hoffman, 345 U.S. 330, 339–340 (1953).

110. *Id.*, discussing *Weber*, 443 U.S. at 193.

111. *Id.* at 309.

112. *Id.* at 313 (Stevens, J., dissenting).

113. *Id.* at 315.

114. *Id.*

115. *Id.* at 316.

116. *Id.*

117. *Id.* at 318.

118. *Id.* at 319 n.14.

119. *See* Selig, *Affirmative Action in Employment: The Legacy of a Supreme Court Majority*, 63 IND. L.J. 301, 345 (1987).

120. *Id.*

121. *Id.* at 346.

122. 478 U.S. 501 (1986).

123. *See supra* note 54.

124. *See* Shield Club v. City of Cleveland, 370 F. Supp. 251 (N.D. Ohio 1972).

125. *See* Headen v. City of Cleveland, No. C73–330 (N.D. Ohio, April 25, 1975), cited at 478 U.S. at 506.

126. *See* Fed. R. Cir. P. 24(a)(2).

127. 478 U.S. at 510–512.

128. *See* Vanguards of Cleveland v. City of Cleveland, 753 F.2d 479 (6th Cir. 1985), *aff'd*, 478 U.S. 501 (1986). The Sixth Circuit also found that the decree was fair and reasonable to nonminority firefighters, noting that the plan did not require the hiring of unqualified minority firefighters, did not create an absolute bar to the advancement of

nonminorities, and was short. *Id.* at 485. Further, the court reasoned that *Stotts* did not affect the outcome of the case because *Stotts* involved an injunction and not a consent decree. *Id.* at 486.

129. 478 U.S. at 515 (footnote omitted).

130. *Id.* at 517 (footnote omitted).

131. Section 706(q) of Title VII; *see supra* note 54.

132. 478 U.S. at 518.

133. *Id.* at 519–521.

134. *Id.* at 521.

135. *Id.*

136. Justice Brennan rejected the union's and government's arguments set forth at note 132 and accompanying text.

The fact that a consent decree *looks* like a judgment entered after a trial obviously does not implicate Congress' concern with limiting the power of federal courts unilaterally to require employers or unions to make certain kinds of employment decisions. The same is true of the Court's conditional power to modify a consent decree; the mere *existence* of an *unexercised* power to modify the obligations contained in a consent decree does not alter the fact that those obligations were created by agreement of the parties rather than imposed by the court. Finally, we reject the argument that a consent decree should be treated as an ''order'' within the meaning of § 706(g) because it can be enforced by a citation for contempt. There is no indication in the legislative history that the availability of judicial enforcement of an obligation, rather than the creation of the obligation itself, was the focus of congressional concern. *Id.* at 523 (emphasis in original and footnote omitted).

137. *See supra* notes 48–55 and accompanying text.

138. The Court also rejected the union and government argument that the union's consent was required before the court could approve a consent decree. ''[W]hile an intervenor is entitled to present evidence and have its objections heard at the hearings on whether to approve a consent decree, it does not have power to block the decree merely by withholding its consent.'' 478 U.S. at 529 (citations omitted). In so ruling, the Court acknowledged that an approved consent decree cannot dispose of the valid claims of nonconsenting intervenors or impose obligations on a party that did not consent to the decree. ''However, the consent decree entered here does not bind Local 93 to do or not to do anything. It imposes no legal obligations on the Union at all; only the parties to the decree can be held in contempt of court for failure to comply with its terms.'' *Id.* at 529–530.

139. *Id.* at 530 (O'Connor, J., concurring).

140. *Id.* at 533 (White, J., dissenting).

141. *Id.* at 535 (White, J., dissenting).

142. *Id.* at 541 (Rehnquist, J., dissenting).

143. *Id.* at 544 (emphasis in original) (Rehnquist, J., dissenting).

144. *Id.* at 545.

145. *See generally* Schwartz, *The 1986 and 1987 Affirmative Action Cases: It's All Over but the Shouting*, 86 MICH. L. REV. 524, 532 (1987).

146. *Id.* at 533.

147. Rutherglen and Ortiz, *Affirmative Action Under the Constitution and Title VII: From Confusion To Convergence*, 35 UCLA L. REV. 467, 476 (1988).

148. *Id.* at 478.

149. *Firefighters*, 478 U.S. at 517 n. 8.

150. 478 U.S. 421 (1986).

151. *Id.* at 426.

152. *See* State Commission for Human Rights v. Farrell, 43 Misc. 2d 958, 252 N.Y.S. 2d 649 (1964).

153. 478 U.S. at 428.

154. The district court made four findings. First, the union had adopted discriminatory procedures and standards for admission into the apprenticeship program. Second, the union had restricted the size of its membership to deny access to minorities. Third, the union had selectively organized nonunion sheet metal shops with few, if any, minority employees and admitted only white employees to membership. The union also refused to organize sheet metal workers in the blowpipe industry because a large percentage of those workers were minorities. Finally, the union discriminated in favor of white applicants seeking to transfer from sister locals. *Id.* at 429–431.

155. *See* EEOC v. Local 638, 532 F.2d 821 (2d Cir. 1976).

156. *See* EEOC v. Local 638, 565 F.2d 31 (2d Cir. 1977).

157. This program included union liaisons for vocational and technical schools, the creation of part-time and summer sheet metal jobs for qualified minority youths, and financial assistance to needy apprentices. 478 U.S. at 437.

158. *See* EEOC v. Local 638, 753 F.2d 1172 (2d Cir. 1985).

159. The Court held that the district court did not use incorrect statistical evidence in evaluating the union's membership practices, 478 U.S. at 440–442; that the contempt fines and establishment of a fund ordered by the district court were proper remedies for civil contempt, *id.* at 442–444; and that the district court's appointment of an administrator to supervise the union's compliance with court orders was proper and within the court's discretion. *Id.* at 481–482.

160. As noted by Justice Brennan, the EEOC challenged the membership goal and final order even though the EEOC had joined the plaintiffs in asking the court to order numerical goals, ratios, and timetables. *Id.* at 444 n. 24.

161. *Id.* at 445.

162. *See supra.*

163. *Id.* at 447 (citations omitted).

164. *Id.* at 448–449 (citations omitted).

165. *Id.* at 452–465, 466–470.

166. The cases relied upon by the union and the EEOC are cited at page 471 of Justice Brennan's plurality opinion.

167. *See supra* notes 43–67 and accompanying text.

168. 478 U.S. at 474.

169. *Id.* (footnote omitted).

170. *Id.* at 476.

171. *Id.* (footnote omitted).

172. *Id.* at 479; *see Weber*, 443 U.S. at 208–209, 216.

173. *See* U.S. Const., Am. V.

174. The Court subsequently held that strict scrutiny analysis was the proper test. *See* City of Richmond v. J. A. Croson Company, 109 S. Ct. 706 (1989).

175. 478 U.S. at 480–481.

176. *Id.* at 483 (Powell, J., concurring in part and concurring in the judgment).

177. *Id.* (Powell, J., concurring in part and concurring in the judgment).

178. *Id.* at 483–484 (Powell, J., concurring in part and concurring in the judgment).

179. *See supra* notes 74–89 and accompanying text.

180. 478 U.S. at 485 (Powell, J., concurring in part and concurring in the judgment).

181. 448 U.S. 448 (1980) (discussed in Chapter 5). In his *Fullilove* concurrence, Justice Powell set forth four factors to be applied to race-conscious hiring remedies: (1) the efficacy of alternative remedies; (2) the planned duration of the remedy; (3) the relationship between the percentage of minorities to be employed and the percentage of minorities in the relevant population or work force; (4) the availability of waiver provisions if the hiring plan could not be met; and (5) the effect of the remedy upon innocent third parties. 448 U.S. at 510–511, 514 (Powell, J., concurring).

182. *See* § 703(j), quoted at note 18 *supra*.

183. 478 U.S. at 491 (O'Connor, J., concurring in part and dissenting in part).

184. *Id.* at 495 (O'Connor, J., concurring in part and dissenting in part).

185. *Id.* at 497 (citation omitted) (O'Connor, J., concurring in part and dissenting in part).

186. *Id.* at 498 (O'Connor J., concurring in part and dissenting in part).

187. *Id.* at 499 (White, J., dissenting).

188. *Id.* at 500 (White, J., dissenting).

189. *See supra*.

190. 478 U.S. at 500 (Rehnquist, J., dissenting).

191. Scolia, *The Disease as Cure*, WASH U.L.Q 147 (1979).

192. 480 U.S. 147 (1987).

193. *Id.* at 153 (plurality opinion).

194. The United States Court of Appeals for the Fifth Circuit upheld the hiring order. NAACP v. Allen, 493 F.2d 614, 621 (5th Cir. 1974).

195. *See* Paradise v. Prescott, 585 F. Supp. 72 74 (M.D. Ala. 1983).

196. 480 U.S. at 165 n. 15 (plurality opinion).

197. Paradise v. Prescott, 767 F.2d 1514 (11th Cir. 1985).

198. 480 U.S. at 167 (plurality opinion) (footnote omitted).

199. *Id.* at 170 (plurality opinion) quoting *Sheet Metal Workers*, 478 U.S. at 485 (Powell, J., concurring in part and concurring in the judgment).

200. *Id.* at 175 (plurality opinion).

201. *Id.* at 179 (plurality opinion).

202. *Id.* at 182–83 (plurality opinion).

203. *Id.* at 184 (plurality opinion).

204. *See supra*.

205. 480 U.S. at 189 (Powell, J., concurring).

206. 402 U.S. 1 (1971).

207. 480 U.S. at 193 (Stevens, J., concurring) (footnote omitted).

208. *Id.* at 196 (O'Connor, J., dissenting).

209. *Id.* at 198 (O'Connor, J., dissenting).

210. *Id.* at 199 (O'Connor, J., dissenting).

211. *Id.* at 196 (White, J., dissenting).

212. *Id.* (White, J., dissenting).

213. 480 U.S. 616 (1989).

214. *Id.* at 619.

215. *Id.* at 623.

216. *Id.* at 623.

217. *Id.*

218. Joyce testified in the district court that one of the interviewers had been her

supervisor when she began as a road maintenance worker. Joyce stated that she had not been issued coveralls as had male employees, that she had complained to the supervisor, and that she filed a grievance before being issued coveralls. Another interviewer had dealt with Joyce when she chaired a roads operation safety committee. Joyce testified that she had differences of opinion on implementation of safety measures. In addition, a "panel member had earlier described Joyce as a 'rebel-rousing, skirt wearing person'. . . . " *Id.* at 624 n. 5.

219. The agency's affirmative action plan was adopted in 1978. Among other things, the plan provided that the agency was authorized to consider the sex of a qualified applicant in making promotions to positions within a traditionally segregated job classification in which women had been significantly underrepresented. *Id.* at 620–621.

The agency's plan noted that women constituted 36.4 percent of the area labor market and 22.4 percent of agency employees. Women made up 76 percent of office and clerical workers; 7.1 percent of agency officials and administrators; 8.6 percent of professionals; 9.7 percent of technicians; and 22 percent of service and maintenance workers. Of 238 skilled craft worker positions, none was held by a woman. *Id.* at 621. The plan provided that women had not been traditionally employed in these positions, and that women had not been strongly motivated to seek training or employment in these occupations. *Id.*

To evaluate progress under the plan, the agency stated that its long-term goal was to attain a work force whose composition reflected the proportion of minorities and women in the area labor force. *Id.* at 621–622.

220. *Id.* at 625.

221. 443 U.S. 193 (1979).

222. *See* 748 F.2d 1308 (9th Cir. 1984), *modified*, 770 F.2d 752 (9th Cir. 1984).

223. 480 U.S. at 625.

224. *Id.* at 631.

225. *Id.*

226. *Id.* at 632 (citation omitted).

227. *Id.* (footnote omitted).

228. *Id.* at 633 (citation omitted).

229. *Id.* at 633 n. 11 (citation omitted).

230. *Id.* at 637.

231. *See supra.*

232. *See supra.*

233. 480 U.S. at 638.

234. *Id.* at 639–640.

235. *Id.* at 642.

236. In a separate opinion, Justice Stevens wrote that the "only problem for me is whether to adhere to an authoritative construction of the Act that is at odds with my understanding of the actual intent of the author of the legislation." *Id.* at 644 (Stevens, J., concurring). Because *Weber* is "now an important part of the fabric of our law," *id.*, Justice Stevens decided to adhere to the construction of Title VII adopted by the *Weber* Court. Justice Stevens also expressed his view that an employer may find it more helpful to focus on the future instead of "retroactively scrutinizing his own or society's possible exclusions of minorities in the past. . . . " *Id.* at 646 (Stevens, J., concurring). In support of this view, Justice Stevens quoted from Sullivan, *The Supreme Court—Comment, Sins of Discrimination: Last Term's Affirmative Action Cases*, 100 HARV. L. REV. 78, 96 (1986).

237. 480 U.S. at 648 (O'Connor, J., concurring in the judgment).

238. *Id.* at 649 (O'Connor, J., concurring in the judgment). Justice O'Connor wrote that *Weber* and *Wygant* properly resolved the conflicting concerns of minority and non-minority workers. *Id.* at 650.

239. *Id.* at 653.

240. In a significant passage, Justice O'Connor repeated her view, first expressed on *Sheet Metal Workers*, 478 U.S. at 494 (O'Connor, J., concurring in part and dissenting in part), which would assume added significance in subsequent Court decisions:

[I]t is completely unrealistic to assume that individuals of each [sex] will gravitate with mathematical exactitude of each employer . . . absent unlawful discrimination. . . . Thus, a goal that makes such an assumption, and simplistically focuses on the proportion of women and minorities in the work force, without more, is not remedial. Only a goal that takes into account the number of women and minorities qualified for the relevant position could satisfy the requirement that an affirmative action plan be remedial. 480 U.S. at 659 (citation omitted) (O'Connor, J., concurring on the judgment).

241. *Id.* at 656–657 (O'Connor, J., concurring in the judgment).

242. *Id.* at 657 (White, J., dissenting).

243. *Id.* at 658 (Scalia, J., dissenting).

244. Justice Scalia agreed with Justice O'Connor that the prohibitions of Title VII are at least as stringent as those in the Constitution. *Id.* at 664 (Scalia, J., dissenting).

245. *Id.* at 668 (Scalia, J., dissenting).

246. *Id.*

247. *Id.* at 670 (citation omitted) (Scalia, J., dissenting).

248. For decisions discussing *stare decisis, see* Patterson v. McLean Credit Union, 109 S.Ct. 2363 (1989); Welch v. Texas Dept. of Highways and Public Transportation, 483 U.S. 468 (1987); Vasquez v. Hillery, 474 U.S. 254 (1986); Boys Markets, Inc. v. Retail Clerks, 398 U.S. 235 (1970).

249. 480 U.S. at 672–673 (Scalia, J., dissenting).

250. *Id.* at 676 (Scalia, J., dissenting).

251. *See infra* Chapter 3.

252. 480 U.S. at 677 (Scalia, J., dissenting).

253. *Id.*

254. *See* post-*Johnson* decisions discussed *infra.*

255. *See, e.g.,* Schwartz, *supra* note 145.

256. *See generally* R. BORK, THE TEMPTING OF AMERICA: THE POLITICAL SEDUCTION OF THE LAW (1990); E. BRONNER, BATTLE FOR JUSTICE: HOW THE BORK NOMINATION SHOOK AMERICA (1989).

257. *Id.* at 335.

258. *See* H. SCHWARTZ, PACKING THE COURTS: THE CONSERVATIVE CAMPAIGN TO REWRITE THE CONSTITUTION 149 (1988).

259. 109 S. Ct. 706 (1989).

260. *See infra* Chapter 5.

261. *See* J. A. Croson Co. v. Richmond, 822 F.2d 1355 (4th Cir. 1987), *aff'd,* 109 S. Ct. 706 (1989). The Fourth Circuit initially held that the plan was constitutional. J. A. Croson v. Richmond, 779 F.2d 181 (4th Cir. 1985). The Supreme Court remanded the case to the Fourth Circuit for further consideration in light of Wygant v. Jackson Board of Education, 476 U.S. 267 (discussed *supra*).

262. 109 S. Ct. at 721.

263. *Id.*
264. *See Wygant,* 476 U.S. at 279–280.
265. 109 S. Ct. at 721 (citation omitted).
266. *Id.* at 722 (citation omitted). In concluding, Justice O'Connor addressed and rejected the argument that Equal Protection Clause concerns are not implicated when the white majority places burdens on itself. This argument was made in J. ELY, DEMOCRACY AND DISTRUST 170 (1981).
267. 109 S. Ct. at 724.
268. 109 S. Ct. at 728. *See also id.* at 734–735 (Kennedy, J., concurring in part and concurring in the judgment) (agreeing with Justice O'Connor that strict scrutiny should be applied to any racial preference).
269. *Id.* at 735 (Scalia, J., concurring in the judgment).

In dissent, Justice Marshall, joined by Justices Brennan and Blackmun, argued, *inter alia,* that the Court's adoption of strict scrutiny as the standard for race-conscious remedial measures was an unwelcome development. "A profound difference separates governmental actions that themselves are racist, and governmental actions that seek to remedy the effects of prior racism or to prevent neutral governmental activity from perpetuating the effects of such racism." *Id.* at 752 (Marshall, J., dissenting) (citations omitted). In his view, the Court's ruling "signals that it regards racial discrimination as largely a phenomenon of the past, and that government bodies need no longer preoccupy themselves with rectifying racial injustice." *Id.*

270. 109 S. Ct. 2180 (1989).
271. The collateral attack doctrine generally involves the right of a third party to collaterally attack a judgment. *See id.* at 2189 and 2189 n. 5 (Stevens, J., dissenting); *see generally* J. FLEMING and G. HAZARD, CIVIL PROCEDURE § 12.15 (3d ed. 1985).
272. 109 S. Ct. at 2183.
273. *See* U.S. v. Jefferson County, 28 FEP Cases 1834 (N.D. Ala. 1981).
274. *See* U.S. v. Jefferson County, 720 F.2d 1511 (11th Cir. 1983).
275. 109 S. Ct. at 2184.
276. *See* In re Birmingham Reverse Discrimination Employment Litigation, 833 F.2d 1492 (11th Cir. 1987), *aff'd,* 109 S. Ct. 2180 (1989).
277. 109 S. Ct. at 2184 (citation omitted).
278. *Id.,* quoting Hansberry v. Lee, 311 U.S. 32, 40 (1940).
279. *See* Striff v. Mason, 849 F.2d 240, 245 (6th Cir. 1988); Marino v. Ortiz, 806 F.2d 1144, 1146–1147 (2d Cir. 1986), *aff'd by an equally divided Court,* 484 U.S. 301 (1988); Thaggard v. City of Jackson, 687 F.2d 66, 68–69 (5th Cir. 1982), *cert. denied sub nom.* Ashley v. City of Jackson, 464 U.S. 900 (1983); Stotts v. Memphis Fire Department, 679 F.2d 541, 558 (6th Cir. 1982), *rev'd on other grounds sub nom.* Firefighters v. Stotts, 467 U.S. 561 (1984); Dennison v. City of Los Angeles Department of Water & Power, 650 F.2d 694, 696 (9th Cir. 1981); Goins v. Bethlehem Steel Corp., 657 F.2d 62, 64 (4th Cir. 1981), *cert. denied,* 455 U.S. 948 (1982); Society Hill Civic Association v. Harris, 632 F.2d 1045, 1052 (3d Cir. 1980). *Contra* Dunn v. Carey, 808 F.2d 555, 559–560 (7th Cir. 1986).
280. 109 S. Ct. at 2185 (citation omitted).
281. *See* Fed. R. Civ. P. 24.
282. *See* Rule 19(a) of the Federal Rules.
283. *See* Rule 19(b) of the Federal Rules.

284. 109 S. Ct. at 2186 (footnote omitted).

285. *Id.* at 2187.

286. *Id.* at 2188.

287. *Id.* at 2189 (Stevens, J., dissenting).

288. *Id.* at 2190 (Stevens, J., dissenting).

289. *Id.* at 2189 (Stevens, J., dissenting).

290. *Id.* at 2196 (Stevens, J., dissenting).

291. *Id.* at 2199 (Stevens, J., dissenting) (citation omitted).

292. *Id.* at 2200 (Stevens, J., dissenting).

293. 820 F.2d 1293 (D. C. Cir.), *reh'g en banc granted*, 833 F.2d 368 (D.C. Cir. 1987), *opinion vacated*, 841 F.2d 400 (D.C. Cir. 1988) (en banc).

294. *Id.* at 1301.

295. *Id.* (citations omitted).

296. *Id.* at 1304 n. 18.

297. *Id.* at 1304 (footnote and citation omitted). In reaching this conclusion, Judge Edwards noted that the plaintiffs had failed to introduce any data at trial that purported to identify individuals in the District of Columbia labor force who possessed the relevant qualifications for the department's higher level positions. *Id.*

298. *Id.* at 1305.

299. The court remanded the case to the district court for application of *Wygant*, which was decided after the district court's decision, and for the "critical factual determination" under the Constitution whether the department had a "strong basis in evidence" for believing that affirmative action was needed to remedy the present effects of past discrimination within the department. *Id.* Judge Edwards stated that the constitutional standard is stricter than the Title VII standard; therefore, "a 'strong basis in evidence' must be *something more* than a 'manifest imbalance in traditionally segregated job categories.' " *Id.* at 1306.

Concurring in part and dissenting in part, Judge Revercomb opined that the plan was inherently invalid because the district court relied on evidence of sex and racial composition imbalance between the department's upper levels and the population of the District of Columbia between the ages of eighteen and sixty-five. *Id.* at 1307 (Revercomb, J., concurring in part and dissenting in part). Revercomb would require a comparison between District of Columbia residents who were qualified to be members of the police department. Accordingly, unlike the majority, Judge Revercomb would require further findings using the qualified labor market.

300. 813 F.2d 412 (D.C. Cir. 1987), *reh'g denied*, 826 F.2d 73 (D.C. Cir. 1987), *reh'g en banc granted*, 833 F.2d 367 (D.C. Cir. 1987), *reh'g order vacated*, 841 F.2d 426 (D.C. Cir. 1988).

301. 826 F.2d at 76.

302. *Id.* at 77.

303. *Id.* at 78.

304. *Id.* at 81; *see also* 813 F.2d at 428–430.

305. Concurring, Judge Silberman interpreted *Johnson* and *Weber* as holding that Title VII permits "temporary race-conscious employment practices by public or private employers to combat job segregation. . . . " *Id.* at 86 (Silberman, J., concurring). He thought that the case had "very little, if anything, to do with remedies for past discrimination—whether general or proximate, recent or long ago." *Id.* at 88. Instead, he argued, the case had a "great deal to do with old-fashioned American politics, which has always had

a strong ethnic flavor.'' *Id.* Blacks, the "political majority" in the District of Columbia, were claiming what predecessor groups in American cities had claimed, stated Silberman, but would be frustrated by the same constitutional protections which protect minorities.

306. *Id.* at 91 (Mikva, J., dissenting from the court's denial of petition for rehearing).

307. *Id.* at 92.

308. 823 F.2d 351 (9th Cir. 1987).

309. Although the plaintiff was ultimately promoted, the court held that the action was not moot because it affected back pay, benefits, and seniority rights. *Id.* at 353 n. 1.

310. *Id.* at 357.

311. *Id.*

312. *Id.* at 359–360.

313. 836 F.2d 1034 (7th Cir. 1987).

314. *Id.* at 1035. A district court had initially held that the affirmative action program was justified by the statistical disparity, *see* 576 F.Supp. 1461 (N.D. Ind. 1983), and the Seventh Circuit reversed. *See* 750 F.2d 557 (7th Cir. 1984). The Supreme Court vacated the Seventh Circuit's judgment and remanded for reconsideration in light of *Johnson* and *Wygant*.

315. 836 F.2d at 1039.

316. *Id.* at 1040.

317. *Id.* (citation omitted).

318. Justice O'Connor's concurrence in *Wygant* (discussed earlier in this chapter) was identified by the Seventh Circuit as critical to *Wygant's* lowest-common-denominator holding and the disposition of *Janowiak*. *See* 836 F.2d at 1041.

319. *Id.* at 1041–1042 (footnote omitted). *See also* Scoggins v. Board of Education of Nashville, Arkansas Public Schools, 853 F.2d 1472 (8th Cir. 1988) (remanding case for ruling on relevant labor market).

320. *See also* McQuillen v. Wisconsin Education Association Council, 830 F.2d 659 (7th Cir. 1987) (discussing *Johnson* and the burden of proof in affirmative action cases), *cert. denied,* 485 U.S. 914 (1988); Barhold v. Rodriguez, 863 F.2d 233 (2d Cir. 1988) (statistical comparison does not provide firm basis for adoption of affirmative action plan where statistics were not linked to past discriminatory practices); Catlett v. Missouri Highway and Transportation Commission, 828 F.2d 1260 (8th Cir. 1987) (portions of district court order establishing female hiring goal is vacated; state had not been given chance voluntarily to bring personnel practices into compliance with anti-discrimination injunction), *cert. denied,* 485 U.S. 1021 (1988); Cunico v. Pueblo School District No. 60, 693 F.Supp. 954 (D. Col. 1988) (employer's affirmative action unlawful where race was the only factor assessed by the employer in choosing among qualified workers); Fountain v. City of Waycross, 701 F.Supp. 1570 (S.D. Ga. 1988) (upholding affirmative action plan as constitutional).

321. 819 F.2d 766 (7th Cir. 1987) (en banc), *cert. denied,* 484 U.S. 925 (1987).

322. *Id.* at 767.

323. *Id* at 770.

324. *Id.* at 771.

325. *Id.* at 772. Judge Flaum, joined by Chief Judge Bauer, concurred in the judgment and concurred in part. *See id.* at 772–774. For the view of the dissenting judges, *see id.* at 774 (Cummings, J., dissenting); *id.* at 778 (Cudahy, J., dissenting); *id.* at 785 (Fairchild, J., dissenting).

326. 1989 U.S. App. LEXIS 18132 (9th Cir. Dec. 4, 1989).

327. The decree and its legal and factual history are discussed in U.S. v. City and County of San Francisco, 696 F.Supp. 1287 (N.D. Cal. 1988).

328. The Ninth Circuit ruled that the district court did not abuse its discretion in approving the consent decree pursuant to Fed. R. Civ. P. 23. *See* 1989 U.S. App. LEXIS 18132 at p. 13.

329. *Id.* at p. 22.

330. *Id.*, citing *Johnson*, 480 U.S. at 637.

331. 1989 U.S. App. LEXIS 18132 at p. 23 (citation omitted).

332. *Id.* at p. 25.

333. Mann v. City of Albany, Georgia, 883 F.2d 999 (11th Cir. 1989).

334. *See Croson*, 109 S.Ct. at 728–729.

335. 883 F.2d at 1006.

3

Executive Order 11246

On September 24, 1965, President Lyndon B. Johnson signed Executive Order 11246,[1] an order which, as amended, bars discrimination on the basis of race, color, sex, or national origin by certain federal government contractors. This Order and its implementating regulations require federal government agencies to include in contracts with businesses an equal employment opportunity clause, which commits those firms to treat job applicants and employees without regard to their status or membership in the aforementioned groups.[2] In addition, the Order required government contractors to take affirmative action to ensure that the nondiscrimination goal is met. Government contractors are also required to prepare and comply with affirmative action programs for handicapped individuals under the Rehabilitation Act of 1973,[3] and for veterans of the Vietnam era under the Vietnam-Era Veterans' Readjustment Assistance Act of 1974.[4]

The reach and coverage of the Order is broad. Apart from governments and educational institutions, one-half of all employees are employed by businesses which file annual statements with the Equal Employment Opportunity Commission which set forth the sex, race, and ethnic distribution in the occupational classifications of their work forces. Approximately 75 percent of employees described in those reports are employed by federal contractors.[5] This chapter details and reviews the requirements of Executive Order 11246; regulations of the Office of Federal Contract Compliance Programs (OFCCP)[6] which were promulgated for the purpose of ensuring compliance with, and enforcing, the Order; and OFCCP compliance procedures and practices followed by the agency in carrying out its regulatory function and mission. The ensuing discussion does *not* detail every aspect of the Executive Order or implementing regulations. Thus, careful research and analysis must always be undertaken and legal counsel sought when a question arises as to the Order or OFCCP enforcement thereof.

THE ORDER

Contractor Agreements

Executive Order 11246, applicable to "every Government contract hereinafter entered into,"[7] mandates that seven specific provisions shall be included in every government contract (with limited exceptions).[8] These requirements follow.

Nondiscrimination Clause. The contractor will not discriminate against employees or applicants because of race, color, religion, sex, or national origin, and will take affirmative action to ensure that applicants and employees are treated without regard to their membership in those protected groups. Affirmative action includes, but is not limited to, "employment, upgrading, demotion or transfer; recruitment or recruitment advertising; layoff or termination; rates of pay or other forms of compensation; and selection for training, including apprenticeship."[9] Notices of this nondiscrimination clause must be posted by the contractor in conspicuous places.

Solicitations or Advertisements. All solicitations or advertisements for employees placed by, or on behalf of, the contractor shall state that "all qualified applicants will receive consideration for employment without regard to race, color, religion, sex, or national origin."[10]

Notice to Unions of Contractor Commitments. The contractor shall send to each labor union or employee representative with which the contractor has a labor agreement "or other contract or understanding,"[11] a notice provided by the agency contracting officer advising the union or worker representative of the contractor's commitments under the Order. Copies of the notice shall be posted in conspicuous places available to employees and applicants.

Contractor Compliance. The contractor shall comply with Executive Order 11246 and the Secretary of Labor's rules, regulations, and relevant orders.[12]

Information and Reports. The contractor will furnish all information and reports required by the Order and by the Secretary of Labor, and will permit access to books, records, and accounts by the contracting agency and the Secretary for purposes of investigation to ascertain compliance therewith.[13]

Noncompliance Penalties. Where a contractor does not comply with the requirements of the Order, a contract "may be cancelled, terminated, or suspended in whole or in part," the contractor may be declared ineligible for further government contracts, and "such other sanctions may be imposed and remedies invoked" as provided in the Order, or by the Secretary of Labor's rules, regulations, or orders, or as otherwise provided by law.[14]

Inclusion of the Foregoing Provisions. The contractor will include the foregoing paragraphs in every subcontract or purchase order (unless exempted) "so that such provisions will be binding upon each subcontractor or vendor."[15]

In addition to the responsibilities noted above, the Order requires contractors and their subcontractors to file compliance reports with information as to their practices, policies, programs, and employment statistics.[16] Where the contractor or subcontractor is party to a collective bargaining agreement or other contract or understanding with a labor union or agency referring workers or providing or supervising apprenticeship or worker training, the compliance report shall include information regarding the union's or agency's practices and policies affecting compliance.[17] If the union or agency has exclusive possession of such information and refuses to furnish it to the contractor, the Order provides that the contractor shall so certify to the Secretary of Labor as part of the report and shall set forth the efforts made by the contractor to obtain the information.[18]

Secretary of Labor Powers and Duties

Under the Order, the Secretary of Labor may investigate the employment practices of a government contractor or subcontractor to determine whether the seven provisions noted above have been violated. The Secretary is empowered, *inter alia*, to establish procedures governing such investigations, to review and investigate employee or prospective employee complaints of discrimination violative of the Order; to hold hearings for compliance, enforcement, or educational purposes; and to hold hearings prior to imposing or recommending penalties and sanctions under the Order.[19] No order for debarment shall be made without affording a contractor an opportunity for a hearing.[20]

Sanctions and Penalties

As sanctions and penalties for contractor noncompliance, Executive Order 11246 provides that the Secretary of Labor (acting in accordance with issued or adopted rules, regulations, or orders) may take the following actions, among others:

1. Publish the names of noncomplying contractors or unions.

2. Recommend to the Department of Justice that appropriate proceedings be brought to enforce the Order.

3. Recommend the institution of proceedings under Title VII of the Civil Rights Act of 1964.

4. Recommend to the Department of Justice that criminal proceedings be brought where contractors furnish false information to a contracting agency or to the Secretary of Labor.

5. Direct a contracting agency to cancel, terminate or suspend any contract, or portion thereof, for the contractor's failure to comply with the equal opportunity provisions of the contract.

6. Provide that a contracting agency shall refrain from entering into further contracts, or contract extensions or modifications, until the contractor has satisfied the Secretary that the contractor will comply with the Order.[21]

Prior to instituting proceedings against a contractor or cancelling or terminating a contract in whole or in part, the Order states that the Secretary must seek to ensure compliance by conference, conciliation, mediation, and persuasion.[22]

Federally Assisted Construction Contracts

The Order also provides for nondiscrimination in federally assisted construction contracts (defined as any contract for the construction, rehabilitation, alteration, conversion, extension, or repair of buildings, highways, or other improvements to real property).[23] OFCCP regulations applicable to the construction industry are discussed below.[24]

THE OFCCP'S REGULATIONS

As noted above, the OFCCP has issued rules and regulations for the purpose of achieving the aims of, and compliance with, Executive Order 11246. These regulations apply to all government contracting agencies, to contractors and subcontractors who perform under government contracts, and to all agencies and contractors and subcontractors involved in construction contracting.[25]

A description of the principal sections of the regulations is set forth below.

Basic Requirements

Equal Opportunity Clause. Section 60–1.4(a) of the regulations provide that the equal opportunity clause contained in Section 202 of Executive Order 11246 discussed above shall be included by each contracting agency in government contracts. Section 60–1.4(b) provides that similar language shall be included by each administering agency in any grant, contract, loan, insurance, or guarantee involving federally assisted, non-exempt construction. In addition, nonexempt prime contractors and subcontractors must include the equal opportunity clause in each nonexempt subcontract.[26]

Exemptions. The foregoing section refers to "non-exempt" contracts. Exemptions from the requirements of the equal opportunity clause are set forth in 41 C.F.R. § 601.5.

Generally, contracts and subcontracts not exceeding $10,000 (other than government bills of lading and other items) are exempt from the requirements of Executive Order 11246.[27] However, a contractor's contracts or subcontracts in any twelve-month period which have (or can reasonably be expected to have) an aggregate total value exceeding $10,000 are subject to the Order and OFCCP regulations, regardless of whether any single contract exceeds $10,000.[28] Where contracts and subcontracts are for indefinite quantities (e.g., open-ended contracts or requirement-type contracts), the equal opportunity clause shall be included "unless the purchaser has reason to believe that the amount to be ordered in any year under such contract will not exceed $10,000." [29] Notwithstanding the above, the regulations provide that the equal opportunity clause shall be applied to such contracts whenever the amount of a single order exceeds $10,000, and the contract shall be subject to the Order for its duration. [30]

Additional exemptions noted in the regulations are available for "special circumstances in the national interest" which may be determined by the director of the OFCCP; [31] groups or categories of contracts or subcontracts when the director "finds it impracticable to act upon each request individually or where group exemptions will contribute to convenience in the administration of the order"; [32] facilities not connected with the contracts; [33] and national security reasons as determined by the head of an agency. [34]

The OFCCP director may withdraw an exemption for a contract or subcontract (or groups of contracts and subcontracts). [35]

Reports and Information. Contractors and subcontractors must file EEO-1 reports on or before March 31 of each year if, *inter alia*, they (1) are not exempt from the regulations, (2) have fifty or more employees, (3) are prime contractors or "first tier subcontractors" (defined as subcontractors holding subcontracts with a prime contractor), [36] and (4) have a contract, subcontract or purchase order amounting to $50,000 or more. [37] Reports must be filed within thirty days after the award of a contract or subcontract, unless a report has been submitted within the twelve-month period preceding the date of the award. Where complete and accurate reports are not timely filed, the contractor or subcontractor shall be deemed in noncompliance with its obligations under the equal opportunity clause and will be subject to sanctions. [38]

Under the regulations, a contractor may be required to keep employment or other records and to furnish information, upon request, to facilitate the administration of the Order.

Segregated Facilities. Prime contractors or subcontractors are required to insure that none of its facilities segregate employees. [39] "Facilities" means waiting rooms, work areas, restaurants, other eating areas, time clocks, restrooms, workrooms, locker rooms, storage or dressing areas, parking lots, drinking fountains, recreation or entertainment areas, transportation, and housing facilities provided for employees. [40]

Prior to the award of a nonexempt government contract or subcontract or federally assisted construction contract or subcontract, prospective prime contractors and subcontractors shall be required to submit a certification that (1) segregated facilities are not, and will not be, maintained, and (2) employees will not be permitted to perform services at any location controlled by the contractor or subcontractor where segregated facilities are maintained. [41] A similar certification must be obtained prior to the award of any nonexempt subcontract. [42]

Compliance Review and Complaint Procedures

Compliance Reviews. The OFCCP regulations provide for compliance reviews to insure that contractors are meeting the requirements of Executive Order 11246. Such reviews consist of "a comprehensive analysis and evaluation of each aspect of . . . practices, policies, and conditions resulting therefrom,"[43] and, where necessary, recommendations for sanctions shall be made. The OFFCP's procedures in conducting compliance reviews is detailed below.[44]

Deficiencies revealed by a compliance review are to be addressed through conciliation and persuasion. Contractors will be required to make specific written commitments to correct any deficiencies before they will be deemed to be in compliance with the Order.[45] This aspect of the regulations, and the OFCCP's procedures relative thereto, are discussed *infra.*[46]

Pre-award compliance reviews of prospective contractors of contracts, and subcontractors of contracts and subcontracts, exceeding $2 million are required by the regulations, and no such contract will be awarded unless a pre-award compliance review has been conducted by the compliance agency within twelve months prior to the award.[47] The awarding agency is to notify the OFCCP and request the pre-award review, and the OFCCP is to provide written reports of compliance with the regulations within thirty days following the requests.[48]

Complaints. Complaints of violations of the Order and regulations shall be filed with the OFCCP in Washington, D.C., or any regional or area office within 180 days of the alleged violation unless the agency or the OFCCP director extends the filing period for good cause shown.[49] Complaints may be referred to the Equal Employment Opportunity Commission for processing under Title VII.

When the OFCCP concludes the investigation of a complaint, any indication of a violation of the Equal Opportunity Clause shall be resolved by informal means, if possible, including the holding of a compliance conference. If not resolved at this stage, the complaint shall be processed under the enforcement proceedings detailed in the regulations (as discussed below). Within sixty days of the complaint (or additional time as allowed by the director), a report is to be remitted to the director which includes, *inter alia,* a summary of findings, statement of contractor compliance or noncompliance, and statement of disposition of the case.[50]

Show Cause Notices. The OFCCP may issue a notice requiring a contractor to show cause, within thirty days, why monitoring, enforcement proceedings, or other action to ensure compliance with the Order should not be instituted.[51]

Conciliation Agreements. The OFCCP regulations permit written conciliation agreements as a mechanism to correct deficiencies or violations revealed by a compliance review, complaint investigation, or other review. Such agreements shall provide for remedial action to correct noted violations or deficiencies, including back pay and retroactive seniority.[52] Violation of a conciliation agreement will result in written notice of violation(s) to the contractor which the contractor shall respond to within fifteen days from receipt of the notice. In certain circumstances, the OFCCP may initiate enforcement proceedings without issuing a show cause notice or following other requirements contained in the regulation.[53]

Affirmative Action Programs

Section 60–1.40 of the regulations sets forth the requirements of written affirmative action compliance programs which a contractor and subcontractor must develop for each of its establishments within one hundred and twenty days from the commencement of a contract. Contractors and subcontractors covered by this section include those with fifty or more employees and government bills of lading, which in any twelve-month period total or can be reasonably expected to total $50,000 or more.[54]

The regulations define affirmative action programs as a "set of specific and result-oriented procedures to which a contractor commits himself to apply every good-faith effort."[55] Required contents and ingredients of such plans are specifically noted in the regulations.

Utilization Analysis. The OFCCP regulations state that minority groups are most likely to be underutilized in the following departments listed on the EEO–1 report: officials and managers, professionals, technicians, sales workers, office and clerical, and craft workers (skilled).[56] The regulations further state that women are likely to be underutilized in the following departments: officials and managers, professionals, technicians, sales workers, and skilled and semi-skilled craft workers.[57] Calling for contractors to "direct special attention to such jobs" in their analysis and goal setting, the regulations require that work force and utilization analysis must be included in an affirmative action program.

The work force analysis is a listing of each job title in an applicable collective bargaining agreement or payroll records, ranked from the lowest-paid to the highest-paid employee within each department or organizational unit, including supervision.[58] This analysis must also include listings of separate work units, or "lines of progression," within a department, including supervisors. Lines of progression must show the "order of jobs in the line through which an employee could move to the top of the line."[59] In the absence of formal progression lines or promotional sequences, the regulations provide that job titles should be listed by department, job families, or discipline, in order of wage rates or salary ranges. The total number of male and female incumbents must be given, including the total number of Black, Spanish-surnamed American, American Indian, and Oriental incumbents.[60] Wage rates or salary ranges for each job title must be given, and all job titles (including managerial job titles) must be listed.

With respect to the utilization analysis, all major job groups (one or a group of jobs having similar content, wage rates, and opportunities) at a facility must be analyzed to determine if "minorities or women are currently being underutilized (defined as "having fewer minorities or women in a particular job group than would reasonably be expected by their availability").[61] In determining whether minorities are underutilized, the regulations provide that the contractor must consider at least all of the following factors:

• The minority population of the labor area surrounding the facility;
• The size of the minority unemployment force in the labor area surrounding the facility;
• The percentage of the minority work force as compared with the total work force in the immediate labor area;
• The general availability of minorities having the requisite skills in the immediate labor area;
• The availability of minorities having requisite skills in a reasonable recruitment area;
• The availability of promotable and transferable minorities within the contractor's organization;
• The existence of training institutions capable of training persons in the requisite skills;
• The degree of training the contractor is reasonably able to undertake as a means of making all job classes available to minorities.[62]

Female underutilization analysis must consider the following factors:[63]

• The size of the female unemployment force in the labor area surrounding the facility;
• The percentage of the female work force as compared with the total work force in the immediate labor area;
• The general availability of women having requisite skills in the immediate labor area;
• The availability of women having requisite skills in an area in which the contractor can reasonably recruit;
• The availability of women seeking employment in the labor or recruitment area of the contractor;
• The availability of promotable and transferable female employees within the contractor's organization;
• The existence of training institutions capable of training persons in the requisite skills;
• The degree of training which the contractor is reasonably able to undertake as a means of making all job classes available to women.

Goals and Timetables. Contractors are also required to develop goals and timetables which can be attained from "putting forth every good-faith effort" to make the overall affirmative action program work.[64] The contractors' determination of the levels of goals should consider the utilization factors noted above.

Among other things, the regulations provide that goals and timetables should be "significant, measurable, and attainable"; should be "specific for planned results, with timetables for completion"; may not be "rigid and inflexible quotas which must be met" but must be "targets reasonably attainable by means of applying every good-faith effort"; must be designed to correct identifiable deficiencies, with separate goals and timetables for minorities and women; and shall be part of the written affirmative action program.[65]

Additional Required Ingredients. Affirmative action programs must also contain the following items:

- Development or reaffirmation of the contractor's equal opportunity policy as reflected in a policy statement by the contractor's chief executive officer. This statement should indicate his or her attitude on the subject matter, assign overall responsibility, and provide for reporting and monitoring procedures. The statement should also mention nondiscrimination in recruitment, hiring, training, and promotion; employment decisions which will further equal employment opportunity, insure that only valid requirements are imposed for promotions, and insure that all personnel actions are administered in a nondiscriminating fashion.[66]

- The equal employment policy should be disseminated internally through the contractor's policy manual, company newspaper or magazine, meetings with management and other employees, etc.[67] External dissemination should be undertaken by informing recruitment sources of company policy both verbally and in writing; notifying minority and women's organizations, agencies, leaders, etc. of company policy (preferably in writing); communicating with prospective employers as to the existence of the affirmative action program; and other measures.[68]

- A contractor executive should be appointed director or manager of equal opportunity programs with sufficient staffing and support, and should be identified both internally and externally.[69] That individual's responsibilities should include the development of policy statements, affirmative action programs, communication techniques, identification of problem areas, serving as liaison between the contractor and enforcement agencies, designing audit and reporting systems, and other duties listed in the regulations.[70]

- They must identify problem areas by organizational units and job groups, including analysis of work force composition by minority group status and sex, transfer and promotion practices, etc.[71] Corrective action will be reflected under the regulations where the analysis reveals underutilization in specific job groups; lateral or vertical movement of minorities or women at a lesser rate than non-minority or male employees; the elimination of a significantly higher percentage of minorities or women than non-minorities or men by a selection process; and other areas listed in the regulations.[72]

- The contractor should conduct a detailed analysis of promotion descriptions and validate worker specifications by division, department, location or other organizational unit and by job title using job performance criteria. "Where requirements screen out a disproportionate number of minorities or women, such requirements should be professionally validated to job performance."[73] In addition, contractors are required to observe the requirement of the OFCCP's Uniform Guidelines on Employee Selection Procedures.[74]

- The affirmative action guidelines should set forth suggested techniques to improve recruitment and increase the flow of minority and female applicants. Lists of specific organizations which refer minority or female applicants (e.g., the Urban League, Job Corps, the National Organization for Women, and sororities) should be made available.[75]

Community leaders and minority and female employees should also be identified as recruiting sources, and it is suggested that contractors participate in job fairs, special employment programs, and other activities.[76]

• Equal opportunity for promotions are to be addressed in the guidelines, with suggestions that contractors initiate remedial job training and work study programs; require written justification when "apparently qualified" minority or female employees are passed over; encourage child care, housing, and transportation programs to improve employment opportunities; and other actions.[77]

• Internal audit and reporting systems which would monitor records of referrals, placements, transfers, promotions, and terminations are discussed in § 60–2.25. The contractor should require formal reports from unit managers on a scheduled basis to monitor the degree to which goals or timetables are attained and met.[78] Results of such reports should be reviewed with top management.[79]

Sex Discrimination and Religion and National Origin Discrimination Guidelines

In 1970, the Department of Labor issued sex discrimination guidelines (codified as 41 C.F.R. Part 60–20). Generally, these guidelines provide that employers must not discriminate on the basis of sex in employment matters (including wages, hours, and fringe benefits), and requires affirmative action to recruit women to apply for jobs when they have been previously excluded.[80]

Similarly, the OFCCP's religion and national origin discrimination guidelines (41 C.F.R. Part 60–50) set forth an employer's obligations with respect to prohibited discrimination against ethnic groups, and observing the religious observances and practices of employees and prospective employees. With respect to the latter, an employer is required to accommodate employee religious practices unless it can demonstrate that it is unable to reasonably accommodate the employee's or applicant's religious observance or practice without undue hardship on the conduct of the employer's business.[81]

Construction Industry Guidelines

Executive Order 11246 mandates nondiscrimination in federally assisted construction contracts in excess of $10,000.[82] Implementing regulations are set forth at 41 C.F.R. Part 60–4.

Among other things, all solicitations for offers and bids on construction contracts must contain a notice which sets forth specified goals and timetables for minorities and women for each year.

The Equal Opportunity Clause is published at 41 C.F.R. §§ 60–1.4(a) and (b) and must be included in federal and federally assisted construction contracts and subcontracts.[83] In addition, all covered contracts shall include specifications found at 41 C.F.R. § 60–4.3(a).

It should also be noted that the OFCCP previously had approved affirmative action programs (commonly known as "Hometown Plans"), had promulgated "Imposed Plans," and had approved "Special Bid Conditions." A detailed explication of these plans will not be set forth here. However, construction industry employers should be aware of these types of plans.

The OFCCP director has issued goals and timetables for minority and female utilization in specific geographical areas. The goals and timetables are applicable to each construction trade in a covered contractor's or subcontractor's entire work force working in the area covered by the goals and timetables, and shall be inserted by the contracting officers and applicants in the notice required by § 60–40.2. Covered construction contractors performing construction work in geographical areas in which they do not have a federal or federally assisted construction contract shall apply the goals established for the geographical area where the work is being performed.[84]

AFFIRMATIVE ACTION FOR THE HANDICAPPED AND VETERANS

Separate regulatory parts cover a contractor's affirmative action obligations relating to § 503 of the 1973 Rehabilitation Act[85] and veterans.[86]

Affirmative Action Regulations Governing Handicapped Workers

41 C.F.R. Part 60–741 sets forth the affirmative action obligations of contractors and subcontractors for handicapped workers. These regulations apply to all government contracts and subcontracts for $2500 or more.[87]

The regulations set forth an affirmative action clause (see 41 C.F.R. § 60–741.4) which must be included in covered contracts or subcontracts, including modification, renewals, or extensions thereof.

Within one hundred and twenty days of the commencement of a contract, each contractor or subcontractor holding a contract of $50,000 or more and having fifty or more employees shall prepare and maintain an affirmative action program which may be integrated or kept separate from the contractor's other affirmative action programs. If modifications of personnel procedures are needed, contractors are required to include and develop new procedures in the program.[88] Further, the program must provide for a review of all physical or mental job qualification requirements; accommodation of physical and mental limitations of employees; outreach, positive recruitment, and external dissemination of contract policy regarding the handicapped; internal dissemination of the policy; the contractor executive designated as responsible for implementation; and other matters.[89] The enlistment and support of recruiting sources and contracts with appropriate entities are cited as part of the required effort to be undertaken by contractors. Programs are to be reviewed and updated annually.

Employees or applicants may file a written complaint with the OFCCP alleging a violation of the Rehabilitation Act or the regulations within one hundred and eighty days from the date of the alleged violations (unless the time for filing is extended by the OFCCP director for good cause shown). If the contractor has an internal review procedure, the complaint shall be referred to the contractor for processing on a confidential basis. Where the complaint is not resolved under the internal procedure to the satisfaction of the complainant, within sixty days of the referral, the Department of Labor will investigate and process the complaint.[90] If the investigation shows no violation, the complainant is notified and may request review by the director within thirty days.[91]

If the investigation indicates that the regulations or statute have been violated, efforts to conciliate the matter shall be made. Compliance will be satisfied where the contractor or subcontractor makes a specific written commitment to take corrective and precise action by a specified date.[92] If a complaint is not resolved informally, a formal hearing will be held as required by 41 C.F.R. Part 60–30 (discussed below). Noncompliance can result in judicial action to enforce the affirmative action clause (§ 60–741.4); withholding of payments; termination or cancellation of a contract or subcontract; and debarment.[93]

Affirmative Action for Veterans

OFCCP regulations on affirmative action for veterans apply to all government contracts and subcontracts for $10,000 or more (including construction contracts). As in the previous sections, each agency and contractor shall include the affirmative action clause set forth at 41 C.F.R. § 60–250.4 in each of its covered contracts or subcontracts within one hundred and twenty days of the commencement of a contract; every government contractor or subcontractor holding a contract of $50,000 or more and having fifty or more employees shall prepare and maintain an affirmative action program. This program may be integrated into, or kept separate from, other contractor affirmative action programs, and shall be reviewed and updated annually.

The affirmative action obligation of the contractor is to employ and advance qualified disabled veterans and veterans of the Vietnam era. Affirmative action program requirements include contractor review of personnel procedures to ensure consideration of the job qualifications of known disabled veterans and Vietnam-era veteran applicants; a review of all physical or mental job qualification requirements; accommodation to the physical and mental limitations of a disabled veteran, unless the contractor can demonstrate that the accommodation would impose an undue hardship on the conduct of the contractor's business; outreach, positive recruitment, and external dissemination of policy; internal dissemination of policy; and executive responsibility for implementation.[94]

Applicants or employees may file written complaints with the Department of Labor's Veterans' Employment Service (or designee at the local state employment office) alleging a violation of the regulations or the Veteran-Era Veterans' Readjustment Assistance Act. Confidential processing of complaints by contractors shall be required where the contractor has an internal review procedure. If the complaint is not resolved to the satisfaction of the complainant within sixty days of the referral, the complaint will be forwarded to the Department of Labor for investigation. If no violation of the Act or regulations is shown, the complainant is notified and may appeal to the OFCCP director.[95]

Investigations which indicate that a violation has occurred will result in efforts to secure compliance through conciliation and persuasion. The director may approve a contractor's compliance commitments if those commitments are specific, in writing, and indicate the precise action to be taken and dates for completion.[96] Complaints not resolved by informal means shall be resolved by formal hearing under 41 C.F.R. Part 60–30 (discussed below).

Noncompliance can result in appropriate judicial action, withholding of payments, termination or cancellation of contracts or subcontracts, and debarment.[97]

ENFORCING THE ORDER

As noted above, the OFCCP has issued rules of practice for administrative proceedings to enforce Executive Order 11246. This section sketches the main requirements of these rules (codified at 41 C.F.R. Part 60–30).

Complaint and Hearing Procedures

Complaints alleging violations of the Order, implementing regulations, or contractual obligations may be issued by the Department of Labor upon referral from the OFCCP. The defendant must file an answer to the complaint within twenty days after service thereof.[98] The answer shall contain (1) a statement of facts constituting a ground of defense, and shall admit, explain, or deny each of the complaint's allegations unless the defendant is without knowledge, or (2) state that the defendant admits all the allegations of the complaint. Waiver of, or request for, a hearing should be set forth in the answer. If the complaint allegations are admitted (or an answer is not filed) the hearing is waived and an administrative law judge (ALJ) may decide the case, based on the material facts alleged in the complaints. Exceptions to the decision, and a supporting brief, may be filed by the parties.

The rules of practice provide for discovery. Interrogatories, written requests for admissions of facts, and requests to produce may be served upon an opposing party, and must be answered, objected to, or responded to within twenty-five days after service.[99] Depositions may also be taken upon reasonable notice or administrative subpoena.[100]

The rules provide for motions for summary judgment by the government, the defendant, or other parties. If there is no genuine issue as to any material fact and the movant is entitled to judgment as a matter of law, the motion will be granted.

Parties have the right to be represented by counsel at OFCCP hearings. Formal rules of evidence of the Department of Labor's Office of Administrative Law Judges apply.[101] Witnesses shall give oral testimony and are subject to cross-examination. Objections to the admission or rejection of evidence may be made by the parties, with formal exception to an adverse ruling not required. Upon request, any party is entitled to oral argument.[102]

"Interested persons" may petition for and participate as a party in OFCCP hearings. Labor organizations may participate where the proceedings involve employees covered by a collective bargaining agreement which may be revised as a result of compliance. Other persons or organizations shall have participation rights if a final administrative order "could adversely affect them or the class they represent" and participation may contribute materially to the proper disposition of the complaint.[103]

Post-hearing procedures are as follows. Briefs may be filed within twenty days after receipt of the hearing transcript, with extensions of time available on timely request.[104] Thereafter, the ALJ shall make recommended findings, conclusions, and a decision which will be certified (with the record) for recommended decision to the Secretary of Labor for final administrative order.[105] Exceptions may be filed within fourteen days of receipt of the ALJ's ruling, and responses to the exceptions may be submitted within fourteen days of their receipt by other parties. All exceptions and responses shall be filed with the Secretary.

Subsequent to the expiration of the time for filing briefs and exceptions, the Secretary of Labor will make a final decision (the final administrative order)[106] on the basis of the record. A conclusion by the Secretary that a contractor violated Executive Order 11246, the Equal Opportunity Clause, or regulations will result in the issuance of an order enjoining the violations and requiring appropriate remedies and sanctions. Failure to comply with the final administrative order shall result in immediate cancellation, termination and suspension of contracts and/or debarment from further contracts,[107] and other sanctions.

Expedited Hearings

Expedited hearings may be used when a contractor or subcontractor has violated a conciliation agreement; has not adopted and implemented an affirmative action program; has refused to give access to or supply required records or information; or has refused to allow an on-site compliance review.[108]

Interrogatories may not be served; depositions may only be taken with the ALJ's permission. Among other things, the ALJ must make recommended findings, conclusions, and decisions within fifteen days after a hearing is concluded. Exceptions may be submitted within ten days after receipt of the decision, with responses to be submitted within seven days after receipt of the exceptions. The Secretary of Labor shall then issue a final administrative order. Unless the Secretary issues that order within thirty days after the expiration of the time for filing exceptions, the ALJ's recommended decision shall become a final administrative order effective on the thirty-first day after expiration of the time for filing exceptions.[109]

COMPLIANCE REVIEWS

This section details audit procedures of the OFCCP as set forth in the agency's compliance manual.[110]

Desk Audits

A percentage of establishments are randomly selected for compliance reviews as generated by the Equal Employment Data System (EEDS). After a contractor has been selected for a compliance review, the Equal Opportunity Specialist (EOS) will contact the contractor and seek to obtain the name of the chief executive officer, the name of the person responsible for preparing and implementing the affirmative action program, and the correct mailing address of the establishment. Outside counsel or consultants will be identified at the initial stage.

A "scheduling letter" will be sent to the contractor scheduling a compliance review and requesting the affirmative action program and supporting documentation. A follow-up contact with the contractor should occur. At the time the scheduling letter is sent, the EOS will contact the EEOC, state and local fair employment agencies, and the Veterans Employment and Training Service requesting information on any complaints filed against the contractor or other pertinent information.

The request for affirmative action programs must be complied with by the contractor. If not submitted to the EOS, a show cause notice may be issued, or the director of the OFCCP may proceed directly to administrative enforcement.[111]

The compliance manual provides that the EOS should evaluate the contractor's performance on goals, its good-faith efforts, personnel activity, etc. for at least the last full affirmative action program year, and the current plan year if the contractor is six months or more into its current plan year.

The EOS will review the submitted materials. The submission will be automatically considered unreasonable, the desk audit suspended, and a show cause notice issued if one or more of the following items of the Order plan is missing.

- A work force analysis
- A utilization analysis
- Goals for underutilized areas

If these items are included, the EOS will evaluate these ingredients for reasonableness under 41 C.F.R. Part 60–2 (see supra). If the Order plan does not meet the reasonableness standard, the desk audit will be suspended and a show cause notice issued. If the reasonableness standard is met, the plan will be evaluated for acceptability under the Order and regulations. Further, handicapped and veteran's plans are also reviewed for acceptability under 41 C.F.R. Parts 60–741 and 60–250, respectively. The EOS will evaluate the contractor's good-faith efforts to meet its goals, including an overall assessment of the contractor's goals and affirmative action performance. The EOS will seek to identify any goal areas needing further evaluation.

OFCCP policy is to follow Title VII principles in analyzing potential discrimination issues. In addressing potential discrimination issues, the EOS will review the contractor's work force analysis and look for evidence of concentrations and underrepresentations of minorities and females. In auditing personnel activity, a method known as the Impact Ratio Analysis (IRA) is used. The IRA is a ratio between selection rates for minorities and women and others. Selection rates for minorities or women less than 80 percent of the selection rate for nonminorities or men may be investigated in an on-site review.

Additionally, the EOS will be alert for wage and salary disparities shown in underrepresented areas as compared to those in areas of concentration. The EOS may attempt to obtain from the contractor actual salary information and/or keys to any wage codes used by the contractor.

This sketch does not detail all of the factors and items addressed by an EOS during a desk audit. Careful consultation with counsel, and review of a contractor's plan and supporting documentation, are required whenever the OFCCP advises that it has selected the contractor for a compliance review and audit. For a helpful review and understanding of the issues relative to the audits, the OFCCP's standard Compliance Review Report should be examined.[112]

On-site Review Procedures

On-site reviews are not conducted in all instances. The major purpose of the on-site review, according to the OFCCP, is to investigate potential problem areas identified by a desk audit, to verify contractor implementation of affirmative action programs, and to resolve violations.

During the on-site review, the EOS will review applications, personnel files, labor agreements, policy and compensation manuals, posted job openings, company newsletters, etc. Visual confirmation of the posting of EEO posters, policy statements, and other items will be undertaken by the EOS during a facility inspection.

A typical on-site review will begin with an entrance conference with the facility's chief executive officer and/or his/her representative(s). The purpose of the review, information needed, length of the review, and need to conduct employee interviews will be discussed. After the entrance conference, the EOS will seek to meet with personnel who are knowledgeable about the contractor's personnel policies and practices. Compliance with any prior conciliation agreements or letter of commitment will be discussed.

Formal or informal interviews may be conducted by the EOS and documented in writing. The OFCCP manual states that management representatives do not have the right to be present during on-site interviews with nonmanagement personnel. As set forth in the manual, interviews with management personnel may be attended by the contractor's attorney or other management representative, except when the manager is not speaking for management. In formal interviews, interviewees may be asked to read, sign, and date interview notes taken by the EOS, and the EOS should seek to confirm quotes or paraphrasing.

The EOS will usually inspect the Immigration and Naturalization Service Forms I-9[113] maintained by the contractor. Any unresolved deficiencies in the contractor's affirmative action program and required ingredients will be discussed with those individuals charged with developing and maintaining the program. The EOS will seek to identify deficiencies and recommend corrective action. Furthermore, the contractor's compliance with the OFCCP sex discrimination guidelines[114] will be addressed. Maternity leave issues under the Pregnancy Discrimination Act of 1978[115] and 41 C.F.R. § 60–20.3(g) will be reviewed, as well as fringe benefits and sexual harassment issues.

Good-faith efforts by the contractors will also be reviewed. In this regard, applicant flow records, employment activity audits, and verification of correspondence, job orders, bid lists, and other documentation will be sought. Compliance with OFCCP religion and national origin guidelines will also be explained.

Affirmative action programs for the handicapped and veterans will be investigated. The EOS will explore the contractor's performance as required by OFCCP regulations. Interviews with individuals identified as handicapped or disabled, or observed by the EOS as such, may be taken, as well as a description of any accommodations made or needed.

At the conclusion of the on-site review, an exit conference will typically be held with the CEO or his/her representative. The EOS will discuss, *inter alia*, any identified deficiencies and recommend corrective actions. Discussion of whether the OFCCP will require a letter of commitment or a conciliation agreement may be scheduled. Moreover, the EOS may indicate an estimated time within which the contractor can expect to receive written results of the on-site review.

After the review, the contractor may receive a letter which sets forth deficiencies in its affirmative action programs or compliance with OFCCP regulations. The contractor shall respond to the OFCCP letter and attempt to convince the OFCCP that the asserted deficiencies either do not exist or have been remedied. Negotiations between the OFCCP and the contractor may commence. All agreements (and rejected demands) should be put in writing and confirmed by letter to the OFCCP. If a final agreement is reached, the contractor will be ordered to execute a letter of commitment or a conciliation agreement. Because a conciliation agreement waives certain procedural rights employed by contractors, contractors should always attempt to obtain a letter of commitment.

A show cause notice may be issued where a contractor refuses to submit a plan and supporting documents to the OFCCP, refuses to permit an on-site review, harasses an EOS, violates a conciliation agreement, or engages in other conduct.

CONCLUSION

It should be noted that the OFCCP is currently engaged in the process of rewriting and revising its enforcement manual, with final review of chapters on how to reach resolutions, a glossary of terms, and good-faith efforts undergoing legal review by its Department of Labor.[116] Thus, further developments in that area must be monitored.

Enforcement of Executive Order 11246 promises to be vigorous. Current OFCCP director Cari Dominguez has indicated that she will so enforce the Order, and has stated that her agenda includes expanding compliance reviews to examine senior management selection practices and mapping out a plan for determining the agency's agenda beyond the year 2000.[117]

Again, this chapter merely sketches the basic requirements and provisions of Executive Order 11246 and implementing regulations issued by the OFCCP. At all times, contractors must take special care in analyzing issues arising under the Order and should seek counsel when dealing with the OFCCP.

NOTES

1. 3 C.F.R. 339–348 (1964–1665 Comp.). The Order is reprinted in the Affirmative Action Compliance Manual (BNA), at pp. 101–104, as amended by Executive Order 11375 (Oct. 13, 1967), and Executive Order 12086 (effective Oct. 8, 1978).

2. *See generally* CCH 1989 GUIDEBOOK TO FAIR EMPLOYMENT PRACTICES 127 (Apr. 27, 1989); C. SULLIVAN, M. ZIMMER, and R. RICHARDS, EMPLOYMENT DISCRIMINATION, VOL. II 547–567 (1988).

3. 29 U.S.C. § 701 *et seq.*

4. 38 U.S.C. § 2021 *et seq.*

5. *See* F. Welch, *Affirmative Action and Discrimination*, in THE QUESTION OF DISCRIMINATION: RACIAL INEQUALITY IN THE U.S. LABOR MARKET 154 (S. Shulman and W. Darity, eds., 1989).

6. Executive Order 11246 delegated enforcement power to the United States Secretary of Labor who, in turn, delegated power to the Office of Federal Contract Compliance (OFCC), an agency within the Department. C. SULLIVAN, et al., *supra* note 2 at 549–550 n. 14. The OFCC delegated part of its enforcement authority to federal agencies. Thereafter, the OFCC was reorganized and renamed the OFCCP, and all responsibilities for compliance matters were consolidated into the OFCCP. *Id.*; *see also* 2 CCH EMPL. PRAC. GUIDE ¶ 4380.

7. Executive Order 11246, § 202.

8. Section 204 of the Order provides that the Secretary of Labor may exempt a contracting agency from the requirements of the Order "when he deems that special circumstances in the national interest so require. . . . " The Secretary may also purchase orders (1) with respect to work which is to be (or has been) performed outside the United States, and no recruitment of workers within the United States is involved; (2) for standard commercial supplies or raw materials; (3) involving less than specified amounts of money or numbers of workers; or (4) involving subcontracts below a specified tier. The Secretary may also exempt contractor facilities which are separate and distinct from the contractor's

activities related to the contract, provided that the exemption will not interfere with the purposes of the Order and, in the absence of the exemption, all facilities shall be covered by the Order.

9. Section 202.

10. *Id.*

11. *Id.*

12. *Id.*

13. *Id.*

14. *Id.*

15. *Id.*

16. Section 203(1).

17. Section 203(c).

18. *Id.*

19. Sections 206–208.

20. Section 208(b).

21. Section 209(a)(1)–(6).

22. Section 209(b).

23. Sections 301, 302(1).

24. *See infra* at notes 82–84 and accompanying text.

25. 41 C.F.R. § 60–1.1.

26. 41 C.F.R. § 60–1.4(c).

27. 41 C.F.R. § 60–1.5(a)(1).

28. 41 C.F.R. § 60–1.5(a)(2).

29. 41 C.F.R. § 60–1.5(a)(1).

30. *Id.* The regulations also discuss work performed outside the United States; contracts with state or local governments; contracts with certain educational institutions; and work on or near Indian reservations. *See* 41 C.F.R. § 60–1.5(a)(3)–(6).

31. 41 C.F.R. § 60–1.5(a)(1).

32. *Id.*

33. *Id.*, § 60–1.5(b)(2).

34. *Id.*, § 60–1.5(c).

35. *Id.*, § 60–1.5(d).

36. *See* 41 C.F.R. § 60–1.3.

37. 41 C.F.R. § 60–1.7(a)(1).

38. *Id.*, § 60–1.7(a)(4).

39. *Id.*, § 60–1.8(a).

40. *Id.*

41. 41 C.F.R. § 60–1.8(b).

42. *See also* 41 C.F.R. §§ 60–1.9 and 1.10 (discussing compliance by labor unions, recruiting and training agencies, and foreign government practices).

43. 41 C.F.R. § 60–1.20(a).

44. *See infra* notes 110–15 and accompanying text.

45. 41 C.F.R. § 60–1.20(b).

46. *See* p, 103.

47. 41 C.F.R. § 60–120(d).

48. *Id. See also* 41 C.F.R. § 60–1.29 (preaward notices).

49. 41 C.F.R. §§ 60–1.21–1.22. For required contents of complaints, *see* 41 C.F.R. § 60–1.23.

50. 41 C.F.R. § 60–1.24(d).

51. 41 C.F.R. § 60–1.28.

52. *Id.*, § 60–1.33. Conciliation agreements must be distinguished from "letters of commitment" which are used to resolve minor technical deficiencies. *See* § 60–1.33(b).

53. Section 60–1.34(a)(1)–(3). *See also* 41 C.F.R. § 60–2.2(c) and 41 C.F.R. § 60–4.8 (violations of letters of commitment and procedures related thereto).

54. 41 C.F.R. § 60–1.40; 41 C.F.R. § 60–2.1(a).

55. 41 C.F.R. § 60–2.10.

56. 41 C.F.R. § 60–2.11.

57. *Id.*

58. 41 C.F.R. § 60–2.11(a).

59. *Id.*

60. *Id.*

61. 41 C.F.R. § 60–2.11(b).

62. 41 C.F.R. § 60–2.11(b)(1).

63. 41 C.F.R. § 60–2.11(b)(2).

64. 41 C.F.R. § 60–2.12.

65. *Id.*

66. 41 C.F.R. § 60–2.20.

67. Section 60–2.21.

68. Section 60–2.21.

69. Section 60–2.22.

70. *Id.*

71. Section 60–2.23.

72. *Id.*

73. Section 60–2.24(b).

74. Section 60–2.24(d)(2).

75. Section 60–2.24(e)(1). *See also* § 60–2.26 (discussing contractor support for community bonds and organizations).

76. Section 60–2.24(e)(4)–(11).

77. Sections 60–2.24(f)(1)–(8), 60–2.24(h).

78. Section 60–2.25(b).

79. Section 60–2.25(c) and (d).

80. 41 C.F.R. §§ 60–20.3(c), 60–20.5, and 60–20.6.

81. 41 C.F.R. § 60–50.3.

82. Executive Order 11246, §§ 301–304.

83. 41 C.F.R. § 60–4.3(a).

84. 41 C.F.R. § 60–4.6.

85. *See* 29 U.S.C. § 706.

86. 38 U.S.C. § 2012 *et seq.*

87. 41 C.F.R. § 60–741.1. If a single order of a contract is $2,500 or more, the affirmative action clause shall be applied. 41 C.F.R. § 60–741.3(a)(2). With respect to indefinite contracts and subcontracts, the affirmative action obligations apply unless the contracting agency has "reason to believe that the amount to be ordered in any year under such contract is less than $2,500." *Id.* Waivers of coverage may be granted by the head of an agency with concurrence of the OFCCP director. Section 60–741.3(b).

"Handicapped individual" is defined as a person who (1) has a physical or mental impairment which substantially limits one or more of such person's major life activities,

(2) has a record of such impairment, or (3) is regarded as having such an impairment. 41 C.F.R. § 60–741.2 and Appendix A.

88. An example of such procedures are set forth at 41 C.F.R. Part 741, Appendix C.

89. 41 C.F.R. § 60–741.6(b)–(j).

90. 41 C.F.R. § 60–741.26(a), (b), and (e).

91. 41 C.F.R. § 60–741.26(g)(1).

92. 41 C.F.R. § 60–741.26(g)(2).

93. Section 60–741.28.

94. 41 C.F.R. § 60.250.6.

95. 41 C.F.R. § 60–250.26(b)–(g)(1).

96. Section 60–250.26(g)(2).

97. Section 60–250.28.

98. 41 C.F.R. § 60–30.6

99. 41 C.F.R. §§ 60–30.9 and 60–30.10.

100. Section 60–30.11.

101. Section 60–30.18, as amended by 55 Fed. Reg. 19069 (May 8, 1990).

102. Section 60–30.21.

103. Section 60–30.24.

104. Section 60–30.25.

105. Sections 60–30.26, 60–30.27.

106. Section 60–30.29.

107. Section 60–30.30.

108. 41 C.F.R. §§ 60.31–60.37.

109. 41 C.F.R. § 60–30.37.

110. The compliance manual is reprinted in the *Affirmative Action Compliance Manual* published by the Bureau of National Affairs.

111. *See* 41 C.F.R. § 60–1.26(a)(2).

112. Affirmative Action Compliance Manual (BNA), at pp. 2:0073–2:0153.

113. These forms are used to record the citizenship status of new employees.

114. *See* 41 C.F.R. § 60–2.13(h).

115. 42 U.S.C. § 2000e(k).

116. *See Affirmative Action Compliance Manual* (BNA), News and Developments (Nov. 28, 1989), at p. 4.

117. *Id.* at 3.

4

The EEOC'S Affirmative Action Guidelines

Title VII of the Civil Rights Act of 1964[1] (Title VII) established the Equal Employment Opportunity Commission (EEOC or Commission), a five-member body, to enforce and administer the provisions of that statute. Generally, Title VII prohibits discrimination against individuals on the basis of race, color, religion, sex, or national origin by employers, employment agencies, and labor organizations.[2]

As noted in the preceding chapters, affirmative action initiatives and reverse discrimination claims resulting therefrom often involve questions, as to the meaning and application of Title VII. Addressing those questions, the EEOC has determined that Congressional enactment of Title VII was not intended to expose those who comply with the statute to Title VII liability. "Such a result would immobilize or reduce the efforts of many who would otherwise take action to improve the opportunities of minorities and women without litigation, thus frustrating the Congressional intent to encourage voluntary action and increasing the prospect of Title VII litigation."[3]

In January 1979, the EEOC published its Affirmative Action Guidelines (Guidelines),[4] regulations which constitute the Commission's written interpretation and opinion of Title VII and the issue of affirmative action.[5] This brief chapter discusses the major provisions of those regulations.

THE GUIDELINES

The EEOC's Guidelines make it clear that the Commission views voluntary affirmative action as conduct which "must be encouraged and protected in order to carry out the Congressional intent embodied in Title VII."[6] Such affirmative action, in the view of the EEOC, cannot be measured by the standard of "whether it would have been required had there been litigation, for this standard would undermine the legislative purpose of first encouraging voluntary action without litigation."[7] Rather, stated the Commission, entities subject to Title VII must be allowed flexibility in modifying employment systems and practices to comport with the purposes of Title VII.[8]

Circumstances Calling for Affirmative Action
(Guidelines § 1608.3)

Under the Guidelines, voluntary affirmative action is appropriate in the following circumstances. First, affirmative action may be taken where existing or contemplated employment practices have an adverse impact on those protected by Title VII.[9] Second, affirmative action may be taken to correct the effects of prior discriminatory practices. The Guidelines provide that these effects could be initially identified by a comparison between the work force and an appropriate segment of the labor force.[10]

Finally, the Guidelines state that affirmative action can be taken where there is an "artificially limited" labor pool due to historic restrictions by employers, labor organizations, or others.[11] In that circumstance, the Guidelines encourage affirmative action, including training plans and programs, recruitment activity, elimination of adverse impact caused by invalidated selection criteria, and modification of promotion and layoff procedures.

Required Elements of Affirmative Action Plans
(Guidelines § 1608.4)

Section 1608.4 of the Guidelines provides that an affirmative action plan shall contain three elements: (1) a "reasonable self-analysis"; (2) a "reasonable basis" for concluding that affirmative action is appropriate; and (3) "reasonable action."[12]

Reasonable Self-Analysis. Self-analysis requires a determination of whether employment practices exclude, disadvantage, or result in disparate impact or treatment of protected groups; whether the effects of prior discrimination are left uncorrected; and, if the foregoing determinations are made, the attempt to determine why.[13] No method of self-analysis is mandated by the Guidelines. Techniques which comply with Executive Order 11246 or the regulations of the Office of Federal Contract Compliance Programs (*see supra* Chapter 3), or other federal, state, or local employment discrimination laws may be utilized.[14] In addition, the Guidelines provide that the effects of discrimination by other persons or institutions on the employment practices of an employer, union, or other person subject to Title VII is of concern.[15]

Reasonable Basis. If the "reasonable self-analysis" described above reveals a problem area in employment practices (a problem area which need not establish a violation of Title VII), the Guidelines state that a "reasonable basis for concluding that action is appropriate" exists.[16] This reasonable basis will exist "without any admission or formal finding that the person has violated Title VII, and without regard to whether there exists arguable defenses to a Title VII action."[17]

Reasonable Action. Under the Guidelines, action taken pursuant to an affirmative action plan must be reasonably related to problems disclosed by the self-analysis. Reasonable action, stated the EEOC, may include goals and timetables and the adoption of practices which will eliminate actual or potential adverse impact, disparate treatment, or the effects of past discrimination.

Further, the Commission stated that it would apply the following standards in considering the reasonableness of an affirmative action plan.

The plan should be tailored to solve the problems identified in the self-analysis and to ensure fair employment practices in the future. Provisions of a plan which are race-, sex-, or national origin-conscious should be maintained only as long as necessary to achieve those objectives.[18]

Goals and timetables should be reasonably related to the effects of past discrimination, the need for prompt elimination of adverse impact or disparate treatment, the availability of "basically qualified or qualifiable applicants," and the number of employment opportunities expected to be available.[19]

If an affirmative action plan is challenged as violative of Title VII or is asserted as a defense to a charge of discrimination, the foregoing standards will govern the Commission's investigation as to whether or not the self-analysis and the plan are in writing. Stating that the absence of a written analysis and plan may make it difficult to provide credible evidence regarding the analysis and the plan, the EEOC Guidelines recommend that such analyses and plans be in writing.[20]

Executive Order 11246 and Affirmative Action Compliance Programs (Guidelines § 1608.5)

Commission review of affirmative action compliance programs adopted pursuant to Executive Order 11246 (Order) (*see* Chapter 3) is discussed in the Guidelines. Complaints regarding, or challenges to such programs filed under Title VII, may result in an investigation to determine (1) whether the program was adopted by an entity subject to the Order and pursuant thereto,[21] and (2) whether adherence to the program was the basis of the complaint or was the justification for an action challenged under Title VII.

If those determinations are made and the program has been approved by the Department of Labor or authorized agency, the Commission states that it will issue a determination of no reasonable cause.[22] If the program has not been so approved, the program will be reviewed by the EEOC or will be referred to the Department of Labor for approval under the Order. And, if Commission review

or Department of Labor approval upholds the program, the EEOC will issue a
determination of no reasonable course.[23]

Affirmative Action Required by Court Order
(Guidelines § 1608.8)

The EEOC Guidelines interpret Title VII "to mean that actions taken pursuant
to the direction of a Court Order cannot give rise to liability under Title VII."[24]
Thus, where a judgment or consent order requiring adherence to an affirmative
action plan is the basis of a Title VII complaint or is the justification for an
action challenged under Title VII, the Guidelines call for a determination of no
reasonable cause.[25]

One recent development has resulted in a Commission revision of one aspect
of § 1608.8. As set forth in Chapter 2, the United States Supreme Court, in
Martin v. Wilks,[26] held that claims of discrimination brought by white firefighters
who were neither parties nor privies to affirmative action consent decrees were
not precluded under an "impermissible collateral attack doctrine." Rejecting
that doctrine, the Court held that joinder as a party under the Federal Rules of
Civil Procedure is the required method by which potential parties to a lawsuit
are subjected to the jurisdiction of a court and bound by a judgment or decree.[27]

In light of *Wilks*, the EEOC has issued an interpretive memorandum which
notes that the Guidelines' statement that actions taken pursuant to a court order
cannot give rise to Title VII liability[28] is inconsistent with *Wilks*. Accordingly,
the Commission has determined that that language should not be relied upon or
reiterated.[29] Pending EEOC review of the impact of *Wilks* on the Guidelines,
EEOC personnel were instructed to contact the Commission's Office of Legal
Counsel for guidance. In addition, the memorandum noted that the Commission
may have to defend or attempt to renegotiate agreed-upon or court-ordered plans
which were challenged by nonparties. Therefore, stated the memorandum, the
plan should be evaluated to determine whether it conforms to current legal
standards.[30]

Reliance on the Guidelines as a Defense to a Title VII Charge

Section 713(b) of Title VII[31] provides, in pertinent part, that no person subject
to Title VII shall be subject to any liability for an unlawful employment practice
"if he pleads and proves that the act or omission complained of was in good
faith, in conformity with, and in reliance on any written interpretation or opinion
of the Commission. . . . "[32] To obtain this protection in affirmative action matters,
the Commission Guidelines provide that such protection will be accorded "only
if the self-analysis and affirmative action plan are dated and in writing. . . . "[33]
The Commission therefore recommends that analyses and plans be in writing.

CONCLUSION

This brief chapter is only intended to point out the role played by the EEOC in affirmative action in employment matters. Charges of employment discrimination filed with the agency which challenge an employer's affirmative action plans, and the defense thereof, will be analyzed by the EEOC pursuant to its Guidelines. Although the courts may decline to defer to the Guidelines and the requirements set forth therein,[34] it is clear that the EEOC regulations will govern in administrative investigations which can ultimately result in federal court suits brought by the EEOC on behalf of individuals claiming that an affirmative action plan violates Title VII.

NOTES

1. 42 U.S.C. § 2000e *et seq*.
2. 42 U.S.C. § 2000e-2(a)–(c).
3. *See* EEOC Affirmative Action Guidelines, 29 C.F.R. § 1608.1(a).
4. *See* 29 C.F.R. § 1608.1 *et seq*.
5. *Id.*, § 1608.2.
6. *Id.*, § 1608.1(e) (footnote omitted).
7. *Id.*
8. *Id.*
9. *Id.*, § 1608.3(a). Relative to this provision, one should note the Supreme Court's recent decision in Wards Cove Packing Co. v. Atonio, 109 S.Ct. 2115 (1989) (discussed in Chapter 2). *Atonio* altered the burden allocation scheme applicable to Title VII disparate impact claims. *See* Turner, *The Rehnquist Court and Title VII Disparate Impact Doctrine:* Atonio's *Burden Allocation and the Retreat from* Griggs, OHIO NORTHERN U. L. REV. (forthcoming in 1990). The *Atonio* Court did not reject the disparate impact principle or the application of that principle to employment practices. *See supra* Chapter 2.
10. 29 C.F.R. § 1608.3(b).
11. *Id.*, § 1608.3(c).
12. *Id.*, § 1608.4.
13. *Id.*, § 1608.4(b).
14. *Id.*
15. *Id.*
16. *Id.*, § 1608.4(b)
17. *Id.*
18. *Id.*, § 1608.4(c)(2)(1).
19. *Id.*, § 1608.4(c)(ii).
20. *Id.*, § 1608.4(d)(2).
21. *Id.*, § 1608.5(a).
22. *Id.*, § 1608.5(a)(1).
23. *Id.*, § 1608.5(1)(2).
24. 29 C.F.R. § 1608.8.
25. *Id.*
26. 109 S.Ct. 2180 (1989). *See supra* Chapter 2.
27. 109 S.Ct. at 2186.

28. *See supra* note 25 and accompanying text.

29. *See* EEOC Interpretive Memorandum: Martin v. Wilks, 109 S.Ct. 2180 (1989) (Oct. 17, 1989), *reprinted in* BNA Daily Lab. Rep. No. 220 at pp. D–3–D–4 (Nov. 16, 1989).

30. *Id*. at p. D–4.

31. 42 U.S.C. § 2000e–12.

32. *Id*.

33. 29 C.F.R. § 1608.4(d)(1).

34. The Supreme Court has consistently held that guidelines such as the EEOC's Guidelines on affirmative action are not controlling on the courts, but do "constitute a body of experience and informed judgment to which courts and litigants may properly resort for guidance. . . . '' General Electric Co. v. Gilbert, 429 U.S. 125, 141–142 (1976). *Accord* Meritor Savings Bank, FSB v. Vinson, 477 U.S. 57, 65 (1986); Griggs v. Duke Power Co., 401 U.S. 424, 433–434 (1971).

An additional development of significance is an October 6, 1987 memorandum from EEOC General Counsel Charles Shanor to EEOC regional attorneys concerning goal and timetable provisions in proposed Title VII consent decrees. That memorandum states, *inter alia*, that (1) employers may establish voluntary affirmative action plans without *prima facie* evidence of Title VII violations; (2) goals should be set at, rather than above, current labor market availability levels; (3) consent decrees should set forth a termination date for goals contained therein; and (4) employers have no obligation to select unqualified individuals.

5

Minority Business Set-Asides

In *Fullilove v. Klutznick*,[1] the United States Supreme Court affirmed the constitutionality of the minority business enterprise (MBE) provision of the Public Works Employment Act of 1977 (PWEA)[2] by a 6–3 vote. The PWEA, which authorized the distribution of 4 billion dollars in federal funds to state and local governments for public works projects, provided that 10 percent of those funds were to be expended for MBEs owned by United States citizens who were "Negroes, Spanish-speaking, Orientals, Indians, Eskimos, and Aleuts."[3] An unequivocal affirmation of Congressional power to address and remedy the legacy of racial discrimination, *Fullilove* was correctly viewed as a victory by the proponents of affirmative action[4] and served as an apparent authorization for the creation of MBE programs by state and local governments.[5] Initial application of *Fullilove* by lower federal courts resulted in decisions upholding the constitutionality of MBE programs.[6]

A significant development with implications for minority contracting occurred in 1986. In that year, the Supreme Court decided *Wygant v. Jackson Board of Education*.[7] A plurality of the Court applied strict scrutiny analysis to a collective bargaining agreement provision which essentially tied the layoff of minority teachers to the percentage of minority students in the school district. Invalidating that scheme, the plurality concluded that "societal discrimination, without more, is too amorphous a basis for imposing a racially classified remedy,"[8] and further concluded that the layoff protection provision could not be justified on the theory that minority students needed "role models" to remedy the effects of prior societal discrimination.[9] *Wygant* was applied by lower federal courts in decisions which held that state and local MBE programs were unconstitutional.[10] For example, the United States Courts of Appeals for the Ninth and Sixth Circuits[11] held that MBE programs in Louisville, Kentucky and the City and County of San Francisco, California, respectively, violated the equal protection clause of the Fourteenth Amendment of the United States Constitution.[12]

And, in *J. A. Croson Company v. City of Richmond*,[13] the United States Court of Appeals for the Fourth Circuit held that the City of Richmond, Virginia's MBE plan, which required contractors on city construction projects to subcontract at least 30 percent of the dollar value of the contract to MBEs absent waiver, was unconstitutional. Affirming the Fourth Circuit's decision, the Supreme Court in 1989 held that the city's plan was not justified by a compelling governmental interest, was not narrowly tailored to accomplish a remedial purpose, and was therefore violative of the Fourteenth Amendment.[14]

Apart from its obvious impact on MBE set-aside programs, the *Croson* Court's decision addressed the following matters of import: the unique remedial powers of Congress under § 5 of the Fourteenth Amendment;[15] the level of scrutiny applicable to race-conscious classifications in affirmative action cases; the factual predicate necessary to support race-conscious MBE plans; the requisite narrow tailoring of such plans; and the Court's view with respect to the devices and procedures available to state and local governments which would fall on the constitutional side of the equal protection line.

This chapter examines *Fullilove* and the Court's validation of the PWEA set-aside program; focuses on the treatment of MBE set-asides by the federal courts of appeals, both before and after the Supreme Court's 1986 decision in *Wygant*, and details the cognizable trend developed after *Wygant* in which MBE set-asides did not survive equal protection challenges; and then turns to *Croson* and examines the issues discussed by the Court, and assesses the implications and potential impact of that ruling on numerous MBE ordinances and programs operated by state and local governments.

FULLILOVE

Fullilove v. Klutznick[16] involved a facial constitutional challenge to the PWEA's requirement[17] that, absent administrative waiver, 10 percent of federal funds granted for local public works were to be used by state or local grantees to procure services or supplies from MBEs.[18] That challenge was presented in a suit brought by associations of construction contractors and subcontractors who alleged that they had suffered economic injury due to the enforcement of the 10 percent MBE requirement, and that the MBE provision violated the Equal Protection Clause of the Fourteenth Amendment, the equal protection component of the Due Process Clause of the Fifth Amendment,[19] and various anti-discrimination statutes. The Court upheld the constitutionality of the MBE provision by a 6–3 vote.

The Burger Opinion

Chief Justice Burger, joined by Justices White and Powell, stated that programs employing racial or ethnic criteria call for "close" examination; "yet we are also bound to approach our task with appropriate deference to the Congress, a coequal branch. . . ."[20] Burger then posed a two-part analysis applicable to the case: (1) whether the objectives of the PWEA were within the power of Congress, and (2) if so, whether the limited use of racial and ethnic criteria was a constitutionally permissible means for achieving the Congressional objectives.

With respect to the first issue, Chief Justice Burger concluded that the PWEA was primarily an exercise of the Constitutional Spending Power.[21] "The reach of the Spending Power, within its sphere, is at least as broad as the regulatory powers of Congress."[22] Thus, if Congress could achieve the objectives of the MBE set-aside through its regulatory powers, stated the Chief Justice, it could do so under the spending power.

Chief Justice Burger found further support for the set-aside in the Constitutional Commerce Power.[23] He opined that Congress could have drawn on that clause to regulate the practices of contractors on federally funded public works projects. In his view, the legislative history of the MBE provision[24] showed that there was a rational basis for Congress to conclude that impaired minority business access to public contracts, perpetuated by contractor practices, had affected interstate commerce.

Chief Justice Burger also reasoned that § 5 of the Fourteenth Amendment authorized the MBE program. He concluded that Congress had sufficient evidence from which it could conclude that minority businesses had been denied effective participation in public contracting opportunities by practices which perpetuated the effects of prior discrimination.[25] "Congress, of course, may legislate without compiling the kind of 'record' appropriate with respect to judicial or administrative proceedings."[26] The Chief Justice was satisfied that Congress had an "abundant historical basis from which it could conclude that traditional procurement practices, when applied to minority businesses, could perpetuate the effects of prior discrimination."[27]

Chief Justice Burger made several additional, noteworthy points. First, he rejected the contention that Congress must act in a color-blind fashion in exercising its remedial powers.

It is fundamental that in no organ of government, state or federal, does there repose a more comprehensive remedial power than in the Congress, expressly charged by the Constitution with competence and authority to enforce equal protection guarantees. Congress not only may induce voluntary action to assure compliance with existing federal statutory or constitutional anti-discrimination provisions, but also, where Congress has authority to declare certain conduct unlawful, it may, as here, authorize and induce state action to avoid such conduct.[28]

Second, Chief Justice Burger concluded that the MBE provision was not constitutionally defective because some nonminority businesses would be deprived of access to government contracting opportunities. In his view, the "burden" on nonminorities was relatively light when the scope of the public works program was compared to overall construction contracting opportunities. Moreover, stated Burger, Congress could act on the "assumption" that some nonminority businesses had benefitted from the past exclusion of minority firms, even though the particular nonminorities challenging the MBE provision were innocent of any discriminatory conduct.[29] Third, and finally, Burger found it significant that the PWEA MBE administrative scheme provided for waiver and exemption. In that regard, he noted that the PWEA's implementing regulations and guidelines provided for the elimination of "front" enterprises (MBEs who were not bona fide entities for PWEA purposes); that waivers were available which could be used to avoid unreasonable prices charged by MBEs; and that nonminority grantees could demonstrate that, despite their best efforts, the 10 percent target could not be achieved and that a waiver was required.[30]

The Powell Opinion

In an important concurring opinion, Justice Powell called for a three-part inquiry: (1) whether Congress was competent to make findings of unlawful discrimination; (2) if so, whether sufficient findings had been made to establish that minority business enterprises had been adversely affected by unlawful discrimination; and (3) whether the 10 percent set-aside was a permissible means for redressing identifiable past discrimination. Finding it beyond question that Congress was authorized to identify, prohibit and remedy illegal discriminatory practices,[31] Justice Powell determined that Congress was not required to make specific factual findings with respect to every legislative action. "Such a requirement would mark an unprecedented imposition of adjudicatory procedures upon a coordinate branch of Government."[32] After reviewing the legislative history and materials discussed by Chief Justice Burger, Powell concluded that a court "must accept" the conclusion that purposeful discrimination was a significant contribution to the small percentage of federal contracting funds received by minorities.[33]

Concluding that strict scrutiny (under which government may employ a racial classification only when necessary to accomplish a compelling governmental purpose)[34] was the applicable standard, Powell called for review of four factors when considering the proper scope of race-conscious remedies: (1) the efficacy of alternative remedies; (2) the planned duration of the remedy; (3) the relationship between the percentage of minorities to be employed and the percentage of minorities in the relevant population or work force; and (4) the availability of waiver provisions if the plan requirements could not be met.[35] With respect to the first factor, Powell concluded that Congress knew in 1977 that other remedies had failed to ameliorate the effects of racial discrimination in the construction industry. As support for that conclusion, Powell noted that minority contractors were receiving less than 1 percent of all federal contracts.[36] With regard to the second factor, he concluded that the MBE provision was not permanent, but would terminate as soon as the PWEA ended. "The temporary nature of this remedy ensures that a race-conscious program will not last longer than the discriminatory effects it is designed to eliminate."[37] Applying the third factor, Powell noted that 4 percent of contractors were members of minority groups while approximately 17 percent of the national population were minority group members. "The chance of a 10% set-aside thus falls roughly halfway between the present percentage of minority contractors and the percentage of minority group members in the Nation."[38] As to the final factor (waiver), Justice Powell concluded that the MBE provision may have been unfair if it were applied rigidly in those areas of the country where minorities constituted a small percentage of the population. The waiver provision met this concern, stated Powell, since waivers could be issued based on the availability of qualified minority contractors in a geographic area, the size of an area's minority population, and efforts made to find minority contractors.

An additional factor—the effect of the set-aside on "innocent" third parties—was also discussed by Justice Powell. He did not believe that their burden was so great that the set-aside should not be approved. Citing the Second Circuit's *Fullilove* opinion, Powell noted that the set-aside would not affect 96 percent of the contractors competing for over 99 percent of construction funds.[39] Thus, in Powell's view, the effect of the PWEA set-aside was limited and widely dispersed, and its use was consistent with fundamental fairness.

The Marshall Concurrence

Justice Marshall, joined by Justices Brennan and Blackmun, concurred in the Court's judgment. Relying on his opinion in *Regents of University of California v. Bakke*,[40] Marshall expressed his view that neither the strict scrutiny nor rational basis standards of review should be applied to racial classifications that provided benefits to minorities for the purpose of remedying the present effects of past racial discrimination.[41] He opined that racial classifications used for such purposes could be justified by showing an important and articulated purpose for its use. The "proper inquiry is whether racial classifications designed to further remedial purposes serve important governmental objectives and are substantially related to achievement of those objectives."[42] Under that standard, Justice Marshall reasoned that Congress had a "sound basis" for concluding that MBEs had received a disproportionately small amount of public contracting business because of the continuing effects of past discrimination. In his view, remedying those effects was a sufficiently important governmental interest justifying the use of racial classifications.

Marshall concluded, further, that the means chosen by Congress were substantially related to the achievement of the PWEA's remedial purpose. He stated that the set-aside, which created a "quota in favor of qualified and available" MBEs,[43] was carefully tailored to remedy racial discrimination while avoiding stigmatization of minority and nonminority firms. Accordingly, Justice Marshall concluded that the MBE provisions passed muster under the Equal Protection Clause.[44]

Thus, a solid majority of the Court concluded in *Fullilove* that Congressional enactment of the MBE provision was a constitutional exercise of the legislative power. Although the Court's decision is defensible and analytically sound, the use of MBE set-asides and the policy formulations underlying the enactment of such statutes continued to be points of concern and debate.

WYGANT AND MBE SET-ASIDES

Pre-*Wygant* Rulings

Initial application of *Fullilove* by federal courts of appeals reviewing state and local MBE plans prior to 1986 typically resulted in findings of constitutional set-aside provisions. For example, in *Ohio Contractors Association v. Keip*,[45] the court held that an Ohio MBE program did not violate the Equal Protection Clause of the Fourteenth Amendment.[46] Reversing the district court, the Sixth Circuit concluded that the Ohio legislature, aware of certain facts which supported the enactment of its set-aside program, enacted a constitutional remedial measure which was similar to the federal plan in *Fullilove*.[47] Addressing the issue of the state's competency to use race-conscious remedies to eliminate the effects of past discrimination, the court determined that § 1 of the Fourteenth Amendment applied.[48] "[W]hen a state legislature takes steps in compliance with the Equal Protection Clause it is acting in the same capacity as that of Congress in adopting legislation to implement the equal protection component of the Fifth Amendment's due process clause."[49]

Additionally, the Sixth Circuit held that the Ohio MBE plan did not cast an undue burden on nonminority contractors. "This 'burden' on nonminority contractors—the amount they were excluded from bidding on—was less than 1 percent of the total."[50] The Sixth Circuit opined that it was "clear that members of the majority can be required to bear some of the burden which inevitably results from affirmative efforts to rectify past discrimination."[51] Even if nonminority contractors were innocent parties, "they are part of a group which did reap competitive benefit from past discriminatory practices of the state that have virtually excluded minority contractors from state business."[52] Thus, stated the court, the state had chosen to remedy the effects of its own past discriminatory practices by means of a program which imposed a relatively light burden on the majority group.[53]

Nor was the Ohio plan overinclusive. In that regard, the court noted that the Ohio legislature's inclusion of Hispanics, Orientals, American Indians and Blacks were the same as the groups identified by Congress in the PWEA. "The fact that individual minority enterprises may not be able to establish that they have suffered economically from the past practices of discrimination is of no importance."[54] The state legislature had considered abundant evidence that the designated minority groups suffered from racial discrimination in the state's contracting and procurement policies.

As to the question of less restrictive means of achieving the state's remedial goals, the Sixth Circuit, citing *Fullilove*, concluded that there was no requirement that the least restrictive means must have been chosen, and further concluded that Ohio could lawfully follow the example set by Congress in the PWEA. As to the flexibility of the program, the court noted that the set-aside requirements were approximate; that there was a provision for waiver or modification where the requirements of a particular contract could not be met in good faith; and that nonminority contractors could continue to participate in set-aside contracts by having a 49 percent ownership or control of an MBE establishment, or by taking up to 50 percent participation in a joint venture with an MBE. In addition, the court determined that the absence of a durational limit in the Ohio MBE statute was not fatal. "It is incredible that this popularly elected branch of government would permit the set-asides for minority contractors to continue beyond the time required to achieve the goal of an equal opportunity for minorities to share in the business of the state."[55] Finding that no given end date is required, the court reasoned that it was sufficient that the state recognized the need for reassessment and reevaluation of the program.[56]

An MBE program was also upheld in *South Florida Chapter of the Associated General Contractors of America, Inc. v. Metropolitan Dade County Florida*.[57] Affirming in part the district court's decision,[58] the Eleventh Circuit relied on Chief Justice Burger's *Fullilove* opinion and "the common concerns" of *Fullilove*: (1) that the governmental body have the authority to pass the legislation; (2) that adequate findings have been made to ensure remedial action by the government; and (3) that the use of racial or ethnic classifications extend no further than the need to remedy the effects of past discrimination. First, the court concluded that "state legislative bodies are not without authority to ensure equal protection to persons within their jurisdictions."[59] Although recognizing that the scope of Congressional power to remedy past discrimination may be greater than that of the states, the court reasoned that the references in *Fullilove* to Congress' power were not intended to imply that governmental entities other than Congress could not act to remedy past discrimination.[60] Applying state law, the court concluded that Dade County was competent to make findings of, and remedy, past discrimination under its home rule charter.[61]

Second, the court determined that the county made sufficient legislative findings of past discrimination based on "reliable, substantial information compiled by independent investigations."[62] Although the district court found that the county government had not engaged in discriminatory practices, the Eleventh Circuit opined that there had been identified discrimination against African-American contractors prior to the advent of the set-aside program. Third, the

Eleventh Circuit held that the set-aside program was narrowly tailored to the legitimate objective of redressing racial discrimination. Finding that adequate safeguards existed (administrative review, established criteria, periodic review of the entire program), the court declined to hold the ordinance facially unconstitutional.[63]

Turning to the question of the constitutional application of the ordinance, the court concluded that the set-aside and subcontractor goal were properly adopted pursuant to the ordinance and applicable regulations. As to the set-aside's relationship to the percentage of African-American contractors and its impact on third parties, the court reasoned, *inter alia*, that the estimated cost of the contract at issue ($6 million) was less than 1 percent of the county's annual expenditures on contracts. Noting that African Americans constituted over 17 percent of Dade County's population, the court stated that the "effect of the set-aside and the subcontractor goal is not disproportionate to either the number of blacks and black contractors residing in the county or the goal of increasing black business participation in order to redress past discrimination."[64] Because of the small percentage of contracts offered, the court also found that the set-aside did not unfairly impact on third parties.

Nor was the court persuaded that the set-aside was unconstitutional because of alternative remedies or the absence of a waiver provision. In its view, the county was not required to choose the least restrictive remedy, and the set-aside was chosen only after a formal finding that the set-aside was necessary to redress the effects of past discrimination.[65] And the county's determination that the set-aside was in its best interests, and that a sufficient number of African-American contractors were available, provided the same safeguard as a formal waiver provision which would protect against unfair effects of a rigid application of the set-aside.[66]

Wygant

The analysis applied to MBE plans changed, however, after the Supreme Court's 1986 decision in *Wygant v. Jackson Board of Education*.[67] There, the Court addressed the issue of the constitutionality of a school board's policy of extending preferential protection against layoffs to employees because of their race. *Wygant* involved a provision of a collective bargaining agreement between a school board and teachers' union which provided that the percentage of minority personnel affected by a reduction in force could not exceed the percentage of minorities employed at the time of the layoff.[68] Under this provision, nonminority teachers were laid off while less senior minority teachers were retained.

The Supreme Court held that this provision violated the Fourteenth Amendment. The plurality opinion[69] applied strict scrutiny analysis to the case even though the layoff provision operated against nonminorities. The plurality initially concluded that the contractual provision was not supported by a compelling state purpose. The school board had argued that its interest in alleviating the effects of societal discrimination and providing minority role models for minority students justified the racial classification. Rejecting the societal discrimination theory, the plurality stated that the Court

never has held that societal discrimination alone is sufficient to justify a racial classification. Rather, the Court has insisted upon some showing of prior discrimination by the governmental unit involved before allowing limited use of racial classifications in order to remedy such discrimination.[70]

The plurality also reasoned that the role model theory had no logical stopping point and would allow the school board to engage in discriminatory hiring and layoff practices long past the point required by any legitimate remedial purpose.[71] Tying the percentage of minority teachers to the percentage of minority students "could be used to escape the obligation to remedy such practices by justifying the small percentage of black teachers by reference to the small percentage of black students."[72] Thus, stated the plurality, societal discrimination is "too amorphous a basis for imposing a racially classified remedy."[73] "In the absence of particularized findings, a court could uphold remedies that are ageless in their reach into the past, and timeless in their ability to affect the future."[74]

The *Wygant* plurality opined that the school board would have been able to show a "strong basis in evidence" for affirmative action by demonstrating a significant disparity between the percentage of minority school teachers hired by the board and the percentage of such teachers available in the labor pool. No such proof or demonstration had been made in the record before the Court. With respect to the means chosen to accomplish the school board's purposes, the plurality noted that, under strict scrutiny, the means chosen must be specifically and narrowly framed to accomplish those purposes.[75] The use of layoffs as a means of achieving the school board's asserted purposes was unconstitutionally intrusive, in the plurality's view. "[L]ayoffs impose the entire burden of achieving racial equality on particular individuals, often resulting in serious disruption of their lives. That burden is too intrusive."[76] Therefore, concluded the plurality, the use of the layoff scheme was not sufficiently narrowly tailored to satisfy the demands of the equal protection clause, a result also reached by Justices O'Connor and White in their concurrences.[77]

Wygant thus required that an affirmative action plan had to be justified by a compelling governmental interest, and that the means chosen to effectuate a plan's purpose had to be narrowly tailored. As recognized in recent lower court decisions, a lowest common denominator view can be fashioned from *Wygant* by combining the plurality's ruling with the concurrences of Justices White and O'Connor.[78] Under this view, *Wygant* stands for the proposition that

a statistical comparison upon which an affirmative action plan is based must compare the percentage of minorities in the employer's work force with the percentage of minorities in the relevant qualified area labor pool before it can establish the predicate past discrimination required to justify an affirmative action remedy under the fourteenth amendment.[79]

Post-*Wygant* MBE Decisions

The *Wygant* plurality's rejection of the notions of societal discrimination and its application of strict scrutiny to a policy which adversely affected nonminorities impacted on subsequent cases in the MBE set-aside area. Because set-aside programs typically involve governmental declarations of past discrimination which require remedial measures, *Wygant*'s rejection of an "amorphous" societal discrimination standard as a sufficient predicate for governmental remedial action had obvious implications for set-aside programs. Underlying the plurality's decision was the view that remedial action which is not linked to specific evidence of past discrimination, which does not make proper labor pool comparisons, and which disrupts the concrete expectations of particular individuals for the purpose of remedial assistance to African Americans and other minorities is too intrusive and violates the Fourteenth Amendment.

Lower court MBE set-aside cases decided after *Wygant* illustrate the impact of that decision on set-aside litigation. For example, in *J. Edinger and Son, Inc. v. City of Louisville, Kentucky*,[80] the court held that a city's minority vendors' ordinance was unconstitutional.[81] The sole basis for the ordinance was general population statistics which showed that 54 percent of Jefferson County, Kentucky was female and 28 percent African American or minority. Less than 1 percent of the dollar volume of the city's 1982 business was awarded to minority, female and handicapped-owned businesses, respectively.[82] A constitutional challenge to the ordinance was brought by corporations owned by white, nonhandicapped males. Affirming the district court's summary judgment in favor of the nonminority companies,[83] the Sixth Circuit agreed with the district court that analysis of general population figures was not appropriate. "Thus, a more appropriate analysis would have focused on the number of minority-owned contractors in the county rather than the number of minorities *per se*."[84] In that regard, the court distinguished the case from its decision in *Keip*,[85] noting that in that case the Ohio legislature had compared relevant groups—the percentage of funds awarded to MBEs and the percentage of total MBEs in the marketplace.

Fullilove was also distinguished by the court in two respects. First, stated the court, Congress analyzed statistics focusing on MBEs and did not rely on general population statistics. Second, "the extensive hearings by Congress produced other evidence corroborating the finding of intentional discrimination."[86] In contrast, stated the Sixth Circuit, the City of Louisville "simply rehashed the statistical disparity between the population distribution and the business operation distribution. No other evidence of discrimination was presented."[87]

Applying *Wygant*, the *J. Edinger* court pointed out what it considered to be several deficiencies in the city's program.

• The city's reliance on general population statistics was troubling given that bid systems are inherently nondiscriminatory.

- The city did not show that minority businesses which submitted the low bids on contracts had been denied contracts in the past.
- The city did not show that minority applicants had been excluded from bid pools.
- The city did not show that qualified minority-owned businesses existed.[88]

Moreover, rejecting the city's argument that discrimination hampered the development of MBEs on the basis of *Wygant*'s rejection of the general societal discrimination theory, the court concluded that "[t]here is no showing that actual discrimination has stunted the development of minority businesses. There is a host of social, economic, personal, and demographic factors which may account for the statistical disparity."[89] Thus, the court held that the evidence was insufficient to justify the ordinance.[90]

In a subsequent decision, *Michigan Road Builders Association, Inc. v. Milliken*,[91] the Sixth Circuit invalidated Michigan's MBE program.[92] Although the state admitted that it had engaged in impermissible discrimination in awarding contracts, the court found this admission to be of little relevance.[93] Rather, the court examined the evidence the state assertedly relied on, and concluded that the documentation did not reflect state discrimination. Proposed legislation in 1971 and subsequent years in the Michigan legislature did not expressly address the need for growth of MBEs, or attribute their competitive difficulties to discrimination.[94] Evidence regarding executive action to increase MBE participation was also reviewed by the court. A task force created by the governor conducted hearings wherein witnesses testified that MBE size and lack of expertise prohibited their effective competition.[95] The state further relied on a commissioned study which reported that most state agencies relied on established contracts, and did not actively seek new supply sources when filling new orders; that only three state agencies used MBE directories to seek out minority suppliers; and that some purchasing officials had unfavorable impressions of the quality and reliability of the performance of small and minority businesses.

The court found it significant that the study did not conclude that state purchasing policies were discriminatory. Thus, the court opined that, at best, the evidence suggested that the obstacle to MBE development in Michigan was societal discrimination, which did not prove that Michigan invidiously discriminated against racial and ethnic minorities in awarding contracts. "A finding of prior, purposeful discrimination against members of each of these [favored] minority groups is required. . . . "[96] Accordingly, the court held that the MBE provisions of the statute were unconstitutional.

Associated General Contractors of California, Inc. v. City and County of San Francisco[97] further illustrates the impact of *Wygant*. Deciding a challenge to the city and county of San Francisco's MBE, WBE, and locally owned business enterprise (LBE) ordinance,[98] the United States Court of Appeals for the Ninth Circuit held, *inter alia*, that the provisions of the ordinance granting preference to MBEs were void as violative of the Equal Protection Clause.[99]

In reviewing the MBE program, the court initially determined that the proper

level of review was one of strict scrutiny and applied a three-part test which
examined governmental authority, findings, and methods. As to the governmental
authority factor, the court concluded that a state or its political subdivision has
the authority to "ascertain whether it is denying its citizens equal protection of
the laws and, if so, to take corrective steps."[100] Turning to the factor of the
findings relative to the MBE program, the court reasoned that a city is not like
the federal government with regard to the necessary findings that must be made;
"as the Founding Fathers recognized, the narrower a government's domain, the
greater the likelihood of oppression. . . ."[101] While not deciding the precise
contours of state or local government power to pass preferential laws such as
MBE plans, the court stated that "[a]t a minimum, the state or local government
must be acting to remedy government-imposed discrimination, perpetrated by it
or by one of its departments or divisions."[102] Citing *Wygant*, the court thus
concluded that state or local governments do not have the power to discriminate
on the basis of race to dispel the lingering effects of societal discrimination.[103]

Interestingly, the city of San Francisco had made extensive findings in support
of the MBE ordinance. Its efforts in that regard included hearings, the submission
of written statements and analysis, and a summary of the information in a report
to the city's board of supervisors, which then conducted its own hearings and
received further written reports. The ordinance was passed after these efforts,
and the court opined that the city's procedures were careful, deliberate, and
deserved the greatest deference. But, stated the court, the city did not intimate
that minorities had been discriminated against by city officials or under the color
of the city's authority. Absent such a finding, the court found no compelling
justification for the government's assistance to minorities through the MBE
program.[104] Moreover, stated the court, the relevant statistics were not sufficient
to justify the city's program. The city had found that MBEs and WBEs received
less than 3 percent of prime contracts awarded during the base period of 1981
and 1982, even though MBEs represented over 33 percent of San Francisco-
based firms.[105]

Concluding that these numbers were flawed, the court determined that the
statistics undercounted MBE participation because the amount of subcontracts
awarded to MBEs was excluded from the city's findings. "[S]uch businesses
may be earning a substantial portion of the city's contracting dollars by way of
subcontracts."[106] In addition, the court stated that the 33 percent MBE figure
was over-inclusive because it encompassed businesses which did not provide
goods or services subject to city contracting (e.g., restaurants, beauty parlors,
and so on). "Contract awards should reflect the pool of available contractors,
not the city's ethnic makeup."[107] Further, the court noted that the city contracted
with firms and individuals based outside San Francisco, while the city's findings
pertained to firms within San Francisco. To support the use of racial classifications, stated the court, such findings must be drawn more precisely and based
on finely tuned data. In that regard, the Ninth Circuit found that the city had no
evidence which supported the inclusion of American Indians, Asians, Blacks,

Filipinos and Hispanics in the MBE program. Again relying on the *Wygant* plurality's analysis, the court expressed its inability to uphold such a broad classification for purposes of the affirmative action program.

With respect to the third factor (the means adopted to accomplish race-conscious remedies), the Ninth Circuit called for narrow tailoring, that is, "the classification adopted must 'fit' with greater precision than any alternative means,"[108] and the program must not impose a disproportionate burden. Reading *Fullilove* and *Wygant* as requiring concrete assurances that administrative procedures be made available to correct harsh effects upon contractors, the court stated that the administrative procedures of the city's ordinance provided no mechanism in which contractors could assert that the ordinance was not applicable to their industry, that the impact of the ordinance was excessive, or that the ordinance gave a windfall to MBEs.[109]

Accordingly, the court held that the city could have adopted remedies other than the MBE set-aside with less dramatic effects on individual rights, including the adoption of procurement guidelines, limitations on the scope of departmental discretion, revision of insurance and bonding policies, an increase in resources devoted to advertising opportunities to groups believed to be underrepresented in the procurement process, and educational programs to acquaint minorities with contracting opportunities and bid procedures. In the absence of a finding of unlawful discrimination by the governmental entity adopting the MBE program, the Ninth Circuit found no compelling justification for "inflicting such harm" on nonminorities.[110] Thus, like *J. Edinger*, the Ninth Circuit's ruling relied on *Wygant* as support for the court's analysis of the sufficiency of findings of discrimination, the pool of available contractors, and the legality of the means employed to remedy unlawful discrimination. The Supreme Court subsequently employed similar reasoning in *Croson*.

One notable exception to the aforementioned application of *Wygant* is *H. K. Porter Company, Inc. v. Metropolitan Dade County*.[111] In that case, the United States Court of Appeals for the Eleventh Circuit held that an MBE set-aside program[112] was constitutional under the Equal Protection Clause of the Fourteenth Amendment. Analyzing Porter's claim under the statutes applicable to the Urban Mass Transit Administration (UMTA),[113] the court examined the legislative history of those statutes and concluded that the rule was not facially unconstitutional. "Congress was addressing the need to ensure that minority business firms would be provided with a fair opportunity to participate in federally funded government contracts."[114] Thus, the court concluded that the UMTA had the authority to promulgate the MBE program.

Rejecting Porter's contention that the MBE program was unconstitutional as applied, the court ruled that the county's plan met the test set forth in *Wygant* and the Supreme Court's decision in *U.S. v. Paradise*.[115] First, stated the Eleventh Circuit, the county acted pursuant to Congress' compelling interest in "eradicating the continuing effects of past discrimination against minorities in the participation of government contracts."[116] The court found no record of evidence that the plan was anything more than temporary, and concluded that the procedure was not a policy to maintain a racial or ethnic balance. The availability of waiver contained in the bidding procedure was also noted.

Determining that the 5 percent MBE goal was sufficiently narrowly tailored to achieve the stated goal of increased minority participation in government contracting, the court opined that the county could rely on Congressional legislative findings that minorities were not participating in government contracts. "We hold that under the circumstances of this case, [the county] was not constitutionally required to make additional findings of past discrimination regarding the awarding of this contract. . . . Its findings provide adequate support for such local projects."[117] Finally, the court concluded that the MBE plan did not unnecessarily trammel the interests of nonminority contractors or subcontractors, and did not impose an unacceptable burden on innocent third parties.

In sum, the lower courts' application of *Wygant* generally resulted in an analysis of MBE programs similar to that subsequently applied by the Supreme Court in *Croson*. Actual historical, and not societal, discrimination became the focal point. General population statistics were no longer sufficient to justify and legitimate a program, as the courts began to call for a more refined and particularized comparison of qualified MBEs in a defined geographical area, or those able to perform the work being contracted. Other courts indicated that the government had to find or show that the government itself engaged in discrimination (as in *San Francisco* and *Michigan Road Builders*). And the courts addressed the question of whether MBE programs were narrowly tailored and not structured in a way that gave "windfalls" to minority businesses. These issues and factors were addressed by the Supreme Court in 1989.

CROSON

The City of Richmond, Virginia's Plan

In 1983, the City of Richmond, Virginia adopted a minority business utilization plan which required prime nonminority construction contractors to subcontract at least 30 percent of a contract's dollar amount to one or more MBEs.[118] Qualified MBEs from all areas of the United States could receive consideration under the set-aside plan.

The Richmond plan was adopted after a public hearing before the Richmond City Council. A study placed before the council indicated that the general population of Richmond was 50 percent minority, and that .67 percent of the city's prime construction contracts had been awarded to minority businesses between 1978 and 1983.[119] In addition, many contractor associations had virtually no minority businesses among their members. The city's legal counsel opined that the ordinance was constitutional under *Fullilove*, and a councilperson stated that the "general conduct of the construction industry in this area, and the State, and around the nation, is one in which race discrimination and exclusion on the basis of race is widespread."[120] No direct evidence of discrimination by the city or nonminority contractors was adduced.

Under the Richmond plan, waiver rules were promulgated which provided that no partial or complete waiver of the set-aside requirement could be granted other than in exceptional circumstances. Waivers were justified where it was shown that "every feasible attempt has been made to comply" and it was demonstrated that "sufficient, relevant, qualified Minority Business Enterprises . . . are unavailable or unwilling to participate in the contract to enable meeting the 30 percent goal."[121] The Richmond plan expired on June 30, 1988.[122]

Croson's Bid and the City's Rejection Thereof

In 1983, J. A. Croson Company bid on a Richmond, Virginia project for the provision and installation of specified plumbing fixtures at the city jail. The company initially contacted five or six MBEs regarding the supply of fixtures; no MBE indicated interest in the project. On the day that bids were due, the company contacted Continental Metal Hose, a local MBE which expressed interest in participating in the project. Continental then contacted one supplier of fixtures who refused to quote a price for the items. Another supplier informed Continental that the supplier would require a credit check which would take thirty days to complete. When the sealed bids were opened, it was revealed that Croson was the only bidder, with a bid of $126,530. The company requested a waiver of the set-aside on the grounds that Continental was unqualified and that other MBEs had not responded or were unable to provide quotes. Continental subsequently submitted a bid to Croson which was $6,183.29 higher than the price for fixtures which Croson had indicated in its bid submitted to the city, and was 7 percent over the market price. Informed of Continental's bid, the city denied Croson's waiver request.[123]

Croson then notified the city that Continental's quote was substantially higher than any other quote Croson received, and that Continental's bid was submitted twenty-one days after prime bids were due. The company requested permission to raise the contract price because of the additional costs entailed in using Continental.[124] The city denied both the waiver request and the request to raise the contract price, and notified Croson that the project would be rebid. Challenging the city's actions, Croson brought suit alleging that the set-aside ordinance was unconstitutional both facially and as applied. The district court upheld the plan *in toto*.

The Fourth Circuit's Decision

In 1985, a divided panel of the United States Court of Appeals for the Fourth Circuit affirmed the district court's decision.[125] The Supreme Court granted a writ of *certiorari* from the Fourth Circuit, vacated the 1985 decision, and remanded the case for further consideration in light of *Wygant*.[126]

On remand, a divided panel held that the Richmond plan was invalid under the Equal Protection Clause of the Fourteenth Amendment.[127] Acknowledging that the boundaries of *Wygant* would be a matter of dispute, the Fourth Circuit reasoned that the core of *Wygant*'s holding was undisputed: "To show that a plan is justified by a compelling governmental interest, a municipality that wishes to employ a racial preference cannot rest on broad-brush assumptions of historical discrimination."[128] Reversing its 1985 decision, the Fourth Circuit concluded that the Richmond city council had failed to establish the basis for its remedial action, as the council's debate on the ordinance revealed no record of prior discrimination *by the city*. As to the statistics with respect to the minority population of Richmond and the percentage of contracts awarded to MBEs, the court concluded that the use of general population statistics suggested more of a political than a remedial basis for the racial preference.[129] The appropriate comparison, ruled the court, was between the number of minority contracts and the number of minority contractors.[130] Because the MBE plan "was not supported by any impartial report, any meaningful statistical evidence, or even by anecdotal allegations of prior discrimination,"[131] the court ruled that the plan could not be upheld as a remedial measure under *Wygant*.

In addition, the Fourth Circuit held that the plan was not narrowly tailored. "The thirty percent quota was chosen arbitrarily; it was not tied, for example, to a showing that thirty percent of Richmond subcontractors are minority-owned."[132] The court opined that a record of prior discrimination against African Americans would not justify a remedial plan that favors the other minorities included in the Richmond plan's definition of MBE.[133] Finally, the court determined that the plan's waiver provisions, or *any* waiver, would not cure the constitutional defects of the plan.[134]

The Supreme Court's Decision

By a 6–3 vote, the Supreme Court affirmed the Fourth Circuit's decision. Justice O'Connor authored the opinion of the Court with respect to certain parts of her opinion;[135] a plurality opinion joined by Chief Justice Rehnquist and Justice White with respect to another part;[136] and an opinion with respect to other parts which was joined by Rehnquist, White, and Justice Kennedy.[137] Justices Kennedy, Scalia, and Stevens filed separate concurring opinions. Two dissenting opinions, by Justices Marshall and Blackmun, were also filed. Because the Court addressed significant issues and commented on aspects of the case which shed light on future affirmative action jurisprudence, a detailed examination of the various opinions and analyses of the justices is necessary.

The City's Power to Adopt MBE Legislation. Croson argued that, under *Wygant*, Richmond was limited to eradication of the effects of the city's prior discrimination. The city argued that, under *Fullilove*, the city could legislatively define and remedy the effects of prior discrimination in the local construction industry, without making specific findings of past discrimination.

Justice O'Connor, joined by Chief Justice Rehnquist and Justice White, did not adopt either analysis. In her view, Congress, unlike states or political subdivisions, has a "specific constitutional mandate" under § 5 of the Fourteenth Amendment to enforce that amendment, including the power to define and adopt prophylactic rules. She stated that Congressional power to identify and redress societal discrimination does not mean, *a fortiori*, that states and political subdivisions are free to decide that such remedies are appropriate. State power is constrained by § 1 of the Fourteenth Amendment,[138] stated Justice O'Connor, and state remedial actions must comply with that provision. "The mere recitation of a benign or compensatory purpose for the use of a racial classification would essentially entitle the States to exercise the full power of Congress under § 5 of the Fourteenth Amendment and insulate any racial classification from judicial scrutiny under § 1."[139] That result, she concluded, would be contrary to the intentions of the framers of the Fourteenth Amendment.

Notwithstanding the constraints of § 1, O'Connor determined that a state or local subdivision may exercise authority to remedy the effects of past discrimination within its legislative jurisdiction within certain constraints. She opined that the City of Richmond could use its spending powers to remedy private discrimination, if such discrimination was identified with the particularity required by the Fourteenth Amendment. "Thus, if the city could show that it had essentially become a 'passive participant' in a system of racial exclusion practiced by elements of the local construction industry, we think it clear that the city could take affirmative steps to dismantle such a system."[140]

The Level of Judicial Scrutiny. For the first time, a majority of the Court agreed that the strict scrutiny standard of review should be applied to affirmative action initiatives. As stated in Justice O'Connor's opinion: "We thus reaffirm the view expressed by the plurality in *Wygant* that the standard of review under the Equal Protection Clause is not dependent on the race of those burdened or benefited by a particular classification."[141] Absent such an inquiry, stated O'Connor, there was no way to determine whether a classification was benign, remedial, or motivated by illegitimate notions of racial inferiority or racial politics, notions which troubled O'Connor. She noted that African Americans comprised approximately 50 percent of the population of Richmond, and that five of nine seats on the Richmond city council were held by African Americans. "The concern that a political majority will more easily act to the disadvantage of a minority based on unwarranted assumptions or incomplete facts would seem to militate for, not against, the application of heightened judicial scrutiny in this case."[142]

The Court's Finding of Defects in the City's Factual Predicate Supporting the MBE Plan. In *Wygant*, a plurality of the Court rejected the "role model" and "societal discrimination" theories as adequate bases for race-conscious classifications.[143] Applying *Wygant* in *Croson*, Justice O'Connor concluded that a general assertion of past discrimination in an industry does not provide guidance for a legislature to determine the precise scope of the injury to be remedied by the MBE plan. " 'Relief' for such an ill-defined wrong could extend until the percentage of public contracts awarded to MBEs in Richmond mirrored the percentage of minorities in the population as a whole."[144]

While acknowledging that discrimination has contributed to a lack of opportunities for African-American entrepreneurs, O'Connor opined that the city did not have a "strong basis in evidence for its conclusion that remedial action was necessary,"[145] and concluded that the city had not established a *prima facie* case of a constitutional or statutory violation by anyone in the Richmond construction industry. Although the city had designated its plan as "remedial," "the mere recitation of a 'benign' or legitimate purpose for a racial classification, is entitled to little or no weight."[146] Conclusory statements of discrimination were also deemed insufficient: "A governmental action cannot render race a legitimate proxy for a particular condition merely by declaring that the condition exists."[147] Thus, the statements of proponents of the Richmond plan regarding racial discrimination in the construction industry in the area, state and nation were held to be "of little probative value in establishing identified discrimination in the Richmond construction industry."[148]

O'Connor also found that the statistical disparity between contracts awarded to MBEs and the minority population of Richmond was misplaced. Where special qualifications are necessary, she stated, the relevant statistical pool for purposes of demonstrating discriminatory exclusion must be the number of minorities qualified to undertake a particular task.[149] O'Connor noted that the city did not know the number of qualified MBEs in the relevant market qualified to undertake public construction projects, and did not know the percentage of city construction dollars received by minority firms serving as subcontractors on city contracts.

Evidence of low MBE membership in contractors' associations did not persuade the Court. Past societal discrimination in education and economic opportunities and career and entrepreneurial choices were cited by O'Connor as some of the possible explanations for the dearth of minority participation in the industry. To be relevant, she stated, Richmond would have to link the membership number to the number of local MBEs eligible for membership. If the statistical disparity were great enough, the "city would have a compelling interest in preventing its tax dollars from assisting these organizations in maintaining a racially segregated construction project."[150]

Furthermore, O'Connor found no evidence of past discrimination against Spanish-speaking, Oriental, Indian, Eskimo or Aleut persons in the Richmond construction industry. This "random inclusion" of racial groups "suggests that perhaps the city's purpose was not in fact to remedy past discrimination."[151] She thus determined that the "gross overinclusiveness" of Richmond's program suggested that the plan was not narrowly tailored and impugned the city's claim of remedial motivation.

Narrow Tailoring of a Plan. Even though the Court found that it could not assess whether the Richmond plan was narrowly tailored to remedy past discrimination since the plan was not linked to such discrimination, two further observations were made by Justice O'Connor. First, she determined that there was no apparent consideration of using race-neutral means to increase MBE participation in city contracting. Second, she concluded that the 30 percent quota (which was less than the 50 percent black population of Richmond) was not narrowly tailored, but was "perhaps outright racial balancing. It rests upon the 'completely unrealistic' assumption that minorities will choose a particular trade in lockstep proportion to their representation in the local population."[152] Quoting from her opinion in *Sheet Metal Workers v. EEOC*,[153] Justice O'Connor opined that it is "completely unrealistic to assume that individuals of one race will gravitate with mathematical exactitude to each employer or union absent unlawful discrimination."[154] Indicating that a plan should provide for individual consideration of whether a particular MBE has suffered from past discrimination, O'Connor noted that the waiver in the Richmond plan improperly focused solely on the availability of MBEs. "Under Richmond's scheme, a successful Black, Hispanic, or Oriental entrepreneur from anywhere in the country enjoys an absolute preference over other citizens based solely on their race."[155] In her view, any such program is not narrowly tailored to remedy the effects of past discrimination.

The Plurality's View of Permissible Remedial Efforts by the City. In Part V of her opinion, Justice O'Connor (joined by Chief Justice Rehnquist and Justices White and Kennedy) stated that Richmond could act to end discriminatory exclusion where there was a significant statistical disparity between the number of qualified MBEs willing and able to perform a service, and the number of such contractors actually engaged by the locality or the locality's prime contractors.[156] Where a local government discovers individual cases or a pattern of refusals to employ MBEs because of their race, continued O'Connor, a city could penalize the discriminator and provide relief to the victim or employ broader relief.

Race-neutral devices to increase access to city contracting were also cited as permissible measures, including the simplification of bidding procedures, relaxation of bond requirements, training, financial aid for disadvantaged entrepreneurs of all races, and the prohibition of discrimination in providing credit or bonding by local suppliers and banks.[157] It appeared to Justice O'Connor that the city had not considered the use of such race-neutral means.[158] "If MBEs disproportionately lack capital or cannot meet bonding requirements, a race-neutral program of city financing for small firms would, *a fortiori*, lead to greater minority participation."[159]

The Kennedy and Scalia Concurrences. Justice Kennedy's concurrence set forth his view of racial classifications and the Equal Protection Clause. He reasoned that a state has the power to eradicate racial discrimination and its effects in the public and private sectors, and the duty to do so where a state intentionally causes discrimination. Agreeing that any racial preference must face the "most vigorous scrutiny" by the courts,[160] Kennedy opined that the strict scrutiny standard would forbid the use of narrowly drawn racial classifications except as a last resort; that race-conscious relief may be the only adequate

remedy after judicial determination that a state or its instrumentality violated the
Equal Protection Clause; and that the strict scrutiny ruling was consistent with
the Court's precedents. Finding the reasons for the city of Richmond's ordinance
"unmeasured, unexplored, or unexplained" by the city council, Kennedy concluded that the ordinance was not a remedy, but a preference which would cause
the same "corrosive animosities" which the Constitution forbids.[161] In reaching
that conclusion, Justice Kennedy expressed his agreement with (but did not adopt)
Justice Scalia's view of racial neutrality under the Fourteenth Amendment.[162]

In his concurring opinion, Justice Scalia agreed with the majority's opinion
that "strict scrutiny must be applied to all governmental classification of race,
whether or not its asserted purpose is 'remedial' or 'benign.' "[163] But Scalia
disagreed with what he termed the Court's "dicta" regarding state and local
government "discriminat[ion] on the basis of race in order (in a broad sense)
'to ameliorate the effects of past discrimination.' "[164]

At least where state or local action is at issue, only a social emergency rising to the level
of imminent danger to life and limb—for example, a prison race riot, requiring temporary
segregation of inmates . . . can justify an exception to the principle embodied in the
Fourteenth Amendment that "[o]ur Constitution is color-blind, and neither knows nor
tolerates classes among citizens."[165]

Scalia concluded that *Fullilove* did not control in deciding whether Richmond's
plan was constitutional. He found a sound distinction between federal action
under § 5 of the Fourteenth Amendment and state action governed by § 1 of
that Amendment. Justice Scalia also invoked social reality and governmental
theory (which he did not define) in arguing that dispassionate objectivity and
flexibility (again undefined) needed to mold race-conscious remedies, which
"already doubted in a national legislature," are "substantially less likely to exist
at the state or local level."[166]

The racial and political makeup of Richmond also drew Scalia's attention.
"[T]he enactment of a set-aside [was] clearly and directly beneficial to the
dominant political group, which happens also to be the dominant racial group."[167]
He recognized that the "same thing has no doubt happened before in other cities
. . . and blacks have often been on the receiving end of the injustice. Where
injustice is the game, however, turn-about is not fair play."[168]

Like the majority, Justice Scalia reasoned that a state could permissibly undo
the effects of past discrimination by nonracial means, for example, by preferences
for small businesses or for new businesses. And, he continued, a state could
remedy the effects of discrimination against identified victims.[169] Recognizing
that African Americans have suffered discrimination, Scalia argued that the
"relevant proposition is not that it was blacks, or Jews, or Irish who were
discriminated against, but that it was individual men and women, 'created equal,'
who were discriminated against."[170] Instead of racial classifications, Scalia argued for race-neutral remedial programs for the disadvantaged, reasoning that

such programs would have a disproportionately beneficial impact on African Americans.[171]

The Implications and Potential Impact of the Court's Decision

Croson has been cited as a "major defeat" by advocates of affirmative action.[172] Assuming that that description is accurate, and recognizing that the Court did not invalidate all government-sponsored affirmative action programs, it is clear that the Court has made it more difficult for states, cities and other localities to promulgate and implement MBE programs. It is also clear that *Croson* requires state and local governments to assess the constitutionality of extant MBE plans under the more stringent standards set forth in the Court's decision.

One aspect of the Court's ruling which may have a significant impact on constitutional litigation in this area is the majority's holding that all racial classifications are equally suspect—a result foreshadowed by the plurality decision in *Wygant*. State and local governmental racial classifications and distinctions on the basis of race which are utilized to benefit historically disadvantaged groups will now be subjected to strict scrutiny review, and will therefore require a showing of a narrowly tailored program which is enacted to meet a compelling state interest. Thus, all such racial preferences will be reviewed under a test which, with rare exception,[173] has struck down all governmental classification based on race or ancestry.

Another potential and significant impact of *Croson* is the likelihood of legal challenges to MBE programs throughout the nation because of the economic incentive of nonminorities to eliminate the set-aside of a percentage of contracting dollars to minorities.[174] In light of that expected challenge, state and local governments have determined that their programs must undergo a careful review, assessment, and compilation of evidence of past discrimination, and the effects thereof, in city contracting.[175] Such challenges can, of course, have an adverse effect on MBEs. One such company was established in Richmond, Virginia shortly after the city's MBE ordinance had passed, and nineteen individuals were employed. When the MBE ordinance law was challenged and invalidated by the Fourth Circuit, that company's work force was cut in half.[176] In fact, African-American contractors received less than 1 percent of Richmond's business prior to the ordinance; 30 percent of contracting dollars after the ordinance was passed; and less than 1 percent after the ordinance was subsequently held unconstitutional by the Fourth Circuit.[177]

Despite its admission that African Americans have been subjected to, and suffer from unlawful discrimination, the Supreme Court has now adopted a constitutional analysis which does not distinguish between state and local governmental racial classifications through which the racial majority discriminates against racial minorities, and those classifications which are used for the purpose of remedying discrimination against minorities. The import of this analysis cannot be discounted; when coupled with the economic incentives for the dissolution of MBE programs, the Court's decision will serve as the doctrinal and precedential support for numerous suits claiming that MBE plans are unconstitutional.

The legacy of racial discrimination remains a historical reality. A contemporary reality is minority political empowerment as reflected in the growing number of elected minority officials. That same empowerment in the context of set-aside programs troubled some members of the Court. Justice O'Connor's expression of a suspicion of political motivation for Richmond's MBE plan, which Justice Marshall called an insult,[178] must be considered by other cities with population and political "minority majorities." This notion of minority empowerment as an opportunity for minorities to discriminate (the "pay back") suggests, and suffers from, the same racial classification which the Court condemns, for it assumes that minority legislators who vote in favor of an MBE plan do so because of some intent to discriminate against nonminorities. Thus, the *race* of the minority legislator assumes critical importance and effectively trumps other lawful motivations of MBE legislation, such as the economic and other benefits which flow from increased competition, productivity, and employment opportunities for minorities.

Notwithstanding the Court's view that *individuals* must be viewed apart from their race, the Court suggests that cities which have a "majority minority" population, and/or which are headed by minority chief executives and legislators, may act on racial matters in a manner that calls for a skeptical review of governmental actions. This view of the institutional competence of such cities was expressed by some commentators before *Croson*.[179] Professor Drew Days has noted that this view suggests that "less is at risk when race-conscious plans favoring minorities are instituted by governmental bodies controlled by whites."[180]

There is no reason to fear, the argument runs, that whites will discriminate against themselves, whereas minority officials may not exercise such self-restraint when adopting programs that disadvantage whites. This logic elevates form over substance. There is every reason to expect, in the absence of . . . safeguards . . . that set-asides lacking remedial justification are just as likely to be instituted by white as by minority officials.[181]

While the ultimate impact of *Croson* on MBE set-asides must await future cases in the lower courts, certain principles can be gleaned from the opinions of the majority. First, state and local governments must be able to document and present evidence of historical discrimination in the particular jurisdiction's geographical or governmental area by prime contractors. Second, a set-aside policy or program should be narrowly tailored so that any preference or remedial benefit is enjoyed only by those MBEs and minority groups subjected to unlawful racial discrimination. Third, the percentages established as a goal or quota for MBE participation must have some basis in, and reference to, the evidence of historical discrimination; should be linked to, and reflective of, the percentage of MBEs qualified to perform the work; and should bear some relation to the statistical disparity in the particular jurisdiction between qualified MBEs and MBEs awarded contracts in nonset-aside contracting. Some governments may attempt to foreclose any dispute in this area by eschewing percentages altogether. Fourth, the set-aside should be flexible and reviewed on a regular basis, features which may be helpful in defending against claims that a plan is not narrowly tailored and has been implemented, under ulterior motives, for other than remedial or benign goals or purposes.

POST-*CROSON* DECISIONS

Illustrations of the impact of *Croson* are found in recent cases applying the Supreme Court's decision to MBE plans. Shortly after that case was decided, the Supreme Court of Georgia applied *Croson* in *American Subcontractors Association, Georgia Chapter, Inc. v. City of Atlanta*[182] and held that an Atlanta, Georgia MBE set-aside program was unconstitutional. Challenging the 1985 MBE participation goal of 35 percent,[183] an association of nonminority and nonfemale contractors filed suit alleging, *inter alia*, that the MBE plan violated the Equal Protection Clause of the Georgia constitution.[184]

Assuming that the plan was facially constitutional, the Georgia Supreme Court, citing *Croson* and *Wygant*, applied the strict scrutiny standard of review in analyzing the validity of the program. Turning first to the evidence supporting Atlanta's plan, the court concluded that the evidence was not sufficient to justify the MBE program. City witnesses testified that they were not aware of any instance of discrimination against an African-American (or female) contractor. Although the city argued that it relied on studies, minority participation reports, and public hearings, in the court's view the studies (a 1977 Department of Commerce study and a Voter Education Project study on discrimination against black-owned businesses in Georgia) presented a broad overview of national and state black employment trends and a general underutilization of black contractors in the Atlanta area.[185] The court also noted that witnesses for the city suggested nonracial factors affecting underutilization of black contractors: lack of insurance and bonding capability, lack of cash flow, and information not being made available to all bidders before contracting. "It is likely that these factors face a member of any racial group attempting to establish a new business enterprise."[186]

As to the city's minority participation reports, the court noted that the city's reports for 1980 showed that 29 percent of city contracts went to MBEs in 1980, with 41.3 percent MBE participation in 1981.[187] And, continued the court, the evidence adduced at the public hearings provided no support for the plan. In one hearing, thirty-four persons spoke, most of whom favored the plan. In the second hearing, a councilman stated his view that MBEs were underrepresented, and the city compliance officer's statement assumed discrimination against minorities in city contracting. "The city's 'factual' support for the [plan] consists of little more than generalized assertions of underutilization of black contractors in Atlanta, and no evidence of discrimination against black contractors."[188]

Further, the court found that the Atlanta plan was not "narrowly tailored" to remedy prior discrimination. First, stated the court, the plan was not linked to identified discrimination. Second, the court determined that many of the barriers to minority participation were "race-neutral" and could be ameliorated by alternate remedies such as "improving city purchasing and payment procedures, requiring full disclosure of all bid information, relaxing insurance and bonding requirements, and providing loan assistance. . . . "[189] "It is apparent that the city had available to it less intrusive means of accomplishing the [plan's] race-conscious purposes but had not fully explored those less intrusive means as possibly eliminating any need for the [plan]."[190]

Finally, the court determined that the annual "goal" set by the mayor for MBE participation was not narrowly tailored. Reasoning that the semantic distinction between a goal and a quota was beside the point, the court opined that nonminority and nonfemale contractors could not compete for 100 percent of the work, but were limited to the percentage remaining after the "goals" were met. "[W]hether this limitation is described as a quota or a goal, it is a line drawn on the base of race and ethnic status."[191]

Initial application of *Croson* in the federal courts began with the Supreme Court's affirmance of the Sixth Circuit's 1987 invalidation of the state of Michigan's set-aside,[192] and the Court's remand of the Eleventh Circuit's 1987 decision upholding the Dade County, Florida MBE program.[193] In April 1989, the United States District Court for the Western District of Wisconsin in *Milwaukee County Bowers Assn. v. Fiedler* dissolved a preliminary injunction, entered in February 1989,[194] which enjoined Wisconsin's operation of a "disadvantaged" business set-aside program.[195] Implementing the requirements of the Federal Surface Transportation and Uniform Relocation Act of 1987,[196] Wisconsin enacted its disadvantaged business program. Four million dollars of funds appropriated for highway construction were to be allocated to projects that could be bid on only by disadvantaged prime contractors. The $4 million allocation could be made from state, local, or federal funds or a combination of those sources.

Determining that the operative categories of the disadvantaged business statute were actually race, national origin, and gender, and not disadvantage,[197] the district court found that the Wisconsin program was subsidiary to a federal program, and that the state could therefore rely on Congressional findings of past discrimination. This finding was significant since the court concluded that "if the state program is subsidiary to a federal program, it should be analyzed as a federal program to which *Croson* would not apply."[198] Rather, stated the court, the *Fullilove* standards would govern. In reaching that conclusion, the court rejected the plaintiffs' argument that *Fullilove* cannot be relied on as precedent after *Croson*. "Their contention is refuted by the [Supreme] Court's frequent reliance on *Fullilove* in the *Croson* opinion and its explicit distinction between the standards to be applied to review of federal and state programs."[199]

Applying *Fullilove*, the court held that the federal and Wisconsin programs were totally integrated.

Where . . . a state program is enacted to implement federal legislation imposing specified requirements on the state and the legislative framework, the state program should be considered a subsidiary element of the federal legislation.[200]

Having reached this conclusion regarding the federal-state integration of the program, the court concluded that the state could rely on Congressional findings underlying the federal highway funding act. Because the Wisconsin program was not a purely state program, "*Croson*'s evidentiary requirements are inapplicable. Federal statutes and their subsidiaries are properly supported by Congressional findings of nationwide discrimination."[201] In the court's view, Congressional reliance on the legislative history of the 1977 PWEA and hearings and Senate committee reports preceding the enactment of the Surface Transportation and Uniform Relocation Assistance Act of 1987, provided sufficient evidentiary support for the set-aside.[202]

Finally, the court, applying *Fullilove*, held that the federal and Wisconsin program was lawful: the programs operated prospectively; a waiver was available; the program was of limited duration; the eligibility criteria were rebuttable; and the 10 percent set-aside figure was the same as that upheld in *Fullilove*.[203] Further, the court found that the Wisconsin program was narrowly tailored to meet the state government's end (improvement of Wisconsin's implementation of the federal program). No goal was established, and the set-aside was only one element of Wisconsin's program to improve the skills of disadvantaged businesses. In addition, the court concluded that the program did not unduly burden innocent nonminorities since the $4 million set-aside was less than 1.5 percent of the total construction budget.[204]

Fiedler illustrates the continuing validity of *Fullilove* where a federal program provides some or all of the funding of an MBE program. *Croson*'s heightened scrutiny and more vigorous standards were not applied in that context and saved the Wisconsin plan. This decision also highlights the potential difficulties which may arise where a program for the "disadvantaged," touted by Justice Scalia as an alternative to MBE programs, is found to be a proxy for racial or sexual preferences.

Two more recent decisions further illustrate the impact of *Croson*. In *Cone Corporation v. Hillsborough County*,[205] the court entered a preliminary injunction which prohibited the enforcement of a county's MBE program. In the court's view, it was clear that the MBE program did not meet the tests explicated by the Supreme Court in *Croson*, and "the necessity for suspending the program" should have been recognized.[206] Moreover, stated the court, its "time and the parties' time, fees and expenses would have been better served by suspending this MBE program and working on a new program which conforms to the [*Croson*] plurality's standards for an MBE program."[207]

In another case, granting summary judgment against a school board, the court in *Main Line Paving Co., Inc. v. Board of Education, School District of Pennsylvania*[208] held, *inter alia*, that the board's MBE program failed to meet the *Croson* criteria. First, the court found that the facts relied upon by the school board did not provide a sufficient predicate to support the MBE. Even though a series of hearings by the Philadelphia city council showed that one-half of 1 percent of school district contracts were awarded to minority contractors between 1982 and 1983, the court determined that the school district saw *itself* as the prime source of the discrimination to be cured by the set-aside. In that regard, the court referred to facts stipulated to by the parties. The school district's own employees were in large part responsible for denying contracts to minority low bidders on pretextual reasons, and preferred to deal with other contractors, and bids for projects were solicited from contractors on lists which contained few minority- or female-owned businesses. Equally important to the court was the absence of a factual predicate or specific evidence of current discrimination against those aided by the policy.[209]

Second, the court held that the MBE program was not narrowly tailored to remedy prior discrimination. The court found "nothing in the record to indicate that the Board considered the use of race-neutral means to increase minority business participation in its contracting opportunities before opting for race-conscious alternatives."[210] Better oversight of employees involved in the board's contracting practices and the identification of victims of past discrimination were cited by the court as such alternatives. In addition, the court found that few waivers from the requirements of the MBE program were granted, and that prime contractors were required to guarantee minimum levels of minority and female participation, which indicated that the board had established an impermissible quota system.[211]

An example of the survival of a set-aside program under the *Croson* analysis is found in *Coral Construction Company v. King County*.[212] There, a set-aside ordinance for minority- and women-owned business enterprises (MWBE) passed by the county council of King County, Washington, provided two methods by which MWBE's could receive preferences in bids on county contracts. Contractors with bids within 5 percent of the lowest bid received preferences if the bids showed that the contractors were MWBE's or would use MWBEs on a project. Under the second method, contractors for county contracts of more than $10,000 had (with certain exceptions) to use MWBEs for a percentage of the work on those contracts.

A suit challenging the set-aside ordinance was brought by a low bidder on a construction contract when the contract was awarded to an MBE who had submitted a higher bid. The court held that the King County set-aside program met the requirements of *Croson*. Finding that the program was supported by a strong basis of evidence of past discrimination, the court noted that several dozen people had given written or oral descriptions of such discrimination. "Many of the sources relied upon by the county council provided specific examples of past discrimination in the construction industry in King County."[213] Moreover, stated the court, "nearly all of King County's evidence applies specifically to the construction industry within the County's jurisdiction."[214] Such evidence in other jurisdictions located within the county and metropolitan Seattle, Washington, could also be considered, ruled the court. The county's reliance on evidence of past discrimination in the local private construction industry (and not on evidence of discrimination by the county) was also proper, stated the court, since the county was a passive participant in the discrimination as its construction dollars flowed through the local construction industry.

Turning to the question of whether the county's program was a narrowly tailored remedy for past discrimination, the court concluded that the county had considered race-neutral alternatives and had rejected them because they were barred by state law. Further, the county's program was not a rigid quota system, stated the court; utilization requirements were tied to the availability of qualified MWBE contractors and not to the percentages of minorities or women in the general population, and waiver of the preferences were available.[215] Nor was the program over-inclusive, continued the court, for the benefit of the set-aside program could be denied if a particular group had not been discriminated against.

Accordingly, the *King County* court determined that the set-aside ordinance was constitutional under *Croson*. The court's analysis and the county's approach to the promulgation and implementation of its set-aside program offer a concrete example of how a set-aside program can survive a *Croson*-based challenge.

GUIDELINES

Under *Croson* and its progeny, state and local government MBE plans must be based upon evidence which demonstrates the following:

1. Past or present discrimination, and the injury or adverse effect of such discrimination, on minorities.

2. Evidence, both historical and/or current, which supports the determination that discrimination in contracting has occurred.

3. State or local government actions or inaction which caused or contributed to the adverse effects of such discrimination, and acts of discrimination by contractors (including passive acceptance of or acquiescence in discrimination).

4. The reason(s) why the race-conscious program is necessary and why other alternatives would not be effective to remedy or respond to the identified discrimination.

5. The duration of the program relative to the discriminatory wrong.

6. The percentage of contracts to be awarded to MBE firms are related, at least in part, to the number of qualified MBEs able to perform the particular work, and not the number of minorities in the general population of the state or local government's jurisdiction.

PROGNOSIS

Assembling the evidence of past discrimination through hearings and investigations of past discrimination can be costly, and will require a political commitment to expend the necessary funds or legal and administrative costs. Governmental will to unearth and identify its own discriminatory conduct or passive acceptance of discrimination will also be key, for the essence of that exercise is to accept and confirm that actual discrimination was imposed upon and suffered by minorities.

These concerns and issues may explain the fact that, to date, legislatures have been slow to respond to *Croson*. According to the Minority Business Enterprise Legal Defense and Education Fund, about 236 state and local jurisdictions have been affected by *Croson*.[216] A survey of the National Conference of State Legislatures indicated that few states have moved to study the effects of *Croson*,[217] and Minnesota, Michigan, Wisconsin, San Francisco, and Atlanta have halted all or part of their set-aside programs.[218] Florida, Louisiana, Massachusetts, Maryland, and Oregon continue to study the Supreme Court's ruling, and suits against MBE programs are pending in the District of Columbia, Boston, and Philadelphia.[219] The real world effects of *Croson* are now apparent. MBE contractors in Atlanta, Georgia and Durham, North Carolina report the loss of business at a level which threatens their existence.[220] One company in North Carolina reports that its revenue tripled to $1.5 million a year when Durham, North Carolina started its minority and women business enterprise program, but may lose its business after *Croson*. Whether state and local jurisdictions can promulgate MBE programs which meet the *Croson* criteria is a question of obvious importance to certain minority businesses.

CONCLUSION

The Supreme Court's decision in *Croson* stands as one of the most significant rulings issued in the area of racial discrimination and affirmative action. And *Croson* illustrates the call for the "heightened accountability" of state and local governments adopting MBE plans.[221] As challenges to MBE set-asides wind their way through the lower courts, a more accurate assessment of the impact of *Croson* will, of course, be possible; the discussion set forth above must suffice for now.

It can be said with assurance at this juncture that the subject matter addressed in *Croson* and the standards announced in the Court's decision are, and will continue to be, points of discussion, analysis, and concern for state and local governments, as well as the topic of legislative initiatives.[222] Future developments in this area bear watching.

NOTES

1. 448 U.S. 448 (1980).
2. Pub. L. No. 95–28, 91 Stat. 116 (1977), *codified in significant part at* 42 U.S.C. §§ 6705(e)–6707(j) (1982).
3. Pub. L. No. 95–28 § 103(f)(2), 91 Stat. 116, 117 (1977), *codified at* 42 U.S.C. § 6705(f)(2) (1982).

4. As noted in the introduction, the term *affirmative action* encompasses several initiatives and programs which are utilized to overcome the effects of past or present practices, policies, or barriers to equal employment opportunity. *See* Equal Employment Opportunity Commission Affirmative Action Guidelines, 29 C.F.R. § 1608.1(c) (1985). The term and concept may include recruitment activities, training, and other actions taken to redress discriminatory conduct. *Id.*, § 1608.3(c); Office of Federal Contract Compliance Programs, Affirmative Action Programs, 41 C.F.R. §§ 60–2.1–2.32 (1987). *See generally* D. MCDOWELL, AFFIRMATIVE ACTION AFTER THE JOHNSON DECISION (1988); Daly, *Some Runs, Some Hits, Some Errors—Keeping Score in the Affirmative Action Ballpark from* Weber *to* Johnson, 30 BOSTON COL. L. REV. 1, 3 n. 1 (1988); Cox, *The Supreme Court, Title VII and "Voluntary" Affirmative Action—A Critique*, 21 IND. L. REV. 767, 790 (1988).

Affirmative action includes programs or other efforts undertaken by federal, state, and local governments which grant preferential treatment to individuals on the basis of race (or other protected status) in the procurement of government contracts, jobs, promotions, and so on. In the context of MBE set-asides, affirmative action efforts typically involve governmental establishment of quotas or goals, often expressed in specific percentages, which are applied in awarding public works contracts. These programs generally require that MBEs and women business enterprises (WBEs) will receive a percentage of service contracts awarded by governmental bodies.

5. The Minority Business Enterprise Legal Defense and Education Fund, Inc. (MBELDEF) has reported that at least thirty states have MBE programs for public contracting; three states have implemented other measures to assist MBEs; and over one hundred and sixty local governments have MBE programs. Only three of the nation's thirty three largest cities did not have set-aside programs. *See* REPORT ON THE MINORITY BUSINESS ENTERPRISE PROGRAMS OF STATE AND LOCAL GOVERNMENTS, MINORITY BUSINESS ENTERPRISE LEGAL DEFENSE AND EDUCATION FUND, INC. (1988); Note, *The Nonperpetuation of Discrimination in Public Contracting: A Justification for State and Local Minority Business Set-Asides After* Wygant, 101 HARV. L. REV. 1797, 1797 n. 6 (1988).

6. *See, e.g.*, South Florida Chapter, Associated General Contractors of America, Inc. v. Metropolitan Dade County, 723 F.2d 846 (11th Cir.), *cert. denied*, 469 U.S. 871 (1984); Ohio Contractors Association v. Keip, 713 F.2d 167 (6th Cir. 1983).

7. 476 U.S. 267 (1986).

8. 476 U.S. at 276 (plurality opinion).

9. *Id.*

10. *See infra* at notes 80–110 and accompanying text.

11. Associated General Contractors of California, Inc. v. City and County of San Francisco, 813 F.2d 922 (9th Cir. 1987), petition dismissed, 110 S.Ct. 296 (1989); J. Edinger and Son, Inc. v. City of Louisville, Kentucky, 802 F.2d 213 (6th Cir. 1986).

12. The Equal Protection Clause provides that "no State shall . . . deny to any person within its jurisdiction the equal protection of the laws." U.S. Const., Am. XIV.

13. 822 F.2d 1355 (4th Cir. 1987), *aff'd*, 109 S.Ct. 706 (1989).

14. City of Richmond v. J. A. Croson Company, 109 S.Ct. 706 (1989).

15. Section 5 of the Fourteenth Amendment provides that "Congress shall have power to enforce, by appropriate legislation, the provisions of this article." U.S. CONST., Am. XIV, § 5. *See generally* Katzenbach v. Morgan, 384 U.S. 641 (1966) (Court adopted sweeping view of Congressional authority to define rights protected by Equal Protection

Clause). For a discussion of Congress' power to create substantive rights under § 5 of the Fourteenth Amendment, *see* Cox, *The Role of Congress in Constitutional Determinations*, 40 U. CIN. L. REV. 199 (1971).

16. 448 U.S. 448 (1980).

17. The Public Works Employment Act of 1977, an amendment to the Local Public Works Capital Development and Investment Act of 1976, 42 U.S.C. § 6701 *et seq.*, authorized a $4 billion appropriation for federal grants by the Secretary of Commerce. Administration of the grants was governed by regulations promulgated by the Secretary and by guidelines issued by the federal Economic Development Administration.

For a full description and discussion of the PWEA, *see Fullilove*, 448 U.S. at 456–472; Days, *Fullilove*, 96 YALE L.J. 453, 463–465 (1987).

18.

The PWEA's MBE provision required that no grant shall be made under this Act for any local public works project unless the applicant gives satisfactory assurance to the Secretary that at least 10 percentum of the amount of each grant shall be expended for minority business enterprises. For purposes of this paragraph, the term "minority business enterprise" means a business at least 50 percentum of which is owned by minority group members or, in case of a publicly owned business, at least 51 percentum of the stock of which is owned by minority group members. For the purposes of the preceding sentence minority group members are citizens of the United States who are Negroes, Spanish-speaking, Orientals, Indians, Eskimos, and Aleuts. 42 U.S.C. § 6705(f)(2).

19. "No person shall . . . be deprived of life, liberty, or property, without due process of law. . . . " U.S. CONST., Am. V.

20. 448 U.S. at 472.

21. "The Congress shall have Power To lay and collect Taxes, Duties, Imports and Excises, to pay the Debts and provide for the common Defense and general Welfare of the United States. . . . " U.S. CONST., Art. I, § 8, cl. 1. *See generally* Buckley v. Valeo, 424 U.S. 1, 90–91 (1976).

22. 448 U.S. at 475.

23. "The Congress shall have Power . . . To regulate Commerce with foreign Nations, and among the several States, and with Indian Tribes. . . . " U.S. CONST., Art. I, § 8, cl. 3. *See generally* Katzenbach v. McClurg, 379 U.S. 294 (1964).

24. *See* 448 U.S. at 456–463. The Chief Justice reviewed the legislative history and tracked the MBE provision from its origin as an amendment to the House of Representatives' version of the PWEA (H.R. 11) offered by Representative Parren Mitchell of Maryland. 123 Cong. Rec. 5097–5098 (1977) (remarks of Rep. Mitchell). In proposing the MBE set-aside, Mitchell noted that an ongoing set-aside program was found in § 8(a) of the Small Business Act, Pub. L. 85–536, 72 Stat. 389. *See* 448 U.S. at 460. The amendment, as modified by substitute language offered by Representative Roe of New Jersey, was accepted by the House. *Id.* at 5328, 5332.

S. 427, introduced in the Senate by Senator Brooke of Massachusetts, contained a similar, but not identical, MBE provision. *See* 448 U.S. at 462 n. 34. That proposal was adopted by the Senate without debate. 123 Cong. Rec. 7156 (1977).

The Conference Committee adopted the House version of the MBE provision. After agreement by the Senate and House, the PWEA, with its MBE provision, was signed into law by President Carter on May 13, 1977. *See id.* at 12941–12942, 13242–13257; *supra* note 18.

25. This "evidence" included the Small Business Act's provision regarding assistance

to small businesses owned or controlled by "socially or economically disadvantaged" persons, which included Blacks, American Indians, Spanish-Americans, Orientals, Eskimos, and Aleuts. *See* 13 C.F.R. § 124.8–1(c)(1). In addition, the Chief Justice cited a 1977 House Committee on Small Business report which summarized a 1975 House Subcommittee on the Small Business Administration's (SBA) Oversight and Minority Enterprise report. *See* H.R. Rep. No. 94–1791 (1977); H.R. Rep. No. 94–468 (1975). The Subcommittee Report stated, *inter alia*, that "past discriminatory practices have, to some degree, adversely affected our present economic system." H.R. Rep. No. 94–468 (1975), quoted at 448 U.S. at 465. The Subcommittee Report also relied on 1975 reports by the United States General Accounting Office and by the United States Commission on Civil Rights.

The Chief Justice also noted that the SBA Subcommittee Report indicated that the Department of Commerce's Office of Minority Business Enterprise's efforts to increase opportunities for minority businesses in public contracting were "totally inadequate." *See* 448 U.S. at 467.

26. 448 U.S. at 478.

27. *Id.*

28. *Id.* at 483–484 (citation omitted).

29. *Id.* at 485.

30. *Id.* at 487–488, 492–495. Chief Justice Burger also rejected the argument that the MBE program was underinclusive, in that it limited the statutory benefits to specified minority groups rather than to all contractors affected by disadvantage or discrimination. "Such an extension would, of course, be appropriate for Congress to provide; it is not a function for the courts." *Id.* at 485.

31. Justice Powell relied on the Commerce Clause and the Thirteenth, Fourteenth and Fifteenth Amendments to the Constitution. *Id.* at 499–501 (Powell, J., concurring).

32. *Id.* at 506.

33. *Id.* at 507.

34. The Court generally applies three constitutional standards of review: strict scrutiny, intermediate level, and rational basis. Strict scrutiny is applied where the state uses race to classify an individual. In that circumstance, the state will be required to show that the racial classification serves a compelling governmental interest, and that the means chosen are narrowly tailored to accomplish that purpose. Daly, *supra* note 4 at 15; Palmore v. Sidoti, 466 U.S. 429 (1984); Loving v. Virginia, 388 U.S. 1 (1967). Commenting on the strict scrutiny standard, Professor Randall Kennedy has written that the

use of *race* as a proxy is specially disfavored because, even when relatively accurate as a signifier of the trait sought to be identified, racial proxies are especially prone to misuse. By the practice of subjecting governmentally-imposed racial distinctions to strict scrutiny, federal constitutional law recognizes that racial distinctions are particularly liable to being used in a socially destructive fashion.

Kennedy, *Racial Critiques of Legal Academia*, 102 HARV. L. REV. 1745, 1794 (1989) (footnote omitted and emphasis in original).

Under intermediate review, which is used to evaluate quasi-suspect classifications, a state must show that a classification serves an important government purpose and is substantially related to accomplishment of that purpose. *See* Craig v. Boren, 429 U.S. 190 (1976). *See also* Mississippi Univ. for Women v. Hogan, 458 U.S. 718 (1982); Kirchberg v. Feenstra, 450 U.S. 455 (1981); Weinberger v. Weisenfeld, 420 U.S. 636 (1975); Reed v. Reed, 404 U.S. 71 (1971); Daly, *supra* note 4 at 15.

The most deferential standard, the rational basis test, requires a rational relationship and legitimate end between the means and end of economic and social welfare legislation which does not involve a suspect class or fundamental right. *See* Daly, *supra* note 4 at 15 n. 35; San Antonio Independent School District v. Rodriguez, 411 U.S. 1 (1973); Brown v. Barry, 710 F.Supp. 352 (D.D.C. 1989). Despite the judicial deference given to legislative action under this test, the Supreme Court has invalidated statutes under the rational basis analysis. *See e.g.*, City of Cleburne v. Cleburne Living Center, Inc., 473 U.S. 432 (1985); Williams v. Vermont, 472 U.S. 14 (1985). *See also* Kotch v. Board of River Port Pilot Commissioners, 330 U.S. 552 (1947) (upholding job allotments by nepotism).

35. 448 U.S. at 511.

36. *Id.* at 513.

37. *Id.* at 513–514.

38. *Id.* at 514.

39. *Id.* at 515. *See* 584 F.2d 600, 607–608 (2d Cir. 1978).

40. 438 U.S. 265, 324–379 (1978).

41. 448 U.S. at 518–519 (Marshall, J., concurring in the judgment).

42. *Id.* at 519 (citation omitted).

43. *Id.* at 521.

44. Two dissenting opinions were issued. Justice Stewart, joined by Justice Rehnquist and calling for a colorblind constitutional analysis and the application of a strict scrutiny standard, concluded that the PWEA MBE provision was unconstitutional. "Under our Constitution, any official action that treats a person differently on account of his race or ethnic origin is inherently suspect and presumptively invalid." *Id.* at 523 (Stewart, J., dissenting) (citations omitted). This rule "cannot be any different when the persons injured by a racially biased law are not members of a racial minority." *Id.* at 526. Although Stewart did not dispute the Congressional power under § 5 of the Fourteenth Amendment or the Commerce Clause to regulate federally funded construction projects, he determined that the MBE provision facially violated the Equal Protection Clause.

Stewart did dispute Congress' ability to effectuate a race-conscious remedy, however. "It has neither the dispassionate objectivity nor the flexibility that are needed to mold a race-conscious remedy around the single objective of eliminating the effects of past or present discrimination." *Id.* at 527 (footnote omitted). Stewart also found no evidence that Congress had engaged in past discrimination in disbursing federal contract funds.

In addition, Justice Stewart stated that the MBE provision may have been enacted to compensate for the effects of social, educational and economic disadvantage. "No race, however, has a monopoly on social, educational, or economic disadvantage, and any law that indulges in such a presumption clearly violates the constitutional guarantee of equal protection." *Id.* at 529–530 (footnote omitted). Stewart thus concluded that the federal government "implicitly teaches the public that the apportionment of rewards and penalties can legitimately be made according to race—rather than according to merit or ability," *id.* at 532, and predicted that notions of racial entitlement and the encouragement of private discrimination would be encouraged by the Court's decision.

In a separate dissenting opinion, Justice Stevens argued that the MBE provision created monopoly privileges for the small number of individuals within a racial classification representing the entrepreneurial subclass. *Id.* at 532 (Stevens, J., dissenting). Finding that the reasons for the racial classifications at issue were not identified, Stevens noted that no relevant economic, social, geographical or historical criteria were used for statutory exclusion or inclusion, or to explain why 10 percent of the total appropriation was to be set aside for MBEs. Justice Stevens also reasoned that it did not necessarily follow that each of the subclasses identified by the statute suffered harm of equal magnitude or were equally entitled to reparations from the government. He stated that Blacks were brought to this country during slavery, while the Spanish-speaking subclass came voluntarily "and the Indians, the Eskimos and the Aleuts had an opportunity to exploit America's resources before the ancestors of most American citizens arrived." *Id*. at 538.

Justice Stevens made additional salient points. He noted, *inter alia*, that the legislative history of the PWEA did not indicate when or how often any MBE was denied access, and that the statute granted special preferences to a class including (a) already successful MBE firms, (2) MBE firms that had never attempted to obtain public business, (3) MBE firms formed after the PWEA was enacted, (4) firms that were unsuccessful in obtaining contracts for reasons unrelated to race, and (5) firms that had been subjected to racial discrimination. *Id*. at 540–541. In Stevens' view, the preference for firms in the first four categories could not be justified as remedial, while firms in the fifth category had a judicial remedy under other provisions of the PWEA. *See* 42 U.S.C. § 6727(d).

45. 713 F.2d 167 (6th Cir. 1983).

46. The Ohio MBE law provided that approximately 15 percent of the estimated total value of all state contracts for insurance purchases were to be set aside for bidding by MBEs only. Ohio Revised Code § 125.081(A). Additionally, the state was required to select, from state construction contracts, a number of contracts whose aggregate value was approximately 5 percent of the total estimated value of contracts to be awarded in the fiscal year. *Id*., § 123.151(C)(1). MBEs were defined as businesses owned and controlled by United States citizens and residents of Ohio who were members of "the following economically disadvantaged groups: Blacks, American Indians, Hispanics, and Orientals." *Id*., § 122.71(E)(1).

47. According to the Sixth Circuit, the Ohio legislature was aware of a 1967 district court decision which found that the state had jointly participated with private companies and craft unions in discriminating against black laborers on public construction projects. *See* Ethridge v. Rhodes, 268 F. Supp. 83 (S.D. Ohio 1967). Executive orders issued by the governor of Ohio which dealt with increased participation by minorities in state contracts were circulated to members of the legislature while the MBE law was being considered. The legislators were also given copies of a decision by an Ohio state court which upheld the constitutionality of 1977 Ohio legislation, which some state agencies interpreted as requiring a set-aside for minority bidders on state contracts. Legislators were further informed of a task force report which found that minority businesses, which constituted 7 percent of Ohio businesses, received less than one-half of 1 percent of state contracts during a certain two-year period. An additional study showed that over $1 billion paid out by the state in construction contracts over a sixteen-year period, with less than one-quarter of 1 percent of the payments going to minority businesses.

48. That section provides, in pertinent part, that no state shall "deny to any person within its jurisdiction the equal protection of the laws." U.S. Const., Am. XIV, § 1. *See generally* Shelley v. Kraemer, 334 U.S. 1 (1948).

49. 713 F.2d at 172 (citations omitted). *But see Croson, infra.*

50. *Id*. at 173.

51. *Id*.

52. *Id*.

53. *Id*.

54. *Id.* at 174.

55. *Id.* at 175.

56. *Id.* Dissenting, Judge Engels concluded that the Ohio MBE plan was fatally flawed by the absence of a durational limitation on its operation. In his view, that deficiency was "aggravated by the General Assembly's failure to articulate the Act's objective, thus making it difficult to determine when the objectives have been fulfilled." *Id.* at 176 (Engels, J., dissenting).

Judge Engels argued that it was unrealistic to expect that states would buttress legislation with the sophisticated legislative history Congress could produce in support of federal laws. But "the legislature apparently took great pains to avoid any direct determination that there has been actual past discrimination against minority business enterprises justifying the Act's set-aside provisions." *Id.* at 177. Further, Judge Engels concluded that the majority did not sufficiently emphasize Chief Justice Burger's opinion in *Fullilove* with respect to the unique role created for Congress under § 5 of the Fourteenth Amendment. *Id.* at 179. That view was later endorsed by the Supreme Court in *Croson* (*see infra*).

57. 723 F.2d 846 (11th Cir.), *cert denied*, 469 U.S. 871 (1984). A county ordinance set aside contracts for bidding solely among African-American contractors and contained goals under which the county could require that a percentage of a contract's value could be subcontracted to these contractors."Black contractors" were defined as contracting or subcontracting business entities which were

at least 51 percentum owned by . . . Blacks, or, in the case of a publicly-owned business, at least 51 percentum of the stock of which is owned by one or more Blacks; and whose management and daily business operations are controlled by one or more such individuals.

See Metropolitan Dade County, Florida Ordinance No. 82–67 (July 20, 1982), quoted at 723 F.2d at 847–848 n. 1. The ordinance defined "Black" as "a person who is a citizen or lawful permanent resident of the United States and who has origins in any of the Black racial groups of Africa." *Id.* at 858. The ordinance is quoted in full in an appendix to the Eleventh Circuit's opinion. *See id.* at 858–859.

58. The district court had found that, in response to disturbances in Liberty City, Florida in 1980, Dade County adopted a resolution which recognized that past discrimination had, to some degree, impaired the competitive position of African-American businesses in obtaining county contracts. In 1982, the county adopted an ordinance which expressly noted that Dade County had a compelling interest in stimulating the African-American business community, a community which "is not expected to benefit significantly in the absence of race-conscious measures. . . . " *Id.* at 848, 858. The ordinance required an examination of all county contracts to determine whether race-conscious measures would enhance African-American participation, and further required consideration of set-asides, bid credits and other devices. *Id.* at 848, 860. In 1982, the county received bids for a project. A nonminority contractor submitted the lowest bid, with the next lowest bid tendered by an African-American contractor. Both bids were rejected because they exceeded the county's estimate and because the bid amounts had become public. Adopting a recommendation by its contract review committee, the county passed a resolution which set aside the contract for competitive bidding exclusively among African-American contractors, and required that 50 percent of the contract's dollar value be awarded to African-American subcontractors. *Id.* at 849, 862. The South Florida Chapter of the Associated General Contractors of America, Inc. challenged this set-aside

in a declaratory and injunctive relief action. The district court held that the 100 percent set-aside was unconstitutional, but upheld the 50 percent subcontractor set-aside. *See* 552 F. Supp. 909 (S.D. Fla. 1982).

59. 723 F.2d at 852.

60. For the *Croson* Court's view of this issue, *see* 109 S.Ct. at 717–720.

61. 723 F.2d at 852.

62. *Id.* at 853 (citation omitted.)

63. *Id.* at 854.

64. *Id.* at 855–856 (footnote omitted). For the *Croson* Court's discussion of this point, *see infra.*

65. 723 F.2d at 856, citing *Fullilove*, 448 U.S. at 508 (Powell, J., concurring).

66. *Id.* at 856. For further examples of pre-*Wygant* rulings on set-asides, *see* Schmidt v. Oakland Unified School District, 662 F.2d 550 (9th Cir. 1981), *vacated on other grounds*, 457 U.S. 594 (1982); Southwest Washington Chapter, National Electrical Contractors Association v. Pierce County, 100 Wash. 109, 667 P.2d 1892 (1983); Arrington v. Associated General Contractors of America, Alabama Branch, Inc., 403 So.2d 893 (Ala. 1986); *see also* Central Alabama Paving v. James, 499 F.Supp. 629 (M.D. Ala. 1980).

67. 476 U.S. 267 (1986).

68. 476 U.S. at 270–271.

69. Justice Powell authored the plurality opinion and was joined by Chief Justice Burger and Justice Rehnquist.

70. 476 U.S. at 274. In support of its position, the plurality cited the Court's decision in Hazelwood School District v. U.S., 433 U.S. 299 (1977), wherein the Court held that for purposes of determining whether a *prima facie* case of racial discrimination had been made, the percentage of black teachers in a school district should have been compared to the percentage of Blacks in the school teacher population in the relevant labor market, rather than the percentage of black students in the district. *Hazelwood* was not an affirmative action case, and the "question whether *Hazelwood* should be transferred wholesale to such a plan has been a constant source of division on the Court." Daly, *supra* note 1 at 12. *See also* International Brotherhood of Teamsters v. U.S., 431 U.S. 324 (1977).

71. 476 U.S. at 275.

72. *Id.* at 276.

73. *Id.*

74. *Id.*

75. *Id.* at 279, citing *Fullilove*, 448 U.S. at 480 (Chief Justice Burger's opinion).

76. *Id.* at 283. *See also* Firefighters v. Stotts, 467 U.S. 561 (1979).

77. Concurring, Justice O'Connor agreed that a role model theory and effort to remedy societal discrimination could not be deemed sufficiently compelling to pass strict scrutiny muster. *Id.* at 288 (O'Connor, J., concurring in part and in the judgment). She reasoned that a statistical disparity between the percentage of minorities on a teaching staff and the percentage of minorities in a student body is not probative of employment discrimination. "[I]t is only when it is established that the availability of minorities in the relevant labor pool substantially exceeded those hired that one may draw an inference of deliberate discrimination in employment." *Id.* at 1857, citing Hazelwood School District v. U.S., *supra* note 75, 433 U.S. at 308.

Also concurring, Justice White's one-paragraph opinion stated that the discharge of white teachers to make room for African Americans, "none of whom has been shown to be a victim of any racial discrimination," was impermissible. *Id.* at 295 (White, J., concurring in the judgment). Concluding that the layoff policy had the same effect, he agreed with the plurality that the policy was unconstitutional.

Dissenting, Justice Marshall, joined by Justices Brennan and Blackmun, argued that a public employer should be permitted to preserve the benefits of affirmative action while reducing its work force where its employees agreed to the insulation of minorities from layoffs. *Id.* at 296 (Marshall, J., dissenting).

Justice Stevens, dissenting, argued that, in the context of public education, a school board could reasonably conclude that an integrated faculty would be able to provide benefits to the student body that an all-white faculty could not provide.

78. *See, e.g.,* Cygnar v. City of Chicago, 865 F.2d 827 (7th Cir. 1989); Janowiak v. City of South Bend, 836 F.2d 1034 (7th Cir. 1987), *cert. denied*, 109 S.Ct. 1310 (1989); Britton v. South Bend Community School Corporation, 819 F.2d 766 (7th Cir.), *cert. denied*, 484 U.S. 925 (1987).

79. *See* Janowiak v. City of South Bend, *supra* note 78, 836 F.2d at 1041–1042.

80. 802 F.2d 213 (6th Cir. 1986).

81. The ordinance provided that businesses which were owned by certain minority groups would receive a preference in bidding on certain city contracts. The minority groups covered by the ordinance were racial minorities which comprised at least 2 percent of the population of Jefferson County, Kentucky, as well as women and handicapped persons. *Id.* at 214. Minorities would receive 20 percent of city contract dollars, with 5 percent earmarked to females, and 3 percent to the handicapped. Where the dollar volume of city contracts did not reach the specified percentages in a given year, minority businesses would receive a 5 percent credit on all bids in the following year. *Id.*

82. *Id.*

83. The district court ruled that the city improperly concluded that discrimination occurred solely on the basis that business distribution did not equate general population distribution, and further ruled that the ordinance was unconstitutional because it did not contain a durational limitation. *Id.*

84. *Id.* at 215.

85. *See supra* notes 45–56 and accompanying text.

86. 802 F.2d at 215.

87. *Id.*

88. *Id.* at 216.

89. *Id.*

90. *Id.*

91. 834 F.2d 583 (6th Cir. 1987), *aff'd*, 109 S.Ct. 1333 (1989).

92. The Michigan statute provided that each state department was required to award not less than 7 percent of certain expenditures to MBEs and not less than 5 percent to WBEs. *See* Mich. Comp. Laws § 450.772. The statute defined "minority" as "a person who is black, hispanic, oriental, eskimo, or an American Indian." *Id.*, § 450.771(s). MBEs and WBEs were defined as enterprises of which more than 50 percent of a business was owned, controlled, and operated by minorities or women, and with respect to which more than 50 percent of the net loss or profit attributable to the business accrued to minority or women shareholders. *Id.*, §§ 450.771(f) and (j).

The Michigan Road Builders filed an action seeking declaratory and injunctive relief, charging that the set-aside provisions violated the Fourteenth Amendment and various federal statutes. The district court granted summary judgment to the state. *See* 654 F.

Supp. 3 (S.D. Mich. 1986). Reversing the district court, the Sixth Circuit held, *inter alia*, that the MBE provision was unconstitutional. Relying on *Wygant*, the court determined that a state must make a finding, based on material factual evidence, that it has engaged in past discrimination before employing a racial classification.

If the state had not engaged in discrimination against racial and ethnic minorities in awarding contracts to supply the state with goods and services in the past, then it cannot assert *in praesenti* that it has a compelling interest in preferring MBEs in the award of such contracts. 834 F.2d at 589.

93. *Id.* at 590 n. 7.
94. *Id.* at 590–592.
95. *Id.* at 592.
96. *Id.* at 594–595 n. 14.
97. 813 F.2d 922 (9th Cir. 1987).
98. This ordinance required city departments to set aside 10 percent of purchasing dollars for MBEs and 2 percent for WBEs; gave MBEs, WBEs, and LBEs a 3 percent bidding preference; required city departments to establish yearly percentage goals for MBE, WBE, and LBE contracting dollars; and established a goal of 30 percent of the city's contracting dollars to MBEs and 10 percent to WBEs. *See* 813 F.2d at 924.
99. Interestingly, the court held that the WBE preference was constitutional. "Unlike racial classifications, which must be 'narrowly' tailored to the government's objective . . . there is no requirement that gender-based statutes be 'drawn as precisely as [they] might have been.' " *Id.* at 942, quoting Michael M. v. Superior Court, 450 U.S. 464, 473 (1980) (plurality opinion). Noting that women have suffered historical discrimination and disparate treatment in business and employment, the court found the city's WBE preference troubling. 813 F.2d at 941. "While the city's program may be overinclusive, we believe it hews closely enough to the city's goal of compensating women for disadvantages they have suffered so as to survive a facial challenge." *Id.* The constitutionality of WBE programs is beyond the scope of this chapter. For an interesting discussion of that subject, *see* Scanlan, *Affirmative Action for Women: New Twist on an Old Debate*, LEGAL TIMES at 17–18 (Dec. 5, 1988). *See also* Main Line Paving Co., Inc. v. Board of Education, School District of Philadelphia, 725 F.Supp. 1349 (E.D. Pa. 1989) (court precludes WBE program because of absence of evidence detailing the small number of contracts awarded to women or gender discrimination).
The court also found no constitutional infirmity in the LBE program. It concluded that the city could rationally allocate funds to ameliorate disadvantages suffered by local businesses, particularly where the city created some of the disadvantages. In addition, the court found that the LBE preference did not discriminate against nonresident corporations solely because they were nonresidents. In its view, the preference was an attempt to remove or lighten a burden borne only by San Francisco businesses. 813 F.2d at 942–944.
100. *Id.* at 929 (citations omitted).
101. *Id.*
102. *Id.* at 930 (footnote omitted).
103. The Ninth Circuit recognized that the insufficiency of societal discrimination as a predicate for governmental rac classification commanded only four votes in *Wygant*. Absent more definitive guidance, the court reasoned that a requirement that state and local governments act only to correct their own past wrongdoing reconciled *Wygant* and *Fullilove*. *Id.* at 930.

104. *Id.* at 932.

105. *Id.* at 932–933.

106. *Id.* at 933.

107. *Id.* at 934 (emphasis in original and citations omitted).

108. *Id.* at 935, citing *Wygant*, 476 U.S. at 280 n. 6 (plurality opinion).

109. *Id.* at 937. The city ordinance allowed city agencies to apply for waivers where qualified MBEs could not be found. Another section of the ordinance contemplated procedures for qualifying businesses as bona fide MBEs. *Id.* at 937 n. 29.

110. *Id.* at 932.

111. 825 F.2d 324 (11th Cir. 1987) (*per curiam*), *vacated and remanded*, 109 S.Ct. 1333 (1989).

112. Metropolitan Dade County's 1979 proposal to construct a rapid transit system for metropolitan Miami, Florida was to be financed, at 80 percent of the project cost, by the federal Urban Mass Transit Administration (UMTA) of the Department of Labor pursuant to the Surface Transportation Assistance Act of 1978, Pub. L. No. 95–599, 92 Stat. 2689 (1978). The county would contribute the remaining 20 percent of the required funds. Under UMTA policy, an MBE was defined as a business owned and controlled by socially or economically disadvantaged persons. "Such disadvantage may arise from cultural, racial, chronic economic circumstances or background, or other similar cause." 825 F.2d at 325 n. 2. Persons included within that category included, but were not limited to, Blacks, Hispanics, Asians or Pacific Islanders, American Indians or Alaskan Natives, and women (regardless of race or ethnicity). *Id.*

Under the program reviewed by the court, each bidder was required to involve MBEs in 5 percent of the contract work, or demonstrate that every reasonable effort had been made to achieve the 5 percent goal. In addition, bidders would be allowed to demonstrate that MBE involvement was not possible because MBEs were either not qualified to perform the work or were unavailable. H. K. Porter's bid was approximately three hundred thousand lower than the next lowest bid. However, H. K. Porter was not awarded the contract because it did not comply with the MBE provisions. Porter then brought suit alleging, *inter alia*, that the MBE goal was unconstitutional on its face and as applied.

113. *See* 42 U.S.C. § 2000d ("No person . . . shall, on the ground of race . . . be subjected to discrimination. . . . "); 49 U.S.C. § 1615(a)(1) ("No person . . . shall on the grounds of race . . . be excluded from participation in, or denied the benefits of, or be subject to discrimination" under a program, project or activity funded under the statute).

114. 825 F.2d at 329.

115. 107 S.Ct. 1053 (1987). In *Paradise*, the Court upheld a one-for-one promotion quota imposed to remedy the exclusion of blacks from positions as state troopers. White state troopers had challenged the quota in a reverse discrimination equal protection class suit.

116. 825 F.2d at 330, citing *Fullilove*, 448 U.S. at 497.

117. *Id.* at 331.

118. *See* Ordinance No. 83–69–59, *codified in* Richmond, Virginia City Code, § 12–156(a) (1985); *Croson*, 109 S.Ct. at 713. The Richmond ordinance defined an MBE as a business at least 51 percent of which is owned and controlled by minority group members. Minority group members were defined as United States citizens who were Black, Spanish-speaking, Orientals, Indians, Eskimos, or Aleuts. *See* 109 S.Ct. at 713.

119. *Id.* at 714.

120. *Id.* (citation omitted). Richmond's city manager also commented on the con-

MINORITY BUSINESS SET-ASIDES

struction industry in Pittsburgh, Pennsylvania. *See* J. A. Croson Company v. City of Richmond, 822 F.2d 1355, 1358 (4th Cir. 1987), *aff'd*, 109 S.Ct. 706 (1989).

121. 109 S.Ct. at 714. Under promulgated purchasing procedures, the lowest bidder was required to name MBEs which would be utilized and the percentage of the total contract price awarded to minority firms. The city's human relations commission was to verify that the minority firms were in fact bona fide MBEs. Where waivers were requested, the city commission was required to make a recommendation regarding the request. The city's director of general services was empowered to render final determinations on compliance, with no direct administrative appeal from the director's denial of waiver. *Id.*

122. The June 1988 expiration of the Richmond plan presented the possibility that the Supreme Court would hold that the challenge to the plan was moot. In fact, during oral argument before the Supreme Court, Chief Justice Rehnquist raised the mootness issue. *See* 57 U.S.L.W. 3247 (Oct. 11, 1988). In its decision, the Court held that the expiration of the ordinance did not render the controversy moot, because a live controversy remained with respect to whether the city's refusal to award Croson the contract was unlawful. *See* 109 S.Ct. at 713 n. 1.

123. 109 S.Ct. at 715.

124. *Id.*

125. J. A. Croson Company v. City of Richmond, 779 F.2d 181 (4th Cir. 1985). In that opinion, the panel majority found that national findings of discrimination in the construction industry and a study of the award of prime contracts in Richmond rendered reasonable the city council's view that low minority participation in city contracting should have been addressed. *Id.* at 190 n. 12. The panel majority upheld the 30 percent set-aside after comparing that percentage to the percentage of minorities in Richmond's population (50 percent). *Id.* at 191.

126. *See* 476 U.S. 267 (1986).

127. *See* 822 F.2d 1355 (4th Cir. 1987), *aff'd*, 109 S.Ct. 706 (1989).

128. *Id.* at 1357.

129. *Id.* at 1359.

130. *Id.*, citing J. Edinger & Son, Inc., *supra*, and Associated General Contractors of California, *supra*.

131. *Id.* at 1360.

132. *Id.*

133. *See supra* note 118.

134. *See supra* note 121. Dissenting, Judge Sprouse argued that the Richmond plan was lawful under the *Wygant* plurality's opinion and *Fullilove*. *See* 822 F.2d at 1362–1368 (Sprouse, J., dissenting).

135. Justice O'Connor was joined by Chief Justice Rehnquist and Justices White, Stevens and Kennedy in Parts I, III–B, and IV of her opinion. These parts discuss the facts of the case, the legality of the factual predicate offered in support of the Richmond plan, and the question of the narrow tailoring of the plan, respectively. *See* 109 S.Ct. 712–716, 723–728, 728–729.

136. *See id.* at 717–720 (Part II, discussing the city's power to adopt legislation to address the effects of past discrimination).

137. *See id.* at 720–723, 729–730 (Parts III–A and V, discussing the standard of review of racial classifications, and the array of lawful devices the city could employ to rectify the effects of past discrimination).

138. *See supra* note 48.

139. 109 S.Ct. at 719.

140. *Id.* at 720. Justice Kennedy did not join this Part of Justice O'Connor's opinion. Acknowledging that the ''summary in Part II is both precise and fair,'' Kennedy concluded that the issue discussed therein was not before the Court. *Id.* at 734 (Kennedy, J., concurring in part and concurring in the judgment).

In his concurring opinion, Justice Scalia noted that it is one thing to permit racially based conduct by the federal government, whose legislative powers were ''explicitly enhanced'' by § 5 of the Fourteenth Amendment, and ''quite another to permit it by the precise entities against whose conduct in matters of race that Amendment was specifically directed. . . . '' *Id.* at 736 (Scalia, J., concurring in the judgment).

141. *Id.* at 721. *See Wygant*, 476 U.S. at 279–280; *id.* at 285–286 (O'Connor, J., concurring).

142. 109 S.Ct. at 722 (citation omitted).

143. *See supra* notes 70–73 and accompanying text.

144. 109 S.Ct. at 723.

145. *Id.* at 724, quoting *Wygant*, 476 U.S. at 277.

146. *Id.* (citation omitted).

147. *Id.* at 725 (citations omitted).

148. *Id.* at 724.

149. *Id.* at 725, citing Johnson v. Transportation Agency, 480 U.S. 616, 651–652 (1987) (O'Connor, J., concurring); Hazelwood School District v. U.S., 433 U.S. 299, 308 (1977).

150. *Id.* at 726.

151. *Id.* at 727–728.

152. *Id.* at 728.

153. 478 U.S. 421, 494 (1986) (O'Connor, J., concurring in part and dissenting in part).

154. *Id.* at 494.

155. 109 S.Ct. at 729.

156. *Id.* at 729.

157. *Id.* at 729–730.

158. A majority of the Court noted this consideration in Part IV of Justice O'Connor's opinion. *See id.* at 728–729.

159. *Id.* at 728. Concurring in part and concurring in the judgment, Justice Stevens did not agree with the premise that governmental racial classifications are never permissible except as a remedy for a past wrong. *Id.* at 730 (Stevens, J., concurring in part and concurring in the judgment). He did agree that the Richmond ordinance could not be justified as a remedy for past discrimination.

160. *Id.* at 734 (Kennedy, J., concurring in part and concurring in the judgment).

161. *Id.* at 735.

162. *Id.* at 734.

163. *Id.* at 735 (Scalia, J., concurring in the judgment).

164. *Id.*

165. *Id.* (quoting Plessy v. Ferguson, 163 U.S. 537, 559 (1896) (Harlan, J., dissenting)).

166. *Id.* at 736, quoting *Fullilove*, 448 U.S. at 527 (Stewart, J., dissenting).

167. *Id.* at 737.

168. *Id.*

169. *Id.* at 738.

170. *Id.* at 739. Of course, those "individuals" were discriminated against *because of* their membership in those groups, the very vice that anti-discrimination laws were enacted to address.

171. *Id. See also* Milwaukee County Pavers Assn. v. Fiedler, 707 F.Supp. 1016, 1024–1027 (W.D. Wis. 1989) (granting motion for preliminary injunction, the court opined that Wisconsin set-aside program for "disadvantaged" businesses was, in actuality, based on suspect classifications), *preliminary injunction dissolved as to federally funded contracts,* 710 F.Supp. 1532 (W.D. Wis. 1989).

Dissenting in *Croson,* Justice Marshall (joined by Justices Brennan and Blackmun) stated that the Court's decision marked "a deliberate and giant step backward in this Court's affirmative action jurisprudence." *Id.* at 740 (Marshall, J., dissenting). Justice Marshall was willing to view the local evidence of discrimination in Richmond against the backdrop of nationwide discrimination in the construction industry. Thus, he stated, the Richmond City council was aware of the federal set-aside program; the Supreme Court's *Fullilove* decision; the fact that .67 percent of construction contract funds dispensed by Richmond in a five-year period went to minority-owned prime contractors; testimony that Richmond construction trade associations had virtually no minorities among their members; and testimony from city officials with regard to the exclusionary history of the local construction industry. *Id.* at 742–743.

Justice Marshall also dissented from the Court's adoption of strict scrutiny review of race-conscious remedial measures. In his view, racial classifications used for the purpose of remedying the effects of discrimination should not be subject to such scrutiny. Quoting from his opinion in *Fullilove,* Justice Marshall stated:

Because the consideration of race is relevant to remedying the continuing efforts of past racial discrimination, and because governmental programs employing racial classifications for remedial purposes can be crafted to avoid stigmatization, . . . such programs should not be subjected to conventional "strict scrutiny"—scrutiny that is strict in theory, but fatal in fact. *Id.* at 752 (quoting *Fullilove,* 448 U.S. at 518–519).

As to the Court's view of the racial and political dominance of minorities in Richmond, Justice Marshall argued that the numerical and political dominance of nonminorities in the State of Virginia and the nation "provide an enormous political check against the 'simple racial politics' at the municipal level which the majority fears." *Id.* at 753. Marshall further recognized that an increasing number of cities which recently came under minority leadership will be the cities with the most discrimination to rectify. Moreover, stated Marshall, the city council vote for the set-aside was not purely along racial lines; one of four white council members voted for the measure while another abstained. "The majority's view . . . implies a lack of political maturity on the part of this Nation's elected minority officials that is totally unwarranted. Such insulting judgments have no place in constitutional jurisprudence." *Id.* at 753–754. *See also id.* at 757 (Blackmun, J., dissenting).

172. *See* 14 BNA Daily Lab. Rep. (Jan. 24, 1989), at p. A–8.

173. *See* Korematsu v. U.S., 323 U.S. 214 (1944) (Court sustained a conviction for violation of a military order during World War II which excluded all persons of Japanese ancestry from certain geographical areas). It is ironic that *Korematsu* was the Supreme Court's first decision which explicitly referred to race as a suspect classification. *See also*

Hirabayashi v. U.S., 320 U.S. 81 (1943) (Court upheld military plan which set curfews, established detention in relocation centers, and excluded Japanese from certain areas of the west coast).

174. *See* "Assessing Impact of Case on Race Quotas," WALL STREET JOURNAL (Jan. 25, 1989), at p. B1.

175. *Id.*

176. *See* N.Y. TIMES (Jan. 25, 1989) at p. 10 (national edition).

177. *Id.*

178. *See* 109 S.Ct. at 754 (Marshall, J., dissenting).

179. *See* Wright, *Color-Blind Theories and Color-Conscious Remedies*, 47 U. CHI. L. REV. 213, 236 (1980) ("courts must scrutinize somewhat more carefully those [affirmative action] programs instituted by decisionmakers of the minority race").

180. Days, *supra* note 17 at 480.

181. *Id.* (footnotes omitted).

182. 376 S.E.2d 662 (1989). *See also* Georgia Branch v. City of Atlanta, 253 Ga. 397, 321 S.E.2d 325 (1984) (Atlanta's 1982 set-aside ordinance held void as violative of state legislative requirement that all contracts must be awarded to "lowest and/or best bidder"). The city corrected the deficiency noted in *Georgia Branch* by amending the city charter to redefine the term "lowest and/or best bidder" to include compliance by bidders with the MBE/WBE program. 376 S.E.2d at 663.

183. The minority and female business enterprise program reviewed by the Georgia Supreme Court was set forth in an administrative order announced by the mayor of Atlanta. An MBE was defined as a business entity of which at least 51 percent of the ownership or control was by minority persons, with the same percentage of ownership or control required for female business enterprises. *Id.* The plan did not have an expiration date or geographical limitation, and annual participation goals were to be set by the mayor under specific criteria which included a forecast of eligible projects and the number of MBE firms available. Contracts were not to be awarded if bids did not identify MBEs or WBEs by name, scope, and dollar value of work which met the established goals. *Id.* Waivers were available where a bidder could show a good-faith, but unsuccessful, effort to comply with the plan. *Id.*

184. "Protection to person and property is the paramount duty of government and shall be impartial and complete. No person shall be denied the equal protection of the laws." Ga. Const., Art. I, § 1, ¶II.

185. 376 S.E. 2d at 665.

186. *Id.* (citation omitted).

187. *Id.*

188. *Id.* at 666.

189. *Id.*

190. *Id.*

191. *Id.* at 667, *quoting* Regents of the University of California v. Bakke, 438 U.S. 265, 289 (1978).

192. Michigan Road Builders Association, Inc. v. Milliken, 834 F.2d 583 (6th Cir. 1987), *aff'd*, 109 S.Ct. 1333 (1989), discussed *supra* notes 126–135 and accompanying text.

193. H. K. Porter Company, Inc. v. Metropolitan Dade County, 825 F.2d 324 (11th Cir. 1987) (*per curiam*), *vacated and remanded*, 109 S.Ct. 1333 (1989), discussed *supra* at notes 152–162 and accompanying text.

194. Milwaukee County Powers Assn. v. Fiedler, 707 F.Supp. 1016 (W.D. Wis. 1989).

195. Milwaukee County Powers Assn. v. Fiedler, 710 F. Supp. 1532 (W.D. Wis. 1989). *See* Wis. Stat. § 84.076(1) and (2). This statute provides that Wisconsin would reserve $4 million in construction contracts for disadvantaged businesses as set forth in 49 C.F.R. § 23. Firms were disadvantaged if small and owned and controlled by socially and economically disadvantaged individuals. The regulation presumed that "Black Americans, Hispanic Americans, Native Americans, Asian-Pacific Americans, or Asian-Indian Americans" were disadvantaged. 49 C.F.R. §§ 23.62, 23.69, Appendix A.

196. Pub. L. No. 97–424, 96 Stat. 2097, 2100. Section 106(c) of that act provided that not less than 10 percent of amounts authorized by the statute should be expended with small businesses owned and controlled by socially and economically disadvantaged individuals. Under regulations implementing § 106(c), states seeking federal highway funds were required to meet federal requirements or risk the loss of federal highway funding. *See* 49 C.F.R. § 23.68.

197. The court affirmed its earlier conclusion that "[w]here race, national origin and gender are proxies for socially disadvantaged," a court may not "ignore that the underlying classification is clearly based on invidious categories." *See* 710 F. Supp. at 1539 n.2; 707 F.Supp. at 1026.

198. 710 F. Supp. at 1539.

199. *Id.* at 1540 n. 3 (citations omitted).

200. *Id.* at 1545.

201. *Id.* at 1546 (citation omitted).

202. *Id.* at 1547–1549.

203. *Id.* at 1550.

204. *Id.* at 1551.

205. 723 F.Supp. 669 (M.D. Fla. 1989). *See also* Milwaukee County Pavers Assn. v. Fiedler, 1990 U.S. Dist. LEXIS 2503 (W. D. Wis. Mar. 6, 1990) (ruling on cross-motions for summary judgment, the court holds, *inter alia*, that states are not required to make findings if prior discrimination to ensure that implementation of federal law requirements is narrowly tailored).

206. *Id.* at p. 29.

207. *Id.*

208. 1989 U.S. Dist. 14187 (E.D. Pa. Nov. 29, 1989).

209. *Id.* at p. 36.

210. *Id.* at p. 38.

211. *Id.* at p. 39.

212. 729 F.Supp. 734 (W. D. Wash. 1989).

213. *Id.* at 737.

214. *Id.* (footnote omitted).

215. *Id.* at 739.

216. J. Saddler, "Jobs Set Aside for Minorities, Women are Evaporating," WALL STREET JOURNAL (Dec. 21, 1989), at p. B2.

217. *Id.*, WALL STREET JOURNAL, Dec. 18, 1989 at p. B2.

218. *Id.*

219. Saddler, *supra* note 212.

220. *Id.*

221. *See* 96 YALE L. J. at 478–484. For a discussion of the reach of *Croson* and the

Court's different analysis in federal affirmative action matters, *see* Metro Broadcasting Inc. v. FCC, 58 U.S.L.W. 5053 (1990).

222. On June 22, 1989, Senator Paul Simon (D., Ill.) introduced a bill (S. 1235) which would amend Title VII of the Civil Rights Act of 1964, 42 U.S.C. § 2000e *et seq.*, to allow cities and states to enact reasonable provisions for MBE set-aside programs. *See* 121 BNA Daily Lab. Rep. (June 26, 1989), at p. A–2. Under Simon's bill, which would amend Title VII under the Congress' Fourteenth Amendment powers, state and local governments could "enact reasonable provisions setting aside a percentage of funds for spending on contracts to be awarded to firms that have ownership, control, or employment practices which further the goal of remedying discrimination." *Id.*

6

Conclusion

The foregoing chapters examine the doctrinal underpinnings of affirmative action and judicial and federal agency treatment of various issues which arise as preferential treatment measures are used by employers and state and local jurisdictions. Those chapters reveal that affirmative action is a significant part of the nation's anti-discrimination laws and presents complex questions of law, public policy and morality.

Affirmative action will continue to be recognized as a valid and lawful tool available to employers, governments, and courts. The key question is what types and forms of affirmative action will be permitted as we enter the 1990s. Current trends suggest that affirmative action will be subjected to a much higher level of scrutiny and skepticism by the courts.

Apart from the legal considerations, other trends may affect employer recruitment of minorities and women. According to labor force projections by the Bureau of Labor Statistics for the period 1988 to the year 2000, the labor force is estimated to grow 1.2 percent annually, with 141 million persons in the labor force by the year 2000.[1] By the year 2000, women are projected to be 47 percent of the labor force; African Americans, 12 percent; Hispanics, 10 percent; and Asians and other groups, 4 percent.[2] The Bureau of Labor Statistics projects that 43 million persons will join the labor force between 1988 and 2000. Approximately two-thirds of those entrants are expected to be white non-Hispanics, with Hispanics and African Americans projected to account for 15 percent and 13 percent of such entrants, respectively.[3] Thus, demographics alone may call for an emphasis on minority and female recruitment which would not have otherwise occurred.

Questions and answers regarding the concept and use of affirmative action in employment and public contracting are linked to the broader questions of race and discrimination, and the answers thereto as reflected by the continuing political and social debate over race- and sex-conscious measures. The ultimate outcome of (and conclusion reached in) this debate will have far-reaching and serious consequences for all segments of the nation's populace.

NOTES

1. *See* Fullerton, "New labor force projections, spanning 1988 to 2000," *reprinted in* BNA Daily Lab. Rep. No. 244 (Dec. 21, 1989), at p. F–1.

2. *Id.*

3. *Id.* at p. F–8.

Bibliography

BOOKS

Baldus, D., & J. Cole. *Statistical Proof of Discrimination*. (Shepards McGraw, 1980).

Bell, D. *Race, Racism and American Law*. 2d ed. (Little, 1980).

Bickel, A. *The Morality of Consent*. (Yale University Press, 1975).

Bork, R. *The Tempting of America: The Political Seduction of the Law*. (Free Press, 1990).

Bronner, E. *Battle For Justice: How the Bork Nomination Shook America*. (Norton, 1989).

Bureau of National Affairs. *Affirmative Action Compliance Manual*. (Annual).

Connolly, W., & M. Connolly. *A Practical Guide to Equal Employment Opportunity*. 2 vols. (NY Law Publishers, 1982).

Connolly, W., & D. Peterson. *Use of Statistics in Employment Litigation*. (New York Law Journal, 1989).

Dworkin, R. *A Matter of Principle*. (Harvard University Press, 1986).

Dworkin, R. *Taking Rights Seriously*. (Harvard University Press, 1977).

Ely, J. *Democracy and Distrust: A Theory of Judicial Review*. (Harvard University Press, 1981).

Farmer, J. *Lay Bare the Heart*. (Arbor House, 1985).

Fleming, J., & G. Hazard. *Civil Procedure*. 3d ed. (Little, 1985).

Glazer, N. *Affirmative Discrimination: Ethnic Inequality and Public Policy*. (Basic Books, 1976).

Goldman, A. *Justice and Reverse Discrimination*. (Princeton University Press, 1979).

Gorman, R. *Basic Text on Labor Law, Unionization and Collective Bargaining*. (West, 1976).

Hill, H. *Black Labor and the American Legal System: Race, Work, and the Law*. (BNA, 1977).

Hunsicker, J., J. Kane, & P. Walther. *NLRB Remedies for Unfair Labor Practices*. Rev. ed. (1986).

McDowell, D. *Affirmative Action After the Johnson Decision*. (NFSEP, 1988).

Murphy, B. *Fortas: The Rise and Ruin of a Supreme Court Justice*. (Morrow, 1987).

O'Neill, T., & Bakke. *The Politics of Equality*. (Wesleyan University Press, 1984).

Orwell, G. *Nineteen Eighty-Four*. (1949).

Posner, R. *The Economics of Justice*. (Harvard University Press, 1983).

Report on the Minority Business Enterprise Programs of State and Local Governments. (Minority Business Enterprise Legal Defense And Education Fund, Inc., 1988).

Schlei, B., & P. Grossman. *Employment Discrimination Law*. 2d ed. (BNA, 1983).

Schwartz, H. *Packing the Courts: The Conservative Campaign to Rewrite the Constitution*. (Scribners, 1988).

Shulman, S., & W. Darity, eds. *The Question of Discrimination: Racial Inequality in the U.S. Labor Market*. (Wesleyan University Press, 1989).

Sowell, T. *Civil Rights: Rhetoric or Reality?* (Morrow, 1985).

Stone, G., L. Seidman, C. Sunstein, & M. Tushnet. *Constitutional Law*. (Little, Brown, and Co., 1986).

Sullivan, C., M. Zimmer, & R. Richards. *Employment Discrimination*. (Little, Brown, and Co., 1988).

ARTICLES

Abram. *Affirmative Action: Fair Shakers and Social Engineers*. 99 Harv. L. Rev. 1312 (1986).

Allegreti. *Voluntary Racial Goals After* Weber: *How High is Too High?* 17 Creighton L. Rev. 773 (1984).

Anderson. *The Approval and Interpretation of Consent Decrees in Civil Rights Class Action Litigation*. U. Ill. L. Rev. 579 (1983).

Andritzky and Andritzky. *Affirmative Action: The Original Meaning*. 17 Lincoln L. Rev. 249 (1987).

Assessing Impact of Case on Race Quotas. Wall Street Journal (Jan. 25, 1989).

Belton. *Discrimination and Affirmative Action: An Analysis of Competing Theories of Equality and* Weber. 59 N.C. L. Rev. 531 (1981).

Blumrosen. *The Legacy of* Griggs: *Social Progress and Subjective Judgments*. 63 Chi.–Kent L. Rev. 1 (1987).

Blumrosen. *Affirmative Action in Employment After* Weber. 34 Rutgers L. Rev. 1 (1981).

Blumrosen. *Strangers in Paradise:* Griggs v. Duke Power Co. *and the Concept of Employment Discrimination*. 71 Mich. L. Rev. 59 (1972).

Boyd. *Affirmative Action in Employment—The* Weber *Decision*. 66 Iowa L. Rev. 1 (1980).

Buchanan. Johnson v. Transportation Agency, Santa Clara County: *A Paradigm of Affirmative Action*. 26 Hous. L. Rev. 229 (1989).

Calabresi. Bakke *as Pseudo-Tragedy*. 28 Cath. L. Rev. 427 (1979).

Chambers and Goldstein. *Title VII: The Continuing Challenge of Establishing Fair Employment Practices*. 49 Law and Contemp. Prob. 9 (1986).

Comment. *Walking a Tightrope without a Net: Voluntary Affirmative Action Plans After* Weber. 134 U. Pa. L. Rev. 457 (1986).

Comment. *Affirmative Action and the Remedial Scope of Title VII: Procedural Answers to Substantive Questions*. 136 U. Pa. L. Rev. 625 (1987).

Commerce Clearing House. *Guidebook to Fair Employment Practices*. (1989).

Cox. *The Supreme Court, Title VII and "Voluntary" Affirmative Action—A Critique*. 21 Ind. L. Rev. 767 (1988).

Cox. *The Assertion of "Voluntary" Employment Quotas and Some Thoughts on Judicial Role*. 23 Ariz. L. Rev. 87 (1981).

Cox. *The Role of Congress in Constitutional Determinations*. 40 U. Cin. L. Rev. 199 (1971).

Crenshaw. *Race, Reform, and Retrenchment: Transformation and Legitimation in Antidiscrimination Law*. 101 Harv. L. Rev. 1331 (1988).

Daly. *Some Runs, Some Hits, Some Errors—Keeping Score in the Affirmative Action Ballpark from* Weber *to* Johnson. 30 Boston Col. L. Rev. 1 (1988).

Daly. Stotts' *Denial of Hiring and Promotion Preferences for Non-Victims: Draining the "Spirit" from Title VII*. 14 Fordham Urb. L. J. 17 (1986).

Days. *Fullilove*. 96 Yale L. J. 453 (1987).

Edwards. *The Future of Affirmative Action in Employment*. 44 Washington and Lee L. Rev. 763 (1987).

Edwards. *Race Discrimination in Employment: What Price Equality?* U. Ill. L. F. 572 (1976).

Ely. *The Constitutionality of Reverse Racial Discrimination*. 41 U. Chi. L. Rev. 723 (1974).

Eskridge. *Dynamic Statutory Interpretation*. 135 U. Pa. L. Rev. 1479 (1987).

Fallon and Weiler. Firefighters v. Stotts: *Conflicting Models of Racial Justice*. Sup. Ct. Rev. 1 (1984).

Farber and Frickey. *Legislative Intent and Public Choice*. 74 Va. L. Rev. 423 (1988).

Fullerton. *New Labor Force Projections, Spanning 1988 to 2000*. Reprinted in BNA Daily Lab. Rep. No. 244 (Dec. 21, 1989).

Gold. Griggs' *Folly: An Essay on the Theory, Problems, and Origin of the Adverse Impact Definition of Employment Discrimination and Recommendation for Reform*. 7 Indus. Rel. L. J. 429 (1985).

Greenawalt. *The Unresolved Problems of Reverse Discrimination*. 67 Cal. L. Rev. 87 (1979).

Hooks. *Affirmative Action: A Needed Remedy*. 21 Ga. L. Rev 1043 (1987).

Jones. *The Origins of Affirmative Action*. 21 U. Cal.–Davis L. Rev. 383 (1988).

Jones. *The Genesis and Present Status of Affirmative Action in Employment: Economic, Legal, and Political Realities*. 70 Iowa L. Rev. 901 (1985).

Jones. *"Reverse Discrimination" in Employment: Judicial Treatment of Affirmative Action Programs in the United States*. 25 Howard L. J. 217 (1982).

Kennedy. *Persuasion and Distrust: A Comment on the Affirmative Action Debate*. 99 Harv. L. Rev. 1327 (1986).

Kennedy. *Racial Critiques of Legal Academia*. 102 Harv. L. Rev. 1745 (1989).

Lamber. *Observations on the Supreme Court's Recent Affirmative Action Cases*. 62 Ind. L. J. 243 (1987).

Liebman. *Justice White and Affirmative Action*. 58 Col. L. Rev. 471 (1987).

Meltzer. *The* Weber *Case: The Judicial Abrogation of the Antidiscrimination Standard in Employment*. 47 U. Chi. L. Rev. 423 (1980).

Mishkin. *The Uses of Ambivalence: Reflections on the Supreme Court and the Constitutionality of Affirmative Action*. 131 U. Pa. L. Rev. 907 (1983).

Morris. *New Light On Racial Affirmative Action*. 20 U. Cal.–Davis L. Rev. 219 (1987).

Neuborne. *Observations on* Weber. 54 N.Y.U. L. Rev. 546 (1979).

Norton. *Equal Employment Law: Crisis in Interpretation—Survival Against the Odds.* 62 Tulane L. Rev. 681 (1988).

Note. *Indirect Proof of Discriminatory Motive in Title VII Disparate Treatment Claims After* Aikens. 88 Colum. L. Rev. 1114 (1988).

Note. *Finding a "Manifest Imbalance": The Case for a Unified Statistical Test for Voluntary Affirmative Action Under Title VII.* 87 Mich. L. Rev. 1986 (1989).

Note. *Rethinking* Weber: *The Business Response to Affirmative Action.* 102 Harv. L. Rev. 658 (1989).

Note. *The Nonperpetuation of Discrimination in Public Contracting: A Justification for State and Local Minority Business Set-Asides After* Wygant. 101 Harv. L. Rev. 1797 (1988).

Pattern for Progress: Final Report to President Eisenhower. President's Committee on Government Contracts. (1960).

Posner. *Legal Formalism, Legal Realism, and the Interpretation of Statutes and the Constitution.* 37 Case Western L. Rev. 179 (1986).

Proceedings, 114 F.R.D. 423 (discussing affirmative action).

Reynolds. *The Reagan Administration and Civil Rights: Winning the War against Discrimination.* 1986 U. Ill. L. Rev. 101.

Rigler. *Title VII and the Applicability of Disparate Impact Analysis to Subjective Selection Criteria.* 88 W. Va. L. Rev. 25 (1985).

Rosenfeld. *Decoding* Richmond: *Affirmative Action and the Elusive Meaning of Constitutional Equality.* 87 Mich. L. Rev. 1729 (1989).

Rosenfeld. *Affirmative Action, Justice, and Equalities: A Philosophical and Constitutional Appraisal.* 46 Ohio St. L. J. 845 (1985).

Rutherglen. *Disparate Impact Under Title VII: An Objective Theory of Discrimination.* 73 Va. L. Rev. 1297 (1987).

Rutherglen and Ortiz. *Affirmative Action Under the Constitution and Title VII: From Confusion to Convergence.* 35 UCLA L. Rev. 468 (1988).

Saddler. "Jobs Set Aside for Minorities, Women are Evaporating." Wall Street Journal (Dec. 21, 1989).

Scalia. *The Disease as Cure.* WASH. U. L. Q. 147 (1979).

Scanlan. *Affirmative Action for Women: New Twist on an Old Debate.* Legal Times (Dec. 5, 1988).

Schatzki. United Steelworkers of America v. Weber: *An Exercise in Understandable Indecision.* 56 Wash. L. Rev. 51 (1980).

Schnapper. *Affirmative Action and the Legislative History of the Fourteenth Amendment.* 71 Va. L. Rev. 753 (1985).

Schwartz. *The 1986 and 1987 Affirmative Action Cases: It's All Over but the Shouting.* 86 Mich. L. Rev. 524 (1987).

Schwarzschild. *Public Law by Private Bargain: Title VII Consent Decrees and the Fairness of Negotiated Institutional Reform.* Duke L.J. 887 (1984).

Selig. *Affirmative Action in Employment: The Legacy of a Supreme Court Majority.* 63 Ind. L. J. 301 (1987).

Selig. *The Reagan Justice Department and Civil Rights: What Went Wrong.* U. Ill. L. Rev. 785 (1985).

Shoben. *Differential Pass-Fail Rates in Employment Testing: Statistical Proof under Title VII.* 91 Harv. L. Rev. 793 (1978).

Sobol and Ellard. *Measures of Employment Discrimination: A Statistical Alternative to the Four-Fifths Rule.* 10 Indus. Rel. L.J. 381 (1988).

Spiegelman. *Court-Ordered Hiring Quotas After* Stotts: *A Narrative on the Role of the Moralities of the Web and the Ladder in Employment Discrimination Doctrine.* 20 Harv. C.R.–C.L. L. Rev. 339 (1985).

Strauss. *The Myth of Colorblindness.* 1986 Sup. Ct. Rev. 99 (1987).

Sullivan. *Sins of Discrimination: Last Term's Affirmative Action Cases.* 100 Harv. L. Rev. 78 (1986).

Tribe. *In What Vision of the Constitution Must the Law be Color-Blind?.* 20 J. Marshall L. Rev. 201 (1986).

Tribe. *Perspectives on* Bakke: *Equal Protection, Procedural Fairness, or Structural Justice?* 92 Harv. L. Rev. 864 (1979).

Turner. *The Rehnquist Court and Title VII Disparate Impact Doctrine*: Atonio's *Burden Allocation and the Retreat from* Griggs. Ohio N.U. L. Rev. (forthcoming 1990).

Van Alstyne. *Rites of Passage: Race, the Supreme Court, and the Constitution.* 46 U. Chi. L.Rev. 775 (1979).

Woodside and Mare. *Walking the Tightrope between Title VII and Equal Protection: Public Sector Voluntary Affirmative Action after* Johnson *and* Wygant. 20 Urb. L. 367 (1988).

Wright. *Color-Blind Theories and Color-Conscious Remedies.* 47 U. Chi. L. Rev. 213 (1979).

Index

About the Author

RONALD TURNER is associated with the legal firm of Schiff Hardin and Waite, Chicago. He is also a Research Associate at the Wharton School of Business.